THE ANNALS OF THE TERF WARS
AND OTHER WRITING

Jane Clare Jones

RADICAL NOTION BOOKS

*What would
happen
if the mirror
started to
speak?*

These pieces were all originally written on the dates given. They have been lightly edited in some places for this volume, and some supporting references and footnotes on context have also been added.

CONTENTS

IV – PATRIARCHY, NARCISSISM, AND DOMINATION

V – WOKE CRITICISM

INTRODUCTION
Brighton
APRIL 2022

Owl @UglaStefania · 1d
Trans people: We just want some basic huma-

Bigots: YOU ARE SILENCING WOMEN

Trans people: No, all women can co-exist and-

Bigots: *goes on every national media platform in the country* I AM BEING SILENCED

Trans people: But-

Bigots: *on a megaphone* SILENCED

14   437   1,488

One night in November 2018 this tweet turned up in my feed, and it struck me as a pretty wilful misrepresentation of how the gender war had gone down to date. I was irritated enough to sit down and start writing my own version of what I remembered, from the point I first ran into trans activism online in 2013 through to the build-up of grassroots resistance spurred by the government consultation on the Gender Recognition Act in 2018. I didn't set out to write a satirical play. I was—as I am so frequently—just totally pissed off by the reality-twisting and flat-out lies trans activists tell about this conflict; by their constant evasions about what their ideology actually consists of and what it entails; by their refusal to so much as countenance that women might have 'reasonable concerns' and are not just pretending to sound sensible while secretly planning genocide; and by the bare-faced bullying, smears, guilt-by-association, shit analogies and general all-purpose witch-hunting they have deployed against anyone who does not comply with what they want. I sat down, that is, to try and set the record straight, and to call bullshit. Except it turns out that when you write down—more or less verbatim—what you remember about the kind of things trans activists have said to you on Twitter, it's inadvertently hilarious. Because it sounds completely, utterly bonkers.

7

'The Annals of the TERF-Wars' is a dramatized history of a part of this conflict, but it also serves as a frame for the rest of this collection of threads, essays, presentations, and speeches, which are themselves a historical record—a set of front-line dispatches—from the gender war. I wanted to bring these pieces together for several reasons. First, I hope they present a fairly comprehensive critique of transgender ideology, examining its history, conceptual incoherence, and political implications, as well as dissecting its narcissistic, patriarchal, and totalitarian structure. As many of you reading this will be only too aware, for all its madness, the ideology of the present trans rights movement has been devastatingly successful at capturing 'right-thinking' opinion and the many public institutions eager to jump on the corporate EDI rainbow-washing bandwagon. It is vitally important that we continue to point out—loudly and repeatedly—not only that this ideology is based on a form of batshit reality denial that erases the recognition of sex-based discrimination and the materialist analysis of sex-based oppression and that can only be enforced through authoritarian means, but that its fundamental precepts are profoundly and irrevocably sexist. The project of the present trans rights movement consists, at its core, of the effort to erase the class of female people and redefine us in the gendered image of our oppression, against our political interests, and against our express consent. There is good reason why many women will not accept this axiomatic example of what Andrea Dworkin would call 'the male power of naming.'

Second, by bringing together these pieces—often written in response to particular events or encounters in this conflict—I wanted to capture a small slice of what we have experienced over the last several years. It's become something of a Terven commonplace to note that none of us really believe any of this is happening and suspect we will get to the end of our days without really believing any of it happened at all. Many of us have frequently felt overwhelmed by the barrage of events—from the deeply distressing to the completely preposterous—and I have sometimes felt almost vertiginous at finding myself, by some sort of accident, inside unfolding history. I know I will never remember most of what we have been through. But I wanted to set down some record of part of it, written as it was unfolding.

Lastly, I wanted to make something durable out of a conflict which has, in significant parts, been fought online. The TERF-War has not taken place only on Twitter, but Twitter has been where a great deal of the discursive battle has been waged. In that long summer of 2018, in the months running up to the closing of the consultation, I spent most of my time online, engaged in what felt like intellectual trench warfare, side by side with many women (and a few men). Having been involved since 2013—when no one seemed able to hear a single word we said—that summer was remarkable, and I could feel the once immovable edifice of gender-identity discourse begin to fracture and shift around me. I hope that these pieces—many written on Twitter, in response to Twitter, or about Twitter—will record the role played in this history by this ephemeral, but nonetheless consequential, virtual platform, and document something of the type of political discourse it generated during that mad period in the early 21st century when a bunch of people tried to convince everyone else that humans didn't come in two sexes. I hope also it will serve as a reminder of the time we have spent there together, the many friendships we have forged, and the anguish, hilarity, and insanity of it all.

With love and respect to each and every one of you. It's been an honour to stand alongside you.

The witches struck back!

PUUUUUUUUUUUUUUULLLLLLLLLLLLLLLLLLL!!!!!!!!!!

THE ANNALS OF THE TERF-WARS

janeclarejones.com

NOVEMBER 2018

PROLOGUE: A long time ago in a galaxy far, far away...

Transsexual women: We just want some basic human rights.

Women: Okay.

Transsexual women: We have this condition called gender dysphoria and it's really painful and we need to transition to live as the other sex because it's the treatment for the dysphoria.

Women: Yeah, that sounds tough. Okay, if that's what you need to do.

Transsexual women: We'd like you to treat us as women.

Most women: Um, okay. Sure, we can do that if that helps.

PREQUEL: A long time ago in a lesbian bar that no longer exists

Lesbians: We don't have to treat you as women for sexual purposes, do we?

Many transsexual women: No, that's cool.

Nascent trans activists: Well, actually, if you don't want to fuck us then it invalidates our womanhood and that is misgendering and it's a human rights abuse and you should want to fuck us.

Lesbians: It's a human rights abuse if we don't want to fuck you? What the fuck?

Nascent trans activists: Yes, you should want to fuck us.

Lesbians: Even if you still have dicks?

Nascent trans activists: Even if we still have dicks.

Lesbians: Um yeah, sorry, we don't do dicks. We're LESBIANS.

Nascent trans activists: You are vagina fetishists with unconscious bias and are gatekeeping your vaginas. We are women and our dicks are women's dicks. If you don't want to fuck us, you're bigots.

Lesbians: We're not bigots, it's just you're male, and we fuck female people.

Nascent trans activists: LITERAL VIOLENCE. WE ARE WOMEN. YOU SHOULD WANT TO FUCK US.

Lesbians: Um yeah, we're not really feeling that right now to be honest.

Nascent trans activists: TERF TERF TERF TERF TERF.

Lesbians: HEY PEOPLE! These people are pressuring our sexual boundaries because they say they're women but the way they're pressuring us doesn't make us feel like they're women... in fact, it makes us feel like they're men and we don't fuck men. We're lesbians, we don't fuck men. That's the reason

we did all the marching, so that was okay, right? RIGHT????
(Nascent trans activists: TERF TERF TERF TERF TERF)
Lesbians: HEY PEOPLE!!! Could we get some fucking help here?
Rest of the LGB community and world: Did someone say something?

EPISODE 1: The First War Begins. Scene 1: Cyberspace, around 2013
Trans activists: So, hey, when we said we'd like you to treat us like women that wasn't right, because actually, we ARE women and we demand that you treat us exactly like women because we are women and that you to stop violently excluding us from all your women things.
Women: Um, we thought you were male people who had to transition to help with your dysphoria?
Trans activists: No, that is outdated and pathologizing. Women are women because they have a gender identity which makes them women.
Women: Um, we thought we were woman because we're female?
Trans activists: No, you are women because you have magic womanish essence that makes you women. We have the same magic womanish essence as you, it's just that ours got stuck in the wrong body.
Feminists: That sounds kind of sexist. Can you tell us what this woman-essence is, and how it gets stuck in the wrong body, because that sounds like a weird metaphys...
Trans activists: It's SCIENCE.
Feminists: Science says there's 'magic woman essence'??? Are you sure? Because feminism would...
Trans activists: Shut up, bigots.
Feminists: Sorry? What?
Trans activists: You are our oppressors, you don't get to speak. When you speak you oppress us, and it literally kills us.
Feminists: WHAT?
Trans activists: You are cis women, cis people are our oppressors.
Feminists: We're what?
Trans activists: It's your new name, it comes from Latin, and means you have a magic gender essence that matches your body, and because your magic gender essence matches your body you are privileged...
Feminists: Hang on a minute, women are oppressed because they are women, we're not really sure that's a privilege...
Trans activists: YOU ARE PRIVILEGED BECAUSE YOUR GENDER IDENTITY MATCHES YOUR BODY. Nobody knows the pain of being trapped in the wrong body. It is the greatest pain of all the pains that has ever happened to all of humankind, and everyone who does not know this pain is privileged and is therefore our oppressor.
Feminists: Um, were not really sure we're oppressing you, we don't have much

social power to oppress you, we'd just like to ask you some questions about this gender identity thing...

Trans activists: ARE YOU DEBATING OUR RIGHT TO EXIST???

Feminists: What? No, we just wanted to ask you...

Trans activists: YOU ARE DEBATING OUR RIGHT TO EXIST. THIS IS LITERAL VIOLENCE.

Feminists: No no no hold on, we're just trying to ask you a question...

Trans activists: WE WILL NOT DEBATE OUR RIGHT TO EXIST. YOU ARE TRYING TO EXTERMINATE US. YOU ARE JUST LIKE GENOCIDAL RACISTS

Feminists: What??? We're like genocidal what??? This is fucking crazy. Can we just try and calm down and talk about this?

Trans activists: NO. There is NO DEBATE. Debating is literal violence and makes us unsafe. Repeat after us—Trans women are women. Trans women are women because they have woman essence, just like cis women. You're not women because of your bodies. Bodies have nothing to do with being a woman.

Feminists: Okay, this is sounding nuts now, because we really think our bodies have quite a lot to do with our being women.

Trans activists: Bio-essentialism!

Feminists: What? Essentialism is bad, we agree, but that means thinking people with certain kinds of bodies have to...

Trans activists: No, essentialism is thinking male and female people exist.

Feminists: But male and female people DO exist.

Trans activist: FUCK YOU TERF. DIE IN A FIRE.

Feminists: Woah.

Trans activists: How many fucking times do we need to tell you this, cis-scum? Your body has nothing to do with your being a woman. There is no such thing as female biology.

Feminists: WHAT THE FUCK????

Trans activists: The gender binary was created by white heteropatriarchal colonialism.

Feminists: WHAT THE ACTUAL FUCK???? WHAT DOES THAT EVEN MEAN?? WHICH 'COLONIALISM'????

American trans activists who don't know the rest of the world exists: Colonialism colonialism duh.

Feminists: How the hell is the colonization of North America responsible for the creation of male and female people? And while we're here that sounds kinda racist...

Trans activists: Two-spirit people burble burble sex is a spectrum burble clown fish burble burble intersex people burble burble some women don't have ovaries burble social construct burble Judith Butler

(*Academics with cool-girl syndrome and assorted edgelords and wokebros:* JUDITH

BUTLER!!!!)

Trans activists: …burble burble, there is no such thing as female biology and women are women because they have magic gender essence and therefore some women have penises!

Feminists: Okay, this is batshit. We REALLY need to talk about this.

Trans activists: WE WILL NOT DEBATE OUR RIGHT TO EXIST.

EPISODE 1: The First War Continues. Scene 2: Cyberspace, 2013-14

Enter Intersectional Feminists from top, bottom and side of screen…

Intersectional feminists: THEY WILL NOT DEBATE THEIR RIGHT TO EXIST YOU FUCKING BIGOTS.

Feminists: Hang on, we thought you were feminists. We thought you cared about female people.

Intersectional feminists: Female people are so last century. Only White Feminists care about female people.

Feminists: White what?

Intersectional feminists: All the feminists before us were white middle-class women and they only cared about what white middle-class women care about and they were only interested in getting good jobs for white middle-class women and they didn't care about black women and were dried up whorephobic prudes who didn't realize sex work was liberating and mostly they just wanted to kill trans people.

Feminists: That sounds like some mad-ass caricature.

Intersectional feminists: You would say that, you oppressive old crones. You're just saying that to maintain your power.

Feminists: No, we're not, we don't have much power. We're saying it because it sounds like bullshit. *Starts trying to explain all the things second wave feminism did to help women.*

Intersectional feminists: We're not listening to you, you oppressive bitches. We've hidden all your books in the library to protect young minds from them. You are whorephobes and transphobes and racists. We are intersectional. Only we have learned from the Tumblr-oracle how all the different oppressions have different points on a scale that add up to who is the most oppressed and you are white (so are we mostly but we're pointing at you because somehow that means something, maybe because we have asymmetric haircuts and our profile pics give great side-eye) and you are women and that means that you are the least oppressed and that means that your feminism is shit and that means that you have to centre all these other people in your feminism and if you refuse it's because you're the oppressors and the most oppressed people are trans women and they must be the centre of feminism from now on.

Feminists: You want us to centre male-born people in our feminism?

Intersectional feminists: THAT'S RIGHT BITCHES. And there is no such thing as 'male-born people.' That is cissexism and is literal violence. You need to educate yourselves. We don't have the spoons.

Feminists: Um, yeah, we know quite a lot about the history and practice of feminism and we've thought quite hard about it and I think we're going to carry on centring female people if you don't mind.

Intersectional feminists: OPPRESSORS.

Feminists: Female people are oppressed and our political movement...

Intersectional feminists: SWERF AND TERF. SWERF AND TERF. SWERF AND TERF.

(P.S. – Would you like to try this sourdough bread I made with yeast from my vagina?)

Feminists: Okay. This is getting REALLY fucked up now.

Intersectional feminists: Run away and cry your 'White Feminism™' tears you dried-up old witches. And don't fucking kink-shame us or we'll shank you.

Feminists: Um, this feminism seems not very...

Intersectional feminists with new blue hair: BIG DICK ENERGY.

TERF-blocker descends.

EPISODE 1: The End of the First War. Scene 3: Cyberspace and public sphere, 2014-15

Feminists: *Educate themselves.* *Become increasingly horrified.* *Start writing articles nobody fucking reads.*

HEY PEOPLE! This shit is mental. There are these people saying being female has nothing to do with being a woman, and that they're women because they have magic gender essence, and this sounds pretty sexist, and they also say that sex doesn't exist and given we've always thought that that's the reason we're oppressed we're pretty worried this is a bad idea for women and feminism, and now these other people who say they're feminists are telling us we have to centre people who are not female in our feminism or we're the oppressors and are going on and on about how we shouldn't say anything because we're whorephobic bigots and it's kind of nuts and people are bullying lesbians to have sex with people with penises and they're encouraging young people to take hormones that we don't seem to understand the effects of and we think this is all sketchy as fuck to be honest. What the hell is going on?

Trans activists and intersectional feminists: That woman talking over there is making people unsafe because she is an evil bigot and trans people are the most vulnerable people in the world and she is the oppressor and she is oppressing us by speaking and if she speaks then it is literal violence and it will make people hurt us and we will also hurt ourselves and so you have to stop her speaking and if you don't stop her speaking then you are also an evil bigot and we are going to tell everyone what evil fucking bigots you are and you wouldn't want that now so you better stop her speaking right fucking now.

Civic institution: Um, what now?

Trans activists: *Pickets.* *Inundates with letters and emails and phone calls.* *Goes on Twitter and gets a massive pile of people to bombard institution.*

Civic institution's PR people: This makes us look bad.

Civic institution: Okay, we won't let the bigot speak. I mean, she's just a feminist, right?

Trans activists: Hurray, we are safe! Ding dong, the witch is dead!

Feminists: What the fuck? HEY PEOPLE! I was just trying to say something because I think there are some questions here and I think we should really talk about it. I'm not sure people are women just because they have magic woman essence and I think there might be some not good consequences of thinking this.

Trans activists and civic institutions: SHUT UP BIGOTS.

Misogynist child with column in major left-wing newspaper: SHUT UP BIGOTS. YOU'RE THE KIND OF PEOPLE WHO THOUGHT GAY PEOPLE WERE ALL KIDDY FIDDLERS.

Feminists: Um, lots of us are lesbians actually and the rest of us were totally behind gay rights, like, we've always been allies, what the hell are you going on about?

Misogynist child with column in major left-wing newspaper: *Blocks all the women objecting.* WRONG SIDE OF HISTORY BITCHES.

Woke bros and assorted leftie-misogynists: *Jumping up and down with excitement.* WRONG SIDE OF HISTORY UPPITY BITCHES.

Trans activists and civic institutions and leftie newspapers: REPEAT AFTER US— Trans women are women. Because trans women are women then trans women should be given all the social resources given to other women and if you don't accept this then you are exclusionary bigots and we're going to make damn sure everyone knows what terrible terrible people you are and how you shouldn't be allowed to live or work or speak or write in public. Have you fucking got that???

Feminists: You're intimidating and silencing us.

Trans activists and leftie newspapers: No, we're not. You trigger people by existing and asking questions and having the wrong opinions. You need to shut the fuck up so that everyone is safe. RIGHT NOW.

EPISODE 2: Between the Wars. Scene 1: Public sphere, 2015-17

Feminists: We're feeling pretty demoralized here…

Trans activists: EXCELLENT. You just sit over there and keep your little ladymouths shut. *Organize some more.* *Take over Stonewall and all the LGBT+ organizations.* *Start sending people into school and institutions to explain that people have magic gender essence which sometimes gets trapped in the

wrong body.* *Bully, harass, and no-platform any woman who speaks up.*
Hey, government. We've got this great idea. You know how people think you're
a bunch of assholes who have been driving the economy into the ground and
lining rich people's pockets while you let vulnerable people starve? We've
got just the ticket for you.

Government: *Ears prick up.* Tell us more.

Trans activists: Yeah, all you have to do is change this piece of legislation so we
can get our sex changed more easily. The current legislation is really burdensome, and we're really vulnerable, and it would really help us out, and would
totally make you look like you care about marginalized people while costing
you fuck all.

Government: Well, that does sound like a boon. Is there a catch?

Trans activists: No, not one. It's just streamlining an administrative process
really.

Government: Okay, come and tell us all about it. Is there anyone else we need
to talk to?

Trans activists: No. It doesn't have any effect on anyone, it's just paperwork
really. JUST MAKE SURE YOU DON'T TALK TO THOSE UPPITY WOMEN
OVER THERE THEY'RE ALL EVIL BIGOTS WHO WANT TO KILL US.

Government: Oh yes, they do sound like terrible people, how awful for you.

Trans activists: Yes, they're really horrific. And while we're at it, you might
want to think about removing their rights to single-sex spaces from the
Equality Act because it discriminates against us.

Government: Interesting. Okay, when can you come in?

**EPISODE 2: Between the Wars. Scene 2: The Take Over Continues,
Labour Party, 2016-17**

The left of the left: Austerity sucks! Neoliberalism sucks! WE. WANT. SOCIAL.
DEMOCRACY. NOW.

Some of the feminists: Yeah, we want that, too.

Other of the feminists: We think these people might be wankers.

Some of the feminists: Noted. Let's see what they say…

Momentum: WE. WANT. SOCIAL. DEMOCRACY. NOW.

The new leader of the Labour Party: WE. WANT. SOCIAL. DEMOCRACY. NOW.

Some of the feminists: Okay, great…

Momentum: ANYONE WHO DOESN'T WANT SOCIAL DEMOCRACY NOW IS
A CAPITALIST SHILL.

Some of the feminists: Well, we get what you're saying, but…

Momentum: CAPITALIST SHILL. CAPITALIST SHILL. FUCK THE COLLABO-
RATING CENTRIST BIGOTS…

Some of the feminists: This seems strangely fam…

Momentum: …AND WHILE WE'RE AT IT, TRANS WOMEN ARE WOMEN!

The new leader of the Labour Party: TRANS WOMEN *ARE* WOMEN.

Momentum: TRANS WOMEN ARE WOMEN TRANS WOMEN ARE WOMEN AND ANYONE WHO QUESTIONS IS A BIGOT.

Some of the feminists: Ohhhhhhhhh FUCK...

Other of the feminists: We told you they were wankers.

Misogynist child with column in major left-wing newspaper: Trans women are women and the only people who disagree with me are those centrist-collaborating shills over there...

Some of the feminists: Well, THAT'S bullshit.

Momentum, Labour leadership, misogynist child, and chorus of brocialists: TRANS WOMEN ARE WOMEN. TRANS WOMEN ARE WOMEN. CAPITALIST BIGOT SHILLS BIGOT SHILLS BURN THEM BURN THEM...

Bastardi: Fully automated luxury...

Some of the feminists: Yup. Wankers.

Other of the feminists: Told you.

Labour Party women: So, about this trans women are women thing, we just have a few...

Momentum, misogynist child and chorus of brocialists: SHUT UP YOU FUCKING TERF BIGOTS.

Labour Party women: TERF-what?

Momentum, misogynist child and chorus of brocialists: You are 'Trans Exclusionary Radical Feminists.' That means you're evil and witches and that people can punch you and it's not violence against women because you're witches.

Labour Party women: Um, we're not sure we're radical feminists, or that we're excluding anyone, but we definitely don't think anyone should be punching women and we just wanted to...

Momentum, misogynist child and chorus of brocialists: ZIP IT.

Labour Party women: *In a huddle in the wings, whispering quietly.* What the fuck???? HEY PEOPLE! We're Labour members and this a democratic political party and we think we should...

Momentum, misogynist child and chorus of brocialists: WE TOLD YOU TO ZIP IT.

Labour Party women: But...

Momentum, misogynist child and chorus of brocialists: TSZUP!!!!! *Makes zipping motion.*

Labour Party women: Well, we think we want to talk about this so we're going to go over here and...

Momentum, misogynist child and chorus of brocialists: GREAT. FUCK OFF. WE DON'T NEED SHILLS LIKE YOU IN THE REVOLUTION ANYWAY...

Feminists: This is a fucking clusterfuck.

Momentum: We have this awesome young trans woman who we think would make an awesome Women's Officer because she's awesome and trans women are awesome and trans women are women and there is no difference in any of their life experience which means they might not understand women's political interests and anyone who suggests that is a fucking bigot.

General public: Huh?

Young trans women's officer with variable coloured hair: Hi, I'm Petal, and I'm very petally, and that means I know all about women and their petals and I can represent all the political interests of petals and when I get a womb-transplant I will be even more petally, and if you don't like my petals...

Labour Party women: No, no, your petals are fine, it's just that you're very young, and for most of the time you were alive you were...

Petal: I WAS WHAT? I have *always* been a woman...

Labour Party women: Yeah, we're just not quite sure about that bit...

Petal: FUCK YOU, YOU TRANSPHOBIC BIGOTS.

Labour Party women: Um, we thought you were supposed to be representing us, and actually, it doesn't seem like you're really doing very much...

Petal: FUCK OFF TERFS.

General public: What the hell is going on...?

Feminists: Yeah, we kind of...

Momentum, trans activists, misogynist child and chorus of brocialists: WE THOUGHT WE TOLD YOU WITCHES TO BE QUIET ALREADY.

EPISODE 3: The Second War Begins. Scene 1: Somewhere in Whitehall, 2018

Government: We think we're going to change the law. Just a little administrative clear up to make life less burdensome for the trans population who, as we know, are terribly vulnerable.

Feminists: You're going to do what??? Why didn't you ask us about this?

Government: Yes, well, the trans people said it didn't affect you.

Feminists: THEY SAID WHAT??? Hang on a motherfucking minute.

EPISODE 3: The Witches Strike Back. Scene 2: Cyberspace and public sphere, 2018

Trans activists: REPEAT AFTER US: Trans women are women. Trans women should not be excluded from any spaces women have access to. Anyone who questions that is an exclusionary genocidal racist who is in league with the far right. And, by the way, you're not women anymore, you're cis women, and we want you to stop talking about your bodies, and we're going to change all the words in all the literature that has anything to do with you so that everyone understands that being female is not necessary to being a woman, and from now on you are 'menstruators' and 'cervix havers' and 'pregnant people.' Got that?

Women: WOAH. You fucking what? We're cis-what? And we're not women anymore, we're menstruators? We don't think we like this.

Trans activists: It's inclusive.

Women: Well, it sounds dehumanizing as all hell to us.

Trans activists: Shut up cis people, you are the oppressors. These are the new words for you.

Women: Don't we get to decide which words we use for ourselves?

Trans activists: No, you are the oppressors, if you do not accept these new words you are oppressing us.

Women: We're oppressing you by wanting to be called women??? What the hell is…

Trans activists: BIGOTS! These are your new words. You are cis women, and we are trans women. We are both just different types of women, except we're more oppressed than you so you have to do what we say. Look, there's nothing you can do about it, the government already agrees with us, see?

Women: The government already agrees with you? What?

Trans activists: Yes. REPEAT AFTER US: Trans women are women. The government believes this and is going to change the law so that we can be legally recognized as female if we sign a piece of paper that says we have magic woman essence…

Women: What??? This can't be right. Surely someone would have said something about this? Where are the feminists? Feminists, is this right?

Feminists: U-huh. We were trying to…

Women: What are the implications of this???

Feminists: *Montage of charts and essays.* *Three weeks later.*

Women: Fuck this shit. We need to do something.

Feminists: YES. WE. DO.

Feminists and radicalized women and intersex people and transsexuals and concerned parents and gay men who are realizing something's up and some straight male allies: EVERYONE HOLD HANDS AND PUUUUUUUUUUULLLLLLLLLLLL.

The press: The women seem to be making a shit-ton of noise about something? Why are there stickers of cocks everywhere??? What on earth is going on?

Trans activists and the left-wing press: NOTHING, THEY'RE BIGOTS.

Most of the press: Oh, okay.

A few journalists: *Digging around.* What the actual fuck??????

Feminists and allies: EVERYONE KEEP PUUUUUUUUUULLLLLLLLLLLING. IT'S MOVING.

Trans activists: BURN THE WITCHES BURN THE WITCHES BURN THE WITCHES.

Feminists: Ha, yeah, we're not so scared of you and your words now are we? There's a ton of us here. And people are starting to listen. EVERYONE. C'MON. PUUUUUUUUUUUUULLLLLLLLLLLLLLL.

Trans activists: BURN THE WITCHES BURN THE WITCHES BURN THE WITCHES.

Women and allies: PUUUUULLLLLLLLL.

Feminists watching from around the world: Hell yes! PUUUUULLLLLLLLL.

Women and allies: KEEP FUCKING PUUUUUUUUUUULLLLLLLLLLLLLING.

Trans activists: BURN THE WITCHES BURN THE WITCHES BURN THE WITCHES.

Government: Lah-lah-lah.

A few journalists: Um, actually, we had a little look at this thing, and we think the women might have a point.

Trans activists: NO THEY DON'T THEY'RE WITCHES BURN THEM BURN THEM.

A few journalists: Now, come on, there is a proposed change to law, and this is a democracy, and they have some arguments that seem quite compelling, and there have been some things that have happened recently that seem to suggest that maybe there's some substance to their concerns, and it seems like we should think this through.

Trans activists: NO DEBATE. BURN THEM BURN THEM.

A few journalists: We're not sure that's really helping your case. We think we're going to start covering this in more depth.

Trans activists: YOU CAN'T LISTEN TO THEM THEY'RE WITCHES. IF YOU DON'T GIVE US WHAT WE WANT WE'LL KILL OURSELVES.

Women and allies: PUUUUUUUUUULLLLLLLLL. IT'S MOVING IT'S MOVING!!!!!!!

Feminists watching from around the world: PUUUUULLLLLLLLL!!!!!!!!

Major left-wing newspaper that has been steadfastly quiet: *Ostentatiously clears throat.* Um, actually we think the women might have a point.

Women and allies: *BACKFLIPS.*

Trans activists and allies at home and abroad: OMFG why is the British media so full of evil bigots??????

Women and allies: *Lying in a bundle panting.* Whatfuckingever asshats.

<FIN>

I - SEX AND GENDER

A BRIEF HISTORY OF TRANSGENDER IDEOLOGY

Appendix to The Political Erasure of Sex:
Sex and the Census

OCTOBER 2020

THE CONCEPT OF GENDER AND GENDER IDENTITY

The conceptual kernels of the development of contemporary transgender ideology are to be found in the work with transsexual people and intersex children undertaken by Harry Benjamin, John Money, and Robert Stoller, in the 1950s and 1960s. Harry Benjamin, the first doctor in the United States to champion the cause and treatment of transsexuals, followed his patient—the famed transsexual Christine Jorgensen—in espousing the theory of human 'bisexuality' as an organic explanation of the cause of transsexualism. According to Benjamin "sex is never one hundred per cent 'male' or 'female,'" being rather "a blend of a complex variety of male-female components," which results in a range of "'intersexes' of varying character, degree and intensity," of which transsexuality was one type (cited in Meyerowitz 2002, p. 102). What needs to be underlined here—because it serves as the thread running right through to the present day—is that the notion of transsexuality as a type of intersex condition depends on the idea that humans are *psychically sexed*, often in some kind of innate and immutable way, and that transsexuality arises through the disjuncture between physical and psychological sex (this is the idea commonly expressed as 'a woman trapped in a man's body'). For Benjamin, this model underpinned his belief in performing surgical procedures on transsexuals, arguing that "[i]f it is evident that the psyche cannot be brought into sufficient harmony with the soma then and only then" should we consider "fitting the soma into the realm of the psyche." Or, somewhat less abstrusely, the "person in adult life should live as the sex of his choice. In other words, the psychological sex should be decisive" (cited in Meyerowitz 2002, p. 113).

While Benjamin considered psychological sex to have deeper somatic causes—although he was unable to identify them—the sexologist John Money, working with intersex children at John Hopkins University, developed a model which ascribed the individual's sense of their sex to a combination of biological and sociological factors. Money is responsible for first coining the term 'gender' to describe this internal sense of one's sex, and 'gender

22

role' to denote "all those things that a person says or does to disclose himself or herself as having the status of boy or man, girl or woman" (cited in Meyerowitz 2002, p. 114). In 1964, Robert Stoller then developed the term 'gender identity,' which he used "much as others had used 'psychological sex' to refer to 'one's sense of being a particular sex'" (p. 116). Money then incorporated Stoller's nomenclature, giving an account of 'gender identity' that depends on his notion of the 'critical period of development.' That is, gender identity proceeds by passing through developmental stages, beginning with chromosomal and gonadal differentiation, moving through exposure to hormones in utero, and concluding with socialization into sex-based gender roles. Money argued that once an individual had passed through a particular developmental stage it was impossible, and harmful, to try to reverse it, and that one's gender identity thus became 'fixed' in an immutable way.[1] He conceived the process as similar to language acquisition, a capacity we are biologically primed for that is then given form by social and culturally-specific learning, and which, once acquired, becomes irrevocably set within us. "It is there, in the brain," he explained, that "social customs and traditions" are "assimilated and fused" with the physical sex characteristics that are part of "one's species heritage" (cited in Downing, Moreland & Sullivan, p. 26).

THE MODERN TRANS RIGHTS MOVEMENT

Organized activity to campaign for the rights and recognition of transgender people began in the early nineties, concurrently, on both sides of the Atlantic. In 1992, a trans woman and lawyer called Phyllis Frye established The International Conference on Transgender Law and Employment Policy (ICTLEP), which met in Houston, Texas, for one week per year between 1992 and 1996.[2] At the same time, the lawyer Stephen Whittle, along with veteran trans campaigner Mark Rees, formed the trans lobby group Press for Change (PFC). PFC campaigned and lobbied in earnest from the early nineties until shortly after the passage of the 2004 Gender Recognition Act and set the template for all subsequent trans activism in the United Kingdom, both in terms of methodology and ideology. That ideology, I suggest, was a product of cross-fertilization between ICTLEP and PFC, whose association began in

---

[1] "As you approached each gate's sex-differentiation point, you could have gone in either direction, but as you passed through, the gate locked, fixing the prior period of development as male or female. Your gonads, for example, could have become either testicles or ovaries, but once they became testicles they lost the option of becoming ovaries... In behaviour... at first you drove all over the highway, but as you proceeded you tended to stick more and more to the lanes marked out and specially prescribed for your sex" (cited in Downing, Moreland & Sullivan, p. 24).
[2] Frye's account of the history of ICTLEP is at www.digitaltransgenderarchive.net/files/wd375w32h.

1992, when a PFC briefing on 'The Situation Overseas' appears as an appendix to ICTLEP's first published proceedings (Press for Change 1992).[3]

In addition to keynote lunches and the like, ICTLEP ran a series of workshops charged with considering the situation of trans people and possible interventions in a variety of legal areas. In 1993 and 1994, the moderator for the Health Project was Martine Rothblatt, a trans woman, lawyer, and tech and pharmaceutical billionaire who would come to public prominence in 2014 when *New York Magazine* put them on the front cover as 'The Highest Paid Female CEO in America.' In 1994, Rothblatt delivered a presentation to the Health Project group entitled 'Unisexuality: The Wave of the Future,' a theme later reprised in a plenary presentation of 'The Health Project Report,' and which served as the backbone of the 1995 book *The Apartheid of Sex* (reprinted in 2011 as *From Transgender to Transhuman: A Manifesto on the Freedom of Form*). In these presentations, we can discern the central conceptual plank of the ideology of the present trans rights movement: the claim that sex should properly be conceived as the sex of the mind (or 'gender identity'), and not the sex of the body. Or, as Rothblatt phrases it: "[w]e must finally end the notion that sex is between our legs" and "realize that sex is between our ears" (Rothblatt 1994a, p. 115).[4]

In one sense, Rothblatt's assertion that "[o]ur biological sex is the sex of our minds. Our genitals are simply our genitals, not our sex" (Rothblatt 1994b, p. E2) is simply a more dramatic rendering of the earlier claim made by Benjamin that 'psychological sex' should take priority over the sex of the

---

[3] According to Frye, Stephen Whittle got in touch prior to the organization of the first conference and suggested the possibility of attending using university funding, and this was the reason 'International' was appended to ICTLEP's name. Whittle couldn't attend the first conference and submitted the report in the appendix to the conference proceedings. He did, however, attend the fourth (1995) and fifth (1996) conferences. In 1995, he gave a keynote address with Martine Rothblatt (see n. 4), and also participated, with Phyllis Frye, in the reading of the International Bill of Gender Rights (IGBR). As discussed above, the IBGR includes the assertion that public space should be understood as 'gendered space' and that no trans people should be excluded from any space or activity on the basis of their natal sex. That is, the person with probably the greatest claim to be the originator of trans rights activism in the UK has, since the mid-1990s, been committed to a principle that redefines all sex-based spaces as gender-based spaces, and thus, effectively removes female people's rights to single-sex space. The present, deeply unpleasant, conflict over women's single-sex spaces has thus been coming for a long time. (www.digitaltransgenderarchive.net/files/cn69m416c.)

[4] Notably, this is precisely the same formulation used by Stephen Whittle in a 2006 essay in *The Transgender Studies Reader*, reflecting on his irritation with feminists who challenge the narrative of transgender ideology, and specifically critiquing Janice Raymond's *The Transsexual Empire*. Here, Whittle writes that "what makes a person is what takes place between the ears and not between the legs" (2006, p. 199)—an exhibition of the anti-embodiment mind/body dualism that also characterises Rothblatt's explicitly transhumanist project. With respect to the possible

body. However, what distinguishes Rothblatt's contribution is that these 1994 presentations are the earliest formulation I have encountered in trans activism of what we could call the 'sex-denialist' aspect of contemporary trans ideology—that is, the claim not only that 'psychic sex' or 'gender identity' should take precedence over biological sex, but the claim that the division of humans into male and female types is in some sense *not a material reality*.[5] Rothblatt's presentation on 'Unisexuality' opens with the claim that "[s]exual dimorphism is no longer tenable based on accumulated biochemical, medical and psychological evidence" (p. E1), while the health report asserts that "science is really coming to the conclusion that there is no natural dividing line between the sexes" (Rothblatt 1994a, p. 110).

As those familiar with contemporary trans rights discourse will immediately recognize, Rothblatt here also elaborates the claim that we should be "looking at sex as a continuum instead of an either/or" (p. 112), and that conceiving of people as either male or female is, in and of itself, an oppressive structure that warrants describing as an "apartheid of sex" (p. 111). The aim of transgender activism, Rothblatt suggests, should be to dismantle this "boring, stupid theory and paradigm" that people can be "either put in a male box or a female box" and recognize that "hundreds" or even "thousands of genders" are "possible" in a "post-apartheid gender world" (p. 113).[6] This "gender revolution" (p. 112) will require "an entire new lexicon" or "a new story board

---

transmission of sex denialism between Rothblatt and Whittle, it should also be noted that they were both speakers at the 'Keynote Luncheon,' held at ICTLEP on June 15, 1995. Here, Whittle also outlines his critique of Raymond, prefaced with the classically anti-feminist trope that Raymond is a man-hater who "employs an adversarial approach" and "uses... the discourse of blame directed at men" (Rothblatt and Whittle 1995, p. 26). He is also quite explicit about the fact that the "transgender community has created and exercised its own schools of thought" and have developed a "transgendered ontology" (p. 24). It would be my claim that this 'transgendered ontology' is precisely that outlined here under the rubric of 'transgender ideology' and that its central claim is the prioritizing of gender identity over biological sex in the definition of what constitutes a man or a woman.

[5] While many accounts of the sex denialism in trans ideology trace its origins to Judith Butler's *Gender Trouble*, Rothblatt doesn't reference Butler either in these presentations or in the *Apartheid of Sex*. References to Butler certainly appear in Whittle's later elaborations of sex denialism, and become common—indeed, *de rigueur*—once trans ideology and queer theory start coalescing in an academic context from the late nineties onwards. In the 'Health Law Report' from the previous year, however, Rothblatt derives support for the notion of 'sex is a spectrum' from Anne Fausto-Sterling's 1993 essay 'The Five Sexes' (*The Sciences*, March/April 1993), citing her claim that sex is a "vast, infinitely malleable continuum" (Rothblatt 1992, p. A5-5).

[6] Significantly—given the wide dissemination of trans ideology on the internet and the extent to which digital virtualization has apparently convinced a generation that embodiment is optional—Rothblatt, even at this early stage of the development of the internet, expresses great excitement about the way digital technology allows people to be "any gender that you want to

of life" (p. 113), creating "entire new industries" (p. 112) and "lead[ing] to a need to change family law in every jurisdiction in this country and in fact eventually throughout the world" (p. 113).

In 1993, ICTLEP adopted an 'International Bill of Gender Rights,' affirming the priority of self-determined gender identity over sex, which was refined at successive conferences and given its final form in 1996. The introduction proclaims that, as "the principles of the IBGR are understood, embraced, and given expression by humankind, the acts of legislatures and the pronouncements of courts and related structures will necessarily follow" in a way that "will ultimately determine the course of our culture and civilization" (ICTLEP 1996). The First Principle is 'The Right to Define Gender Identity,' which affirms the individual's "right to define, and to redefine as their lives unfold, their own gender identities, without regard to chromosomal sex, genitalia, assigned birth sex, or initial gender role." The Fourth Principle clearly foreshadows one of the crux issues in the present conflict between trans activism and women's right to single-sex spaces: 'The Right of Access to Gendered Space and Participation in Gendered Activity' reads, "[g]iven the right to define one's own gender identity...no individual should be denied access to a space or denied participation in an activity by virtue of a self-defined gender identity which is not in accord with chromosomal sex, genitalia, assigned birth sex, or initial gender role" (ICTLEP 1996).

In 1994, in Britain, PFC were also engaged in the business of defining their core principles. The Press for Change 'Mission Statement' first formulated in 1994 and revised up until 1996—defines 'transsexual people' as "those whose gender identity is not congruent with their apparent physical gender" (PFC 1994, s. 1.01), and outlines that the "final goal of the campaign is to achieve full legal recognition of transsexual people in their proper gender role" (s. 6.01). Pre-figuring the current debate about gender self-identification, it's notable that at this early stage, and consonant with ICTLEP's 'The Right to Define Gender Identity,' PFC underline that, in their view, "the absolute criterion for transsexual status should be self definition" (s. 6.02), and that they "will resist any definition of transsexual status which relies on an individual having undergone any particular medical or surgical treatment" (s. 6.04).

Significantly, this 'Mission Statement' also reprises Harry Benjamin's belief that transsexual people have "an inherent intersex condition" (s. 7.02). Claims of this kind recur throughout the published material produced by PFC and GIRES—the Gender Identity Research and Education Society, an

---

be and many, many are available," noting that "liberated gender space is being practiced right now in cyberspace" (Rothblatt 1994a, p. 113). It should be noted here that Rothblatt is, explicitly, a transhumanist, and envisions a future in which humanity will achieve digital immortality by uploading our consciousness into cyberspace. (See 'Notes on Digital Transcendence,' p. 232.)

organization also set up in the early nineties in association with Press for Change,[7] whose role has been to disseminate information about the biological underpinnings of gender identity, most of which rests on the assertion of sexed brains.[8] In 2000, Press for Change and GIRES, along with the FTM network (also founded by Whittle), G&SA, the Gender Trust, and Liberty, made a presentation to the Interdepartmental Working Group on Transsexual People, entitled 'Meeting the Needs of Transsexual People,' and reprinted as Annex 2 of their final report (Home Office 2000, p. 30). Here, the authors assert that, "[i]ncreasingly, scientific medicine includes transsexuality as one of the many intersex conditions that exist" (p. 32), a suggestion repeated in GIRES' submission to the Working Group, which makes the classically essentialist claim that "gender represents the psychological and emotional identification within the individual's brain as either male or female" and that "transsexualism is an intersex condition of the brain" (PFC 1999).[9]

Notably, the Working Group's report also includes as appendices an 'Expert Witness Statement' that attributes transsexuality to "errors of the sexual differentiation of the brain" (p. 39) and a submission by Dr Zoe-Jane Playdon entitled 'Transsexualism as an Intersex Condition.' Despite the fact that medical science does not consider transsexuality to be a Difference of

---

[7] The claim that GIRES was established in association with Press for Change was made by Stephen Whittle in a speech he gave at the London School of Economics in January 2017. (www.lse.ac.uk/Events/2017/01/20170110t1830vHKT/Pressing-For-Change.)

[8] The claim that brains are sexed is by no means categorically established, and has been subject to a number of critiques by feminist women working in neuroscience and philosophy of science (Cf. Cordelia Fine, *Delusions of Gender*, 2005; Gina Rippon, *The Gendered Brain*, 2019; Sophie Scott, Speech given at Women's Liberation 2020). Indeed, even if it *were* to be indisputably established that average male and female brains exhibit organic features that can be tied convincingly to certain gendered behaviours, deviations from these averages would still not establish that we were looking at a 'female brain in a man's body.' A brain in a male body is, *a priori*, a male brain. If that brain could be shown to exhibit 'feminine' characteristics, it would demonstrate that some male people exhibit some feminine characteristics, and that the cultural expectation that they should not (i.e. *gender*, in the feminist sense) should be challenged.

[9] One of the starkest versions of this type of 'brain-intersex' claim is made by Lynne Jones MP, who chaired the Parliamentary Committee on Transsexuality (later 'Gender Identity') from the early nineties onwards. On the page on 'Transsexualism' on her personal website, dated to just after the passage of the GRA, she writes, "Transsexualism, or Gender Identity Dysphoria as the syndrome is more correctly known, is thought to be caused by a combination of genetic factors and a hormonal imbalance while the child's body is being formed in the womb. *When the child is born, it has the brain of one sex but the genitalia of the other and so its sex is incorrectly identified at birth*" (my emphasis). In order to counteract the "uninformed opinion" of parliamentarians in the run up to the debate on the 2004 GRA, Jones was also responsible for distributing a document by GIRES explaining "something of the extreme complexity of natural variation in the field of sex differentiation" which rehearsed the details of the 'brain-sex' thesis. (www.gires.org.uk/transsexualism-the-inside-story.)

Sex Development (or DSD, the term now preferred by many advocates partly because of the appropriation of their medical conditions by trans rights discourse), and that, under increasing public criticism, trans rights advocates have now disavowed the claim that transsexuality is a DSD, the function of this claim is to furnish an organic—and hence reifying—basis for the notion of gender identity or psychological sex. Indeed, this is the context in which the Working Group can, in the introduction to their report, reprint a quote from a submission which asserts that trans women have the "brain of a woman" and "think like a woman" (p. 4), without any apparent awareness that many natal women have no concept of what 'thinking like a woman' might mean and would consider such a notion to be fundamentally and irrevocably sexist. In fact, it is our rather startling contention that female people, like all members of our species, 'think like human beings.'

This essentialization of gender identity is one of the two key conceptual moves underpinning transgender ideology, or, in the words of Stephen Whittle, "transgendered ontology" (see n. 4). The key thesis, as expressed by Whittle, is that "to be a man or a woman is contained in a person's gender identity" (Whittle 2002, p. 6), or—as I would frame it, to make the core thought more explicit—'the being of a man or a woman is defined by gender identity and *not by biological sex,*' where 'biological sex' is taken in its conventional sense of 'the division of organisms into male and female types according to their reproductive function.'[10] This axiomatic claim is supported on the one hand by the essentializing of gender identity, and on the other, as we have seen in Rothblatt's signature contribution, by what we can understand as 'sex denialism.'

This sex denialism animates the push to undermine the recording of biological sex on public documents and also surfaces in PFC and GIRES documents, as well as in Whittle's own academic essays. In 1998, Christine Burns published a piece on the PFC website entitled 'Fourth Column Revolutionary,'

---

[10] It is conventional in this argument for advocates of transgender ideology to dismiss the idea that sex can be understood as reproductive capacity using not only intersex people, but also the fact that some humans are infertile. The claim that intersex people undermine the reality of sex as a reproductive classification was dealt with by the developmental biologist Dr Emma Hilton and the evolutionary biologist Dr Colin Wright in the *Wall Street Journal* in February 2020, where they argued that the claim that 'sex is a spectrum' and the classification of male and humans merely a 'social construct' or "arbitrary grouping[s]" that has "no basis in reality" is "false at every conceivable scale of resolution." Intersex individuals, they note, "are extremely rare, and they are neither a third sex nor proof that sex is a 'spectrum' or a 'social construct.' Not everyone needs to be discretely assignable to one or the other sex in order for biological sex to be functionally binary. To assume otherwise—to confuse secondary sexual traits with biological sex itself—is a category error." (www.wsj.com/articles/the-dangerous-denial-of-sex-11581638089.)

which refers to the suggestion that we should "eliminate sex altogether...the UK birth certificate's FOURTH COLUMN...from public records for the whole of Europe" (Burns 1998). Similarly, the GIRES submission to the Interdepartmental Working Group argues that "[t]here is every reason to question why 'sex' should be recorded, at all, on the birth certificate. There are strong scientific, medical and societal reasons to discontinue this requirement." Information "about an individual's 'sexual organs' and predicted 'sexual functions'...deserve privacy and should certainly not appear on any document which the individual might have to show to a non-medical person." GIRES conclude by asserting, without evidence, that "[h]ow individuals see themselves and how they are seen by others, is in terms of 'gender identity,'" a claim that many feminists resist as a sexist concept of 'psychological sex' (GIRES 1999).

Press for Change justifies this attempt to erase the recording and recognition of sex from public life by claiming that it is no longer relevant, given that, apparently, women have now achieved full equality. Burns argues in her 1998 piece that "all around us, changes are already in progress that make the requirement for a legal reference point for sex into an anachronism." In their Working Group presentation, PFC and GIRES claim that as "our knowledge of all sorts of intersex conditions grows, as medicine increasingly admits to there being a significant number of births in which it is impossible to guarantee that the sex designation given is unquestionable, and *as our society increasingly removes the barrier to equality between the sexes*, it may be that 'sex' is no longer something that we should record about an individual" (Home Office 2000, p. 34, my emphasis). Indeed, they continue, should the "government choose to continue its documentation, then we must be aware that we do so, nowadays, for little other reason than to provide demographic data" (p. 34).

In addition to the specific conflict over resources and spaces allocated to women on the basis of sex, these claims point us towards a fundamental point of ideological conflict between the current trans rights movement and those articulating the interests of female people. It is our strong contention—one indeed backed up by data on levels of violence against women, women's income and poverty levels, the amount of unpaid work done by women, and the barriers still faced by women in numerous areas of public life—that our society is still, in fact, *very far away indeed* from a place where the recognition of sex could rightly be considered an irrelevant 'anachronism.' Not only do women continue to experience disadvantage on the basis of sex and need recordkeeping about sex to continue, we have a strong political interest in seeing *far more data disaggregated by sex*, the better to recognize and address outstanding inequalities. Moreover, three decades of trans ideological advocates justifying their political objectives by claiming that discrimination on the basis of sex is no longer a matter of much concern, is, in fact, a tacit admission that activists do on some level—despite disavowals—recognize that there is a conflict of political interests between women and the current form of the trans rights movement.[11]

According to the core thesis of 'transgendered ontology'—that is, that 'the being of a man or a woman is defined by gender identity and not by biological sex'—the quest for 'gender recognition' is not therefore an effort for an individual to *change sex,* but for an individual to be *recognised in their true sex or gender* (hence the change in nomenclature from 'sex-change' surgery to 'gender-affirmation' surgery). As Rothblatt argued in 1994, "we are not changing our sex. We are changing our gender...Our sex is the same as it was when we first entered the doctor's office—the sex of our minds and our soul" (Rothblatt 1994b, p. E3). By this rubric, a trans woman, by virtue of having a female gender identity, has *always* been a woman, one who is only distinguished from a natal female by having been mistakenly assigned the incorrect sex at birth on the basis of their basically irrelevant physical morphology ('born in the wrong body').

This is the thought that underlies the first point in Press for Change's 1997 'Five Principles for the evaluation of legislative proposals covering transgendered people in the United Kingdom,' which suggests that new laws should be judged on whether they are "motivated by a recognition of the need to correct an incorrect or premature assumption of sex or gender identity, subsequently discovered to have been invalid." That is, Press for Change considers

---

[11] Notably, while claiming that it's okay to erase the recognition of sex because women are not really discriminated against on that basis anymore, trans ideological advocates often simultaneously make the contradictory claim that women will be liberated from their millennia long oppression by erasing sex. The basis of this claim is the anti-materialist and incoherent assertion that it is *social categorization* by sex that is the root cause of women's oppression. Rothblatt makes this claim in their 1994 presentations on 'unisexuality' at ICTLEP, as does Burns's 'Fourth Column Revolutionary.' Here Burns suggests that the "fourth column of the British birth certificate is the root of the most enduring and entrenched system of discrimination in modern society." Given that British birth certificates began in 1837, while patriarchy first developed, according to our best understanding, during the agricultural revolution and the subsequent development of Mesopotamian city states (10,000 BCE – 3,000 BCE), this is an epically absurd claim. This is another of the points of the fundamental conceptual contention between trans ideological and feminist analysis. Trans ideology considers that the oppression of women is caused by the mistaken human categorization of sex, and can hence be abolished by pretending that sex does not exist. Feminist analysis thinks that women are oppressed by a hierarchical system of social organization and sex roles that arose historically in order to exploit and control women based on our reproductive capacity. In our view then, women's equality depends on changing this historical social organization, and our very real concern is that if you simply stop recognizing sex while leaving the present forms of social organization intact, what you are doing is denying women the tools to describe, record, and thereby challenge the ways in which they are discriminated against.

their key political objective to be establishing a "fundamental about our case," namely, that the recognition of trans people must not be conceived as a change of a "previously correct record" of sex-designation, but on the basis of correcting a mistaken or 'invalid' attribution. This is perhaps the clearest demonstration of the core aim to change legal conceptualization to posit biological sex as absolutely inferior to, and absolutely overwriteable by, the assertion of gender identity. According to 'transgendered ontology,' people's 'correct' sex/gender is their gender identity, not their anatomical sex. The political objective of a movement based on this ontology, is, therefore, nothing short of the intent to change the meaning of sex in law from a definition based in biology to one based on gender identity. And hence, to recategorize everyone, as GIRES intimated earlier, on the basis of gender identity, whether or not they agree with, consent to, or indeed, are extremely critical of, this new ontology.

Indeed, this is precisely the interpretation given by Stephen Whittle— along with Lewis Turner—of what is undoubtedly the crowning political achievement of the Press for Change campaign: the passage of the 2004 Gender Recognition Act. In "'Sex Changes'? Paradigm Shifts in 'Sex' and 'Gender' Following the Gender Recognition Act' (Whittle and Turner 2007), Whittle puns on the traditional understanding of 'sex change' to suggest that the GRA both upends the idea that trans people *transition* between sexes, and moreover, has presaged a fundamental *change of the meaning of sex in law*. (What "implications" does the GRA have for "what constitutes a 'sex change'?" Has this changed "what constitutes 'male' or 'female'"? "Has the category 'sex' changed?") According to Whittle, the "sex/gender distinction (where sex normatively refers to the sexed body, and gender, to social identity) is demobilised both literally and legally" by the GRA. Referring to the crucial Clause 9 of the Act which asserts, that "if the person's acquired gender is the male [female] gender, the person's sex is that of a man [woman]," Whittle notes, correctly, that the Act uses the words 'sex' and gender' in a manner contrary to their conventional use (that is, the Act transforms 'male' from a sex to a gender designation). He then, however, uses this obdurate legal confusion as the ground for claiming this "suggests that one's gender precedes one's sex," that "gender identity becomes and defines legal sex," and that "[g]ender then, now determines 'sex.'" Whittle points to the passage of the Act to assert that "the body's sex as a taxonomical tool has in some way become redundant." It would be some ten years—when the effort to reform the GRA to remove all forms of gatekeeping brought the issue to public prominence—before most women learned that a law had been passed which was being used as evidence that the category by which they are protected in law now "corresponds with one's acquired gender" and that, therefore, the "theorisation of sex is no longer necessary."

REFERENCES

Downing, Lisa, Iain Moreland, and Nikki Sullivan. 2015. *Fuckology: Critical Essays on John Money's Diagnostic Concepts* (Chicago: University of Chicago Press).

Burns, Christine. 1998. 'Fourth Column Revolutionary,' Press for Change website. (www.webarchive.org.uk/wayback/archive/20060124120000/http://www.pfc.org. uk/gendrpol/4th-col.htm.)

GIRES. 1999. 'Submission by GIRES to the Interdepartmental Working Group on Transsexual People.' (www.webarchive.org.uk/wayback/archive/20060124120000/ http://www.pfc.org.uk/workgrp/gires.htm.)

Home Office. 2000. *Report of the Interdepartmental Working Group on Transsexual People,* April 2000. (http://docs.scie-socialcareonline.org.uk/fulltext/wgtrans.pdf.)

ICTLEP. 1996. *International Bill of Gender Rights.* As adopted at the International Conference on Transgender Law and Employment Policy, 1996. (www.digitaltransgenderarchive.net/files/2z10wq28m.)

Jones, Lynne. 2005. 'Transsexualism,' Statement on official website, 4 January 2005. (www.lynnejones.org.uk/lynne-jones-mp/transsex.htm.)

Meyerowitz, Joanne. 2002. *How Sex Changed: A History of Transsexuality in the United States* (Boston, MA: Harvard University Press).

Press for Change. 1992. 'The Situation Overseas,' *First International Conference on Transgender Law and Employment Policy Proceedings,* Appendix I, pp. 324-333. (www.digital-transgenderarchive.net/files/sn009x85j.)

Press for Change. 1994. 'Mission Statement,' Press for Change website. (www.webarchive.org.uk/wayback/archive/20060124120000/http://www.pfc.org.uk/campaign/pfcaims.htm.)

Press for Change. 1997. 'Five Principles for the Evaluation of Legislative Proposals Covering Transgendered People in the United Kingdom,' Press for Change website. (www.webarchive.org.uk/wayback/archive/20060124120000/http://www.pfc.org. uk/campaign/princpls.htm.)

Rothblatt, Martine. 1993. 'Second Report on the Health Law Project,' *Second International Conference on Transgender Law and Employment Policy Proceedings,* Appendix 5, pp. A5-1 - A5-16. (www.digitaltransgenderarchive.net/files/gq67jr234.)

Rothblatt, Martine. 1994a. 'Your Heath Report Project,' *Third International Conference on Transgender Law and Employment Policy Proceedings*, pp. 107-117. (www.digitaltransgenderarchive.net/files/kw52j810t.)

Rothblatt, Martine. 1994b. 'Unisexuality: The Wave of the Future,' *Third International Conference on Transgender Law and Employment Policy Proceedings*, Appendix E, pp. E1-E6. (www.digitaltransgenderarchive.net/files/3b5918656.)

Rothblatt, Martine and Stephen Whittle. 1995. 'The Apartheid of Sex' and 'Choice and the Human Experience,' speeches given at 'Keynote Luncheon,' 15 June 1995, *Fourth International Conference on Transgender Law and Employment Policy Proceedings*. (www.digitaltransgenderarchive.net/files/kw52j813n.)

Whittle, Stephen. 2002. 'Disembodied Law,' Chapter 1 of *Respect and Equality: Transsexual and Transgender Rights* (London: Cavendish Publishing). First published as 'Becoming Man' in *Reclaiming Genders*, edited by Kate More and Stephen Whittle (London: Cassell, 1999).

Whittle, Stephen. 2006. 'Where Did It Go Wrong? Feminism and Trans Theory – Two Teams on the Same Side?' in *The Transgender Studies Reader*, edited by Susan Stryker and Stephen Whittle (London and New York: Routledge).

Whittle, Stephen and Lewis Turner. 2007. "'Sex Changes'? Paradigm Shifts in 'Sex' and 'Gender' Following the Gender Recognition Act,' *Sociological Research Online*, 12(1), 2007. (www.socresonline.org.uk/12/1/whittle.html.)

WHAT WE BELIEVE

Twitter

1 MARCH 2020

Dear academics,

What we believe:

1. That humans are unambiguously either male or female in well over 99% of cases.[1]

2. That female people exist as a sex class.

3. That female people exist as a sex class because they are subject to structural oppression on the basis of sex.

4. That female people have been historically subjected to oppression on the basis of their sex because male people have positioned them as both a reproductive and sexual resource (i.e. because of their bodies), and secondarily, as a domestic and emotional resource.

5. That gender is the name for the totality of the system which maintains female people in a subordinate position as a sex class.

This includes:

- The coding of personality traits as proper to a sex.
- Sex roles in terms of appropriate behaviour and domestic and social roles.
- Hierarchies of status applied to both of these.
- Inculcated modes of entitlement and lack of entitlement, assertion and boundary-drawing, beliefs about whose needs are prioritized and who is supposed to provide care.

---

[1] For a more detailed discussion of the intellectual development and critique of arguments used to undermine the material reality of sex, please see my essay 'The History of Sex: Sex Denial and Gender Identity Ideology,' forthcoming in *Sex and Gender: A Contemporary Reader*, edited by Alice Sullivan and Selina Todd (London: Routledge).

- The use of male violence to enforce all the above, especially in the mode of aggrieved entitlement when male people do not get their expected needs met by females.
- The gendering of a whole hierarchical edifice of binary cultural values (mind over body, reason over emotion, ideas over matter, etc.).
- The construction of subjecthood as a form of absolute sovereignty. The belief that you exist outside relation and social and material dependence. The belief that your identity belongs to you and is not a material and social process.
- Only, finally, and superficially…whether you have long hair, wear nail-varnish, like pink, or have a fondness for glitter.

6. Because sex is the axis of our oppression, we object to efforts by trans ideologues to stop us describing the world in terms of sex.

We object to being denied the right to think and speak and organize *using the analysis we have developed of our own oppression.*

We object to being told that because male people want female people to stop using words for sex, that we do as we are fucking told.

We object to being demonized because we refuse to comply.

We object to civic institutions and law-making authorities and universities dictating that we have no legitimate interest in the political definition of 'woman,' and no legitimate interest in the words to describe the material reality of our own oppression.

We will not accept or be coerced into accepting the political erasure of sex, the political erasure of the recognition of female people in law, the rights and protections afforded to us on that basis, the removal of the words that describe the historical reality of our oppression, or our right to organize politically in order to advocate for our interests.

Asking—no, *demanding*—on pain of extreme sanction, that we do so falls so far beyond the purview of 'being kind' that it makes my head explode and my blood boil simultaneously.

7. Please explain, in a manner befitting our profession, why female people should accept the political erasure of the axis of their own oppression.

Without calling us names or telling us to 'be kind.'

WHAT IS AT STAKE

janeclarejones.com
SEPTEMBER 2018

Author's Note: A good deal of work has been done on elaborating and evidencing many of the issues raised in this piece since it was originally written. For this edition, I have included some supporting references that were not available at the time of writing.[1]

The core thesis of transgender ideology, as expressed by veteran trans rights activist Stephen Whittle, is that "to be a man or a woman is contained in a person's gender identity" (p. 28) and is *not*, therefore, a matter of one's biological sex. This thesis rests on two fundamental belief complexes:

- *Sex denial:* The view that the classification of humans into male and female types is a cultural construct that is in some way arbitrary.
- *Gender identity essentialism:* The view that whether someone is a 'man' or a 'woman' resides only in their innate, internal sense of 'gender identity,' and that a male person with a gender identity of 'woman' is therefore a woman in fundamentally the same way as a female person is (providing she 'identifies as a woman').

This thought that women and trans women share a fundamental identity is encapsulated in the slogan 'Trans Women Are Women.' It is critical to understanding this debate to grasp that the ideology of the present trans right movement considers self-identification of gender identity to be the sole criterion of whether someone is a man or a woman. A man does not necessarily have to take cross-sex hormones or undergo sex-reassignment surgery to be considered a woman. He simply has to assert that he *identifies* as one.

Leaving momentarily aside the staggering batshittery of the idea that the existence and recognition of human sexual difference is somehow arbitrary. (Burble burble spectrum burble intersex burble burble clownfish burble burble.) And the fact that the erasure of bodies—and specifically *women's* bodies—is the most patriarchal-immortality-project-death-cult-on-crack idea

---

[1] This piece was originally published on *janeclarejones.com* as 'Appendix' to 'Gay Right and Trans Rights: A Compare and Contrast.' It has been rewritten in places for this edition to reflect further clarification of my analysis of the structure of trans ideology.

I have seen in my *entire life*, this has such terrible political and practical implications that it completely fries my brain.

IMPLICATIONS FOR WOMEN

1. If a woman is 'whoever identifies as a woman,' then the **concept of 'woman' is redefined from an objective biological state to a subjective state which has no agreed upon definition.** There are many practical implications of this, but even were there not, it seems to me evident that women have a legitimate right to have opinions about changing the definition of the political and legal class to which we belong.

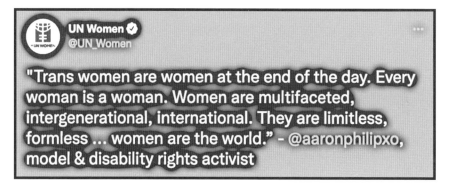

UN Women ✓
@UN_Women

"Trans women are women at the end of the day. Every woman is a woman. Women are multifaceted, intergenerational, international. They are limitless, formless ... women are the world." - @aaronphilipxo, model & disability rights activist

Trans ideologues often claim that redefining women has no impact on us. Which is false. One of the most contentious aspects of this redefinition is calling women 'cis'—which is purportedly 'just descriptive' of someone who is 'not trans.' However, according to transgender ideology, 'trans' is defined as 'someone whose gender identity does not match their sex assigned at birth,' while 'cis,' conversely, is 'someone whose gender identity matches their sex assigned at birth.' There is nothing 'just descriptive' about this. It demands both the acceptance that sex is 'assigned' rather than 'observed and recorded,' and the acceptance that we all have a 'gender identity,' despite the fact that a) 'gender identity' does not meaningfully describe our own experience of being women, and b) we have serious political objections to it.

The concept of 'cis' also does political work to posit 'cis-privileged' women as the 'oppressors' of trans women, and hence to nullify our claims that we are an oppressed class and have a legitimate right to exclude members of the oppressor class in certain instances—a right that is recognized by the single-sex exemptions enshrined in the 2010 Equality Act. The political stakes embedded in women accepting the designation 'cis' are pretty quickly manifested whenever a woman refuses it. (Self-determination and identification are a sacred right for trans women apparently, but no such right is granted to women—for whom the act of self-determination is apparently a hate crime). A particularly notable example of this happened on Twitter recently, when the gay and lesbian icon and general national treasure Alison Moyet[2] declared that she was not 'cis' and was relentlessly piled on and scolded for the temerity of thinking she had a right to self-define.

2. Changing the definition of woman to something that is subjective **undermines the class of women as a conceptual, legal and political category.** Moreover, trans activism demands that 'woman' or words associated with 'woman' never be used in a manner that is 'exclusive' of trans women or not 'inclusive' of trans men, that is, that the word 'woman' is never used to refer to a biological class.[3] The practical upshot of this demand to change language so that it's 'inclusive'[4] has been the erasure of the word 'woman,' and the decomposition of female people into body parts and functions. The Green Party has started calling us 'non-men,' pregnant women become 'pregnant people,' people who have periods become 'menstruators,' women become 'uterus-havers.' This is dehumanizing, othering, and an erasure of women which conceals the structure and reasons for the historic oppression of the class of reproductive persons, and our ability to politically organize to resist that oppression. Gender oppression, sexism, and misogyny, are not incidentally related to women's biology, and are not simply unmotivated 'bad attitudes' towards women that can be remedied by just changing our language. Erasing women as a political class is also an absolute gift for misogynist lefty dude-bros who have been waiting for the last however-many-years to have a reason to tell uppity feminist women to STFU whenever they make a claim about the oppression of women. Now they can just tell us we don't exist—and are being super-oppressive by insisting we do—while burnishing their woke-halos. So, thanks for that.[5]

3. Further, it is a central point of feminist analysis that women are oppressed on the basis of their sex, and because of male investment in appropriating and controlling women's reproductive capacities as a resource. If you cannot name sex, and you decide that naming sex is a hate crime, you effectively **make the feminist analysis of women's oppression unsayable.** Trans ideology has a tendency to claim that we don't need a sex-based analysis of women's oppression, and indeed sometimes to imply that the only possible reason women invented sex-based analysis was to exclude trans women. The utter narcissism of this—not to mention the time-travelling loopiness of

---

[2] Brendan O'Neill, 'Trans Activism Is Now Just Misogyny in Drag,' *Spiked Online*, 10 July 2018.
[3] 'Erasing Female Biology,' *terfisaslur.com*.
[4] Deborah Cameron, 'The Illusion of Inclusion,' *Language: A Feminist Guide*, 5 August 2018.
[5] Jeni Harvey, 'Dear Men on the Left,' *Medium*, 17 November 2017.

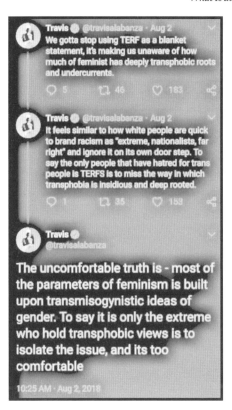

it—is almost beyond comprehension. Hey, guess what, people, maybe we invented feminist analysis for our own liberation, and maybe what you're doing is trying to turn our analysis of our own oppression into hate speech, and maybe we have every right to tell you we're not having it?

4. Following from this is **the importance for feminist analysis of statistical data that tracks the sex-based oppression of women.**[6] The most extreme forms of trans activism are demanding that there should be no statistical documentation of sex except for medical purposes. This would make it impossible for us to say anything about the pay gap, or women's political representation, or violence against women, with any degree of authority. The crimes of males who identify as women are also already being recorded as women's crimes.[7] This has serious implications for the feminist analysis of male-pattern violence. There are also important questions about whether male-born and -socialized people stop committing male-pattern crimes simply because they say they are women.[8]

5. It is impossible to enshrine both gender identity and sex in law as protected characteristics because they are in conflict. I'm not big on 'either/or' thinking because it spatializes and excludes things that are often not spatialized and exclusive. But weirdly, when we are dealing with access to spaces, things *are*

---

[6] A lot of work has been done on this issue subsequent to the writing of this piece, see for example Alice Sullivan, 'Sex and the Census: Why Surveys Should Not Conflate Sex and Gender Identity,' *International Journal of Social Research Methodology*, 23(5), 2020, pp. 517-524, and Jane Clare Jones and Lisa Mackenzie, *The Political Erasure of Sex: Sex and the Census*, October 2020. (www.thepoliticalerasureofsex.org.)

[7] 'These Are Not Our Crimes,' *YouTube*. (www.youtube.com/watch?v=9NpIy-0_esU.)

[8] Rosa Freedman, Kathleen Stock, and Alice Sullivan, 'Evidence and Data on Trans Women's Offending Rates,' Submission to Women and Equalities Select Committee, November 2020. (www.committees.parliament.uk/writtenevidence/18973/pdf.)

spatialized, and they are 'either/or.' *Either* access to spaces is determined on the basis of sex, *or* it's determined on the basis of self-declared gender identity. In the last case, untransitioned male-bodied people will have access to women's space, and **female only space will cease to exist.** It's really that simple.

This will affect toilets, girls and women's changing rooms, rape crisis centres and domestic violence shelters, prisons and women's sports—places that contain partially undressed women, women asleep, and vulnerable women who have experienced a high incidence of male violence. Trans advocates are fond of claiming that our fears about male violence are unfounded and hysterical, or that we think all trans women are perverts or predators. On this point, let's note that if you find yourself in the constant position of telling feminist women that their analysis of male violence and their desires to be protected from male violence are unfounded and hysterical because, y'know, women are violent too, you really should ask yourself: a) why you're using arguments from the MRA-playbook, and b) whether there might be some reason we're not sure you're such great feminist allies.

Trans activists' latest line on this is that we are 'conflating' the proposed new Gender Recognition Act with the Equality Act—because apparently laws exist in total isolation from each other and do not interact.[9] This is all subterfuge and backtracking. Woman's Place UK has compiled a list of trans activist calls to remove the single-sex exemptions from the Equality Act.[10] The present crop of trans activists want access to women's space as a matter of political priority and they seem to give not one shit about whether it exposes women to danger or reactivates their trauma. Let's just be clear about this—women's single-sex spaces do not exist to affirm or validate people's identity. They exist to *meet the needs of women* for privacy or safety or healing from male violence. And refusing to recognize this is a very clear instance of the divergence between women and trans women's interests.

6. This points us towards a more general problem about the **conflict between women's and trans women's political interests.** This is of particular importance with respect to trans women's participation in feminism and their capacity to represent women politically. There has been a ton of talk over the last five or so years about 'trans-inclusive' and 'trans-exclusive' feminism (lo, summon the EVIL TERF). To this, I mostly want to say... feminism is not

---

[9] Rebecca Bull, 'Briefing Note: Impact of Gender Recognition Reform on Sex Based Rights,' *MurrayBlackburnMackenzie*, February 2020. (www.mbmpolicy.files.wordpress.com/2020/02/impact-of-gender-recognition-on-sex-based-rights.-r-bull-11-feb-2020.pdf.)

[10] Woman's Place UK, 'Evidence of Calls to Remove Single Sex Exemptions from Equality Act,' 25 June 2018. (www.womansplaceuk.org/references-to-removal-of-single-sex-exemptions.)

a fucking girl's club. It's a political movement with political objectives and established forms of political analysis. You are welcome to ally yourself with our political projects. You are not, however, welcome to demand access to our political movement, and *then* demand we change our political project and analysis because you find it 'alienating.'

We do a lot of work on reproductive justice, and female bodily autonomy, and reclaiming women's bodies from the darkness and shame that patriarchy has cast them into for millennia, and you may be surprised to discover we don't much fancy casting them back into that darkness because it unsettles your identity and you want to rub out the political relevance of our bodies. It is not even vaguely reasonable to demand this—especially given that we have a long history of understanding why the erasure of embodiment is patriarchy's ground zero. (And it's not an accident Mumsnet is gender-critical central: people who have made and fed other people with their bodies are strangely resistant to the idea that bodies are an irrelevance). We also do a fuckton of work on male violence, which, as we saw above, trans activists have a specific interest in side-lining. The fact that Lily Madigan, in their purported capacity as a Labour Party Woman's Officer, was interested only in shouting 'transphobia' at feminists concerned about women being sexually assaulted by male-bodied people in prison basically tells you the whole story about the non-coincidence of women's and trans activists' interests with respect to male violence. A trans women who is committed to the present formulation of trans ideology is not, therefore, capable of representing the political interests of women. (See 'Female Class Politics,' p. 64.)

IMPLICATIONS FOR FEMINISM AND GENDER-NON-CONFORMING PEOPLE

7. In addition to the erasure of the material reality of sex, **trans ideology is also committed to an essentialist theory of gender.**[11] In this regard trans ideology inverts feminist thought. Feminism thinks sex is real and gender is a social construct that functions as a hierarchy to hold the structure of patriarchal oppression in place. Trans ideology think sex is a social construct and that gender identity is real. What the 'realness' of this identity consists of is undefined. There is the assertion that transgender people have the brains of one sex trapped in the body of another sex—and it should be clear why feminists would raise eyebrows about beliefs in blue and pink brains. There is also the issue that it is entirely unclear how anyone could have an 'internal sense of their own gender' that is not informed in any way by patriarchal gender roles, and which did not amount to the reification of patriarchal gender conventions.

Despite trans ideologues' protestations that there is a distinction between 'gender identity' and 'gender expression,' the un-pin-down-ability of 'gender identity' as a concept—and the inability to define it without reference to gender norms—means that, in practice, trans identity frequently comes to be evidenced by gender-non-conforming behaviour. As we will see below, this is particularly the case in much of the testimony around the identification of 'transgender children.' It is also evident in trans-ing of the gender-non-conforming dead—both gay and straight. (And, people, you cannot both claim the criterion is an internal sense of gender evidenced by self-declaration and then simultaneously trans dead men who never self-identified as trans just because they wore high heels and eyeliner. Which is to say, back away from Prince. Now.)[12]

There are several implications of this:

a) It **serves to naturalize and reinforce patriarchal gender roles.** Trans ideology likes to claim it is challenging patriarchal gender norms. What it is actually doing is saying that everyone who does not conform to patriarchal gender norms is a different 'type' of person and putting them in a separate category. The boxes '(cisgender) man' and '(cisgender) woman' are thus left for the gender-conforming. It does not shatter the gender conventions of the patriarchal definition of 'man' to say that all men who manifest femininity

---

[11] Rebecca Reilly-Cooper, 'Gender Is Not a Spectrum,' *Aeon*, 28 June 2016.
[12] Meghan Murphy, 'Prince Was Not Trans, He Is Proof That Men Need Not Be Masculine,' *Feminist Current*, 23 April 2016.

are thereby not men. It is, in fact, a re-inscription of the definition of patri-archal masculinity as a repudiation of the feminine, and it's conservative as hell.

b) Given that **the gender conventions associated with patriarchal ideas of women are oppressive** and frequently restrict our agency, voices, sub-jectivity, movement, and ability to occupy space or express our needs, rede-fining women as people who 'identify with gender' is harmful to us.

c) Trans-identification often involves putting people on a medical pathway. Changing the criterion of 'being trans' from experiencing sex dysphoria to identifying with 'gender'—especially given the way many young people have been exposed to trans ideology through social media over recent years—is leading to **the medicalization of gender non-conformity** in young peo-ple.

IMPLICATIONS FOR CHILDREN, ESPECIALLY HOMOSEXUAL CHIL-DREN, ESPECIALLY LESBIAN GIRLS

8. Over the last five years there has been a dramatic increase in referrals of young people to gender clinics. The impact of trans ideology on clinical prac-tice—and how this also affects social workers, teachers, mental health ser-vices, and other services that work with young people—has shifted from an approach based on 'watchful waiting' to one based on immediately affirm-ing a child's trans identity, and making moves towards transition, includ-ing prescribing puberty blockers and cross-sex hormones. Previous to this change, the clinical opinion was that most gender-dysphoric children and teens would desist from cross-sex identification by adulthood, and usually grow up to be gay and lesbian. The push to medicalize trans-identifying chil-dren thus constitutes **the medicalization of homosexual children**, in a manner which, effectively, straightens them out.[13]

9. The figures from the UK Gender Identity Service at the Tavistock suggest that a **disproportionate number of the increased referrals of young people are female.**[14] The fact that until recently most cases of trans identi-fication was in males, means that this imbalance is particularly concerning.

---

[13] For further discussion about the potential harms to gender-non-conforming children, see Helen Joyce, *Trans: When Ideology Meets Reality* (London: OneWorld Books, 2021).

[14] 'From Adult Males to Teenage Girls: The Movement from Etiology to Ideology,' *Transgender Trend*, 29 June 2017. (www.transgendertrend.com/from-adult-males-to-teenage-girls-the-movement-from-etiology-to-ideology.)

Were it the case that the recent de-stigmatization of trans identity was simply making it possible for existent trans kids to 'become their authentic selves,' there would be no reason why there would be such a stark increase in the number of female children seeking to transition. Testimony from concerned parents, and from some female desisters, lends support to the new phenomenon known as Rapid-Onset Gender Dysphoria[15]—in which a child who has previously shown no evidence of trans identity announces they are trans, often after spending a great deal of time on the Internet, and often in association with other underlying issues, such as depression, anxiety, social isolation, eating disorders, and, especially, autism.

Feminists would argue that it is imperative to recognize that entering puberty in a patriarchy is, in itself, a traumatic experience for many girls[16] because it involves the experience of your body becoming a sexual object and a target of violence. This, along with the sexual abuse it often occasions, is a significant factor in many of the disorders that affect teenage girls, and it is readily comprehensible to us why teenage girls would be attracted to the idea of avoiding this traumatizing process and regaining control of their bodies by presenting as male. We are not, however, convinced that medicalizing girls is an ideal solution to the trauma of patriarchal violence, especially under conditions in which providing them with alternative feminist analyses that could illuminate their distress has been rendered a thoughtcrime.

IMPLICATIONS FOR LESBIANS

10. Given the power imbalances between men and women, the gay rights movement has been historically weighted towards the representation of the interests of gay men. This tendency is now exacerbated by the fact that the gay rights movement has wedded itself to a political ideology invested in both refusing recognition to female people as a group and refusing to recognize that some people are exclusively same-sex attracted, as opposed to 'same-gender' attracted. The consequence of this is that **many lesbians now feel that the LGBTQI+ movement is no longer their home,**[17] and will not defend their existence as women, their identity as lesbians, and the political interests that follow from that. This was the issue behind the recent protest

---

[15] Lisa Littman, 'Parent reports of adolescents and young adults perceived to show signs of a rapid onset of gender dysphoria,' *Plos One*, 16 August 2018. (doi.org/10.1371/journal.pone.0202330.)

[16] Glosswitch, 'Anorexia, Breast Binding and the Legitimisation of Body Hatred,' *New Statesman*, 24 August 2016.

[17] Danielle Cormier, 'Lesbians Are Being Excluded from the Vancouver Dyke March in the Name of 'Inclusivity,' *Feminist Current*, 13 August 2018.

at London Pride[18] in which lesbian women disrupted the start of the march with banners proclaiming 'Lesbian = Female Homosexual' and 'Transactivism Erases Lesbians.'[19] Both of which are true statements.

One of the main issues here is that there has been a marked tendency over recent years[20] for certain trans women—who previously identified as heterosexual males and remain attracted to women—to redefine themselves as lesbians, even when they are still male-bodied, and to suggest that lesbian women who will not accept them as sexual partners are guilty of discriminatory transphobia.[21] This is, firstly, a ridiculous attempt to legislate people's sexual choices, and to make acts of sexual discrimination equivalent to acts of political discrimination.[22] This is, moreover, a refusal to recognize the existence of homosexuality *as such*, which, in itself, amounts to a profound act of political erasure. And lastly, it absolutely reeks of the kind of rapey male sexual entitlement that patriarchy breeds into straight men. If you want to convince someone that you are a) a woman and b) a lesbian, I assure you that attempting to shame, bully, or otherwise coerce women into having sex with you is about the most ineffective method you could devise in a million years.

> **Homosexual**
>
> This might be considered a more medical term used to describe someone who has a romantic and/or sexual orientation towards someone of the same gender. The term 'gay' is now more generally used.

From Stonewall's 'List of LGBTQ+ Terms'

---

[18] 'Pride in London Sorry after Anti-Trans Protest,' *BBC News Online*, 8 July 2016.

[19] Pippa Fleming, 'The Gender-Identity Movement Undermines Lesbians,' *The Economist*, 3 July 2018.

[20] Get the L Out, 'Shame Receipts.' (www.lesbian-rights-nz.org/shame-receipts.)

[21] Caroline Lowbridge, 'We're being pressured into sex by some trans women,' *BBC News Online*, 26 October 2021.

[22] Magdalen Burns, 'Re: 'Are Genital Preferences Transphobic?' Give it Up, Riley,' *YouTube*. (www.youtube.com/watch?v=F_5FFGrGzJw.)

PATRIARCHY 101

Twitter

18 APRIL 2021

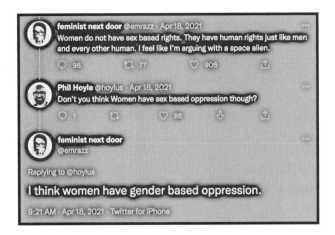

feminist next door @emrazz · Apr 18, 2021
Women do not have sex based rights. They have human rights just like men and every other human. I feel like I'm arguing with a space alien.

98   77   906

Phil Hoyle @hoylus · Apr 18, 2021
Don't you think Women have sex based oppression though?

1   86

feminist next door
@emrazz
Replying to @hoylus
I think women have gender based oppression.

9:21 AM · Apr 18, 2021 · Twitter for iPhone

Women are oppressed *by* gender *on the basis* of sex. How are people so fucking confused?

Let's do Patriarchy 101, shall we?

Patriarchy is a system of *male dominance.*

In this system male people hold most of the power and wealth. In this system, very importantly, we also privilege the needs and interests of male people over those of female people.

The feminist analysis of this situation is that society is structured to serve the interests of males. A significant part of these interests involves positioning female people as a *resource* for males. This includes serving as a reproductive and sexual resource, as well as the exploitation of female people's domestic and emotional labour.

That women have certain reproductive capacities, and that men want to have reproductive and sexual access to women is FUNDAMENTAL to why this system evolved and why men *still have an interest* in maintaining it.

That is, male dominance over women is entirely non-accidentally related to the fact that men want access to WOMEN'S BODIES.

That is, it is SEX-based. And that is why large parts of the system of dominance pertain directly to access to women's bodies or to controlling women's sexuality—abortion, prostitution, surrogacy, sexual violence, female genital mutilation, arranged marriage, etc., etc.

GENDER is the system of sex-based roles AND values that function to position female people as a compliant service class to male needs.

This works through socialization, which rewards female compliance and punishes women who step outside our gender roles. It also involves the entire structure of male violence, which is not a bunch of 'isolated incidents' but is actually an interlocking system for policing women's compliance. (Men don't necessarily understand it like this, they are acting on the basis of inculcated entitlement to women and 'aggrieved entitlement' when they don't get what they think they are entitled to.)

Frankly, I don't even know what you think it means to say women's oppression is 'gender-based.'

Gender is the *mechanism* of women's oppression.

Gender harms women *whether they conform to it or rebel against it.* And female people are subjected to this mechanism *because they are female, and because the mechanism aims at converting them into a resource for males.*

It is true that other gender-non-conforming people get caught in this mechanism, because the mechanism polices both masculinity in males and femininity in females, but that is a side effect of a system structured by male interests in controlling female *bodies.*

I really really want people talking about 'gender-based oppression' to explain:

1. What this actually means with respect to the oppression of female people. Are we oppressed because of how we do gender? Is there a way to do gender that would stop us being oppressed? Can we stop ourselves being the target of male control by doing it differently? Isn't this victim-blaming?

2. Why women are oppressed. Because I have seen no evidence you have a theory of patriarchy that makes any sense.

3. Why gender norms evolved and what function they serve.

> Feminism is a social movement that fights for the equality of all people. Feminists believe that people of all and no genders are equal and should be treated as such. It is also inclusive of all races, religions, cultures, ages etc. You do not have to be a woman to be a feminist.

'Glossary' at *thefamilysexshow.com*.

Because the bottom line is that you are telling us that we must consent to a form of 'feminism' that makes no analytic sense whatsofuckingever, and, moreover, looks a lot like you have somehow decided that the function of feminism is to centre the needs of male people, and for women to compliantly perform their service function, which, um, would actually be nothing more than a performance of the core of patriarchal femininity.

SMASHING THE GENDER BINARY

Twitter

9 MARCH 2022

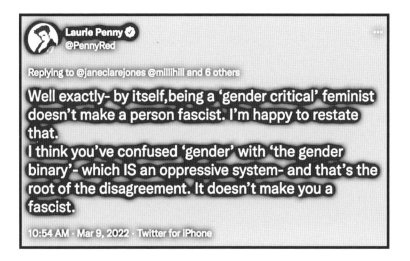

Laurie Penny ✓
@PennyRed

Replying to @janeclarejones @millihill and 6 others

Well exactly– by itself,being a 'gender critical' feminist doesn't make a person fascist. I'm happy to restate that.
I think you've confused 'gender' with 'the gender binary'– which IS an oppressive system– and that's the root of the disagreement. It doesn't make you a fascist.

10:54 AM · Mar 9, 2022 · Twitter for iPhone

Okay, gender is a long-standing feminist concept that denotes the roles and values attached to people of either sex. Second-wave feminism has always considered it to be oppressive, and to be the mechanism of the exploitation of female people.

'The gender binary' is a concept that did not exist until the 1990s and derives principally from the work of Judith Butler. There isn't a coherent account of what 'the gender binary' is and it relies on the conflation of sex/gender, because Butler thinks gender *produces* the perception of sex.

What is expressed by the idea of 'the gender binary' is that what is oppressive is *thinking there are two sexes/genders* and that thinking this is patriarchy.

By this thinking, it's not the gender roles that are oppressive in themselves, it's simply thinking that the roles can only be performed by people of certain sexes.

So, if males can 'woman' and females can 'man' and you add a whole load of extra genders, then everything is all lovely and gender-binary-free, and there's no more oppression.

Just as long as those boring 'cis' women carry on doing most of the reproductive labour and shit work. But they're just gender-conforming and probably are totes okay with it.

What's forgotten here is that gender *exists* to exploit women, and they are exploited by it especially *when* they are gender-conforming. THAT'S WHAT IT'S FOR.

The injunction against being gender-non-conforming is to keep this system propped up, and especially to make sure women carry on fulfilling the 'service' role and men carry on fulfilling the 'dominance' role.

People are discriminated against for being GNC. Women are oppressed for being female.

It is NOT the case that the fundamental structure of patriarchy is 'just stopping people being GNC' because women are oppressed *when they are gender-conforming.*

It is also not the case that by just swapping out which sexed bodies perform which role you have done anything fundamental to undermine the system.

You haven't challenged the roles. You have just decided some people get to opt out or switch.

That reinforces the roles for those who do not opt out and leaves the exploitation of women that those roles facilitate unchanged.

This is especially true given that the people who buy this system have an extremely superficial grasp of how gender works, and have completely forgotten the role it plays in propping up the system of material exploitation.

For them, gender is basically reduced to its performative aesthetic dimensions, and their thinking ends up coming down to the absurd proposition that if males are allowed to perform aesthetic femininity and call themselves women then patriarchy is over.

And they then stick their fingers in their ears and go *lahlahlah* when we repeatedly point out that this will actually do fuck all to alleviate the material exploitation of female people's bodies and labour. Which is what patriarchy is actually about. (P.S. It's not an accident Butler's system does this. She's not remotely interested in the exploitation of female people, or in their experiences of sexual violence. She's interested in the harms to gender-non-conforming people. Fair enough. But that's why queer theory isn't feminism.)

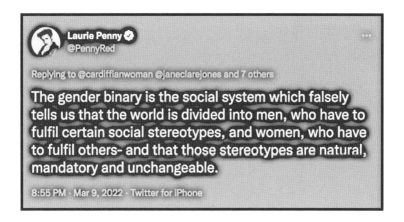

You see, this is where it all goes squiffy.

'Gender' is not the belief that there are men and women, it is the belief that males/men have to do 'man things' and women/females have to do 'woman things.'

Using the concept of 'the gender binary'—instead of the second-wave concept of 'gender'—makes people believe that *the problem is thinking that there ARE men and women*. It conflates the idea of 'male/man/person who does man things' and 'female/woman/person who does woman things,' and now we have a whole generation brainwashed on Tumblr who believe that 'a person who does woman things' IS a woman and a 'female person who doesn't do woman things' IS NOT a woman.

Which is a) bonkers, and b) actually ESSENTIALIZES gender.

The problem is *not* thinking that there *are* men and women.

The problem is thinking men and women have to behave in certain ways.

BOTH / AND: GENDER

The Radical Notion Issue Two

WINTER 2021

There is probably no word in English currently as contested, and as mired in confusion and conflation, as 'gender.' From its origin in linguistics, the term has evolved to be used, variously, as:

a) A polite euphemism for sex (thanks, American puritanism!),

b) To denote the 'masculinity' or 'femininity' of an individual, often taken as a natural property of their being,

c) To describe the hierarchical system of sex-roles, values and status which subordinates women, that is, as the mechanism of patriarchy,

d) As a social identity constituted through repetitive performance of stylized gendered acts or behaviours, which, notably, is also taken to constitute sex, and,

e) As an inner, innate identity, which probably has something to do with sexed brains, or gendered souls, or something ('it's science!'), and which is taken to determine whether someone should be considered male/a man, female/a woman, or, maddeningly, neither.

It would take several volumes to make a decent stab at disentangling this unmitigated mess. My more modest aim here is to begin thinking through how we should best understand the interaction of nature and culture in radical feminist, gender-critical, or gender-abolitionist accounts, and start unpacking how that differs from, on the one hand, conservative notions of gender and, on the other, trans-ideological accounts.

GENDER: NATURE VS. CULTURE?

Traditional or conservative accounts of gender—which existed long before gender was even a concept—consist of the view that males are masculine and do masculine things and females are feminine and do feminine things. They do these things because that's how God and/or Nature made them, and it follows, 'naturally,' therefore, that if men do feminine things and women do masculine things, something unnatural, unholy, and quite possibly sinful is going on. While this is—from a traditional feminist perspective—usually regarded as a conservative account, it is probably fair to say that, when they are not using it as an awkward euphemism for sex, most people's concept of gender comes down to some general thought of male = masculine and female = feminine, and that under the aegis of unstoppable capitalist 'pinkification,' this is probably far more true now than it was in the '70s and '80s, when at least some people seemed to grasp what feminists might be on about.

Because of the alleged givenness of the equations male = masculine and female = feminine, when feminists came to challenge this system, and implicate it in the subordination of women, they addressed themselves directly to the question of whether gender was 'natural.' "One is not born, but rather becomes, a woman," wrote Beauvoir famously, followed immediately by "No biological, psychological, or economic fate determines the figure that the human female [*note!*] presents in society."[1] In her foundational analysis of the *Sexual Politics* of male dominance, Kate Millett partitions gender into 'temperament, role and status,' and likewise maintains that "it must be admitted that many of the generally understood distinctions between the sexes in... role and temperament, not to mention status, have in fact, essentially cultural, rather than biological, bases."[2] "New research," she continues, "suggests that the possibilities of innate temperamental differences seem more remote than ever" and "gives fairly concrete positive evidence of the overwhelmingly *cultural* character of gender, i.e. personality structure in terms of sexual category" (p. 29). Thus, the analysis of the 'social construction of gender' was born, and, back when words still meant what they meant, 'biological determinism' and 'essentialism' became the cardinal feminist sins.

The problem with all this, of course, is that it seems to commit the analysis of male dominance to 'blank slatism,' that is, to the denial that humans have innate temperamental dispositions (if not full personalities), and more specifically, the denial that some of those temperamental dispositions might have something to do with sex. Given that anyone who has met a human infant for more than five minutes will testify that they blatantly have at least rudimentary personalities, this is all a bit implausible. This is made more implausible still given that we know that males and females have different ratios of sex hormones, that hormones are chemicals, and that human consciousness is manifestly impacted by certain types of chemicals, of which hormones are one group. The very existence of 'organic psychoactive chemicals' then points us to a further problem, one already recognized by the feminist analysis of patriarchal metaphysical dualism. That analysis commits us, correctly I think, to denying the neat, hierarchical bifurcation of mind from body, and of culture from nature, which would then seem to

---

[1] Simone de Beauvoir, *The Second Sex*, translated by H. M. Parshley (Middlesex: Penguin Modern Classics, 1983), p. 295.
[2] Kate Millett, *Sexual Politics* (New York: Columbia University Press, 1969), p. 28.

scupper—and much contemporary 'feminism' has run with this, mostly in the wrong direction (hi Judy!)—the sex/gender distinction, on which the 'social construction of gender' argument rests. This is all then, to use a technical phrase, a fucking mess.

To unpick this mess, I want to stop and do a bit of metaphysics, of the type that basically inspired the thought for 'Both/And' as a regular feature in *The Radical Notion*. The human intellect is *spatializing*, which makes sense, seeing as it first developed to help us recognize spatial objects and navigate through space. What this means, however, is that we have an annoying—and distorting—tendency, to *view concepts like they are solid objects*, and the pertinent property of solid objects here is that they can't be *both* one thing *and* another thing *at the same time*. Hence, when we come to think about a concept like 'gender,' we tend to think it must be *either* all one thing *or* all another thing: in this case, that it must be *either* all nature *or* all culture. Which is, um, *stupid.*[3]

To flesh this out a bit, let's look at the various different levels of the gender system in the table overleaf. The first thing to note is that the apparently 'simple' equations male = masculine and female = feminine are not actually so simple at all. The traditional or conservative view includes the thought that certain gendered characteristics arise 'naturally' in each sex (Level 1), *plus* the thought that those characteristics are *proper* to each sex (Level 2). It also includes, usually, the thought that the social roles of each sex just arise naturally directly from the characteristics (Level 5) as does the distribution of status, power and value (Level 6 and 7), and tends to skip neatly over, and dismiss as irrelevant, the entirety of socialization (Level 3 and 4).

There are several things to unpack here. Firstly, contra Millett, it may well be the case that some of the conventionally gendered personality traits, or temperaments, are very loosely distributed by sex (feminist thoughtcrime!). I am, for example, prepared to accept the suggestion, say, that female

---

[3] It is this type of spatializing either/or thinking, which explains why we are also extremely bad at thinking about the relation between binary poles. We tend to flip-flop between poles: 'either it's nature, or it's culture, or it's nature, or it's culture!' When we work out that this is stupid, rather than then thinking it is probably *both* nature *and* culture, we then often decide, because we can't draw a clean line between them (as we could if they were spatial objects), that the poles therefore don't exist and they should be completely collapsed into each other, which, by erasing the existence of one pole, then just reinstates the hierarchy. This is also stupid. It is in fact exactly the type of stupid that leads Judith Butler to collapse sex into gender in *Gender Trouble*, proclaim everything is 'discourse all the way down,' and destroy the sex/gender distinction because that's going to work out great for everyone, thanks. This is how the misconceptions around 'deconstructing binaries'—which should lead to understanding that it's *both* body *and* mind, nature *and* culture, matter *and* idea—have actually resulted in the reinstatement of the patriarchal hierarchy of mind/culture/idea *over* body/nature/matter. (See 'Poststructuralism, Butler, and Bodies,' p. 88, and 'A Note on 'Smashing the Binary,'' p. 113.)

humans have a tendency to be more relational, linguistic, and person-ori-
ented, and male humans have a tendency to be more spatializing, mechanistic, and object-oriented. Something like this would account for *some*, but not
all, of the characteristics subdivided under the first level of our table. It does
not explain, for example, why 'acceptable emotions' should be sexed, why
female people should be thought of as passive, or why male humans and not
female humans get garments with adequate pockets. I think it's important,
however, to accept that there might be some natural distribution of personality traits, and that this might have something to do with organic factors,
such as exposure to hormones in utero.

The first reason to accept this is that it's good intellectual practice to have
the most robust and accurate model that you can. And this is especially important right now, when we find ourselves facing down a tsunami of absolute
bullshit. Secondly, many of the arguments we are currently making about
the dangers of medicalizing gender-non-conforming children more or less
tacitly accept, because it is empirically the case, that gender non-conformity
in children is importantly correlated with adult homosexuality. That there
is a reliable association between gender non-conformity and homosexuality, that this persists from childhood into adulthood, and that it persists
in spite of social conditioning to the contrary, suggests to me that to some
degree or other, humans do have 'gendered' personality traits. The fact that
the phrases 'feminine man' and 'butch woman' *mean* something, and often
mean something with respect to physicality, as well as personality, further
suggests that there is something going on here not reducible to socialization.

From a conservative perspective, this would be game over—viz. 'gender
is natural'—but this is way too fast. By our table, the idea that gendered personality traits might be naturally distributed is only the first level—and the
thinnest conception—of what 'gender' is. The second level, the thought that
such traits are *proper* to each sex, and the system of socialization that inculcates, polices, and reinforces that thought of 'what is proper,' is by no means
'natural.' Social norms about what traits or behaviours are proper to each sex
are, by definition, just that, *social norms*. Moreover, the argument from the association between gender non-conformity and homosexuality I used above
to suggest that we should accept that 'gendered' personality traits might be
natural suggests that it is also evidently natural for those traits to be distributed in the putatively 'wrong' sex. If there are gendered personality traits,
they are distributed between the sexes in an extremely loose, overlapping,
bimodal-type way, and the vast majority of humans have a fairly good distribution of both types of gendered traits. That is, there is nothing 'natural'
about the idea that certain gendered traits are only *proper* to a particular sex,
or that the distribution of those traits needs to be socially policed.

The alleged properness of gendered traits—the thought we often express

	Levels of Gender System
I.	*Sex-role stereotypes: The distribution of characteristics coded as 'masculine' and 'feminine.' Including:*
	a) Personality traits, tastes, preferences
	b) Behaviours congruent with traits/emotions
	c) Aesthetic preferences and presentation
	d) Bodily comportment and vocal presentation
2.	*The belief that characteristics coded as 'masculine' and 'feminine' are **proper** to males and female respectively. Inversely, the belief that gender non-conformity—that is 'femininity' in males and 'masculinity' in women—is aberrant and wrong. **This is a social norm.** This norm leads to:*
3.	*The process of socialization through which proper gendered characteristics are inculcated in males and females. Achieved through 'gender policing,' i.e. punishing and rewarding in/correct traits and behaviours, funnelling individuals into correct gendered activities, and the massive cultural edifice of gendered coding, which begins with children's clothes and toys etc., runs through sex-roles, and extends right up to the hierarchy of metaphysical values.*
4.	*Taking 1-3 together, males are socialized to be active assertive subjects, while females are socialized to see themselves as passive/attractive objects and oriented to nurturing. Male socialization prizes strength and invulnerability and inculcates entitlement, while female socialization penalizes entitlement and inculcates service. I call this the 'deep structure of gender.'*
5.	*The distribution of appropriate social roles justified and enforced through gendered norms and socialization (1-4).*
6.	*The hierarchical distribution of wealth, social status and power, in accordance with these roles.*
7.	*The hierarchical distribution of value to all gendered characteristics up to and including cultural and metaphysical polarities.*

Masculine	Feminine
Active/Subject/Dominant	Passive/Object/Submissive
Active, aggressive, dominant, object-oriented, rational, adventurous, strong, competitive, stoic, independent, etc.	Passive, agreeable, kind, sweet, people-oriented, nurturing, emotional, social, domestic, weak, talkative, etc.
Rough physical activity, competitive sport, fighting, adventures, heroic quests, exploration, technical skill and mastery.	Passivity and compliance, domestic and nurturing activity, attracted to 'prettiness', concern with self-presentation.
Not unduly concerned with self-presentation. Clothes are generally utilitarian and designed to facilitate movement and activity.	Preoccupied with self-presentation. Clothes are elaborate and designed to accentuate attractiveness. Often compromise movement and activity.
Occupy and often 'spread out' into space. Move body as locus of agency and mastery. Direct assertive speech and eye contact.	Fold body up in order to minimize occupation of space. Do not fully use body to express agency. Speech and eye-contact expected to be hesitant/deferential.
Proper: Activity, aggressivity, competitiveness, reason, stoicism, strength, **invulnerability**. '*Hardness*.' '*Traits of subjectivity qua dominance.*' *Improper*: Weakness, emotionality, passivity, dependence, neediness, nurturing. '*Softness*.' '*The repudiation of the feminine.*'	*Proper*: Nurturing, emotionality, prettiness, passivity, selflessness, **compliance**. '*Softness*.' '*Traits of service.*' *Improper*: Rage, defiance, 'selfishness', assertion, intelligence, humour, ambition, power. '*Hardness*.' '*Traits of subjectivity*.'
'Boys don't cry.' 'Man up.' 'Don't be a sissy.' 'What a big strong boy you are.' 'This one is going to be a charmer.' All gendered coding of toys, clothes, activities etc. which reinforce that active, adventurous traits are good and proper to boys.	'That's not ladylike.' 'Aren't you pretty?' 'Smile!' 'You went and got yourself all dirty!' All gendered coding of toys, clothes, activities etc. which reinforce that domestic activity and passive prettiness, unicorns and sparkles are good and proper to girls.
Male socialization inculcates importance of *performing invulnerability* and the *experience, and expectation, of service by females* around material and dependency needs (physical, emotional, sexual). This fosters the illusion of invulnerable in-dependence from need, and hence *entitlement*, and *aggrieved entitlement* when thwarted by female non-compliance.	Expressions of sweetness and compliance are encouraged, assertions of needs discouraged as 'too demanding.' Thus, socialized into under-entitlement. Some rough-and-tumble 'tomboyism' usually tolerated, but frank expressions of desire, wilfulness, defiance, anger, intelligence and competence often either ignored/dismissed (at best) or provoke extreme hostility.
Men traditionally occupy high-status public and professional roles, as well as most roles which require manual or technical labour.	Women traditionally occupy private or domestic roles, or public roles in caring or service-based labour.
Males have traditionally been the property-owning class. The vast majority of wealth and social power is still accumulated in the hands of males, and they still occupy the majority of high-status/paid roles.	Females were traditionally barred from owning property. Women still do far more unpaid domestic labour than men, and disproportionately occupy low-status/paid roles. When an area of labour is 'feminized', its status and remuneration decrease.
Activity, strength, invulnerability, independence, solid, hardness, rationality, mind, culture, ideality, immateriality, universality, singularity, one, eternity, stasis, transcendence, sky/sun, light, civilized, human, white.	Passivity, weakness, vulnerability, dependence, penetrability, softness, emotion, body, nature, sensibility, materiality, particularity, plurality, many, change, process, immanence, earth, dark, primitive, animal, black.

by referring to gender as 'boxes'—and the associated mechanism of social-izing people *into* those boxes and punishing them when they digress, is far more key to the core mechanism of 'what gender is' than the thought that hu-mans might have natural personality traits, which is, in fact, evident. What this clarifies, I hope, is that commitment to 'gender abolitionism' does not then necessitate an untenable commitment to 'blank slatism.' The problem is not that humans have personalities, but that the natural distribution of those personalities means that most of them, to greater or lesser degrees, do not fit neatly into the gendered boxes, because the boxes—the thought that certain traits are proper only to one sex—are a bullshit social norm—one that serves social and political purposes. 'Gender abolition' is not, therefore, a wilful, ideologically naïve demand that humans erase their personalities or some such nonsense, but the demand that those personalities are allowed to develop free from gendered normativity.

The other important reason for framing things this way is that it proofs the feminist analysis of male dominance against the endless efforts by con-servatives to dismiss it by pointing at human personality traits and scream-ing 'they're natural.' Personality traits are natural, to some degree. What is emphatically not natural is thinking they are only, and *must be*, proper to each sex, and the entire structure of socialization and policing that props that up. If, indeed, the distribution of personality traits fell as neatly into their box-es as the conservative thought says they should, then the entire mechanism of socialization would be redundant, which it evidently is not. The function of socialization remains to reinforce the boxes, and, as feminism claims, to serve the social and political purposes of amplifying the hierarchy of male activity/dominance and female passivity/compliance.

Moreover, fundamental aspects of these boxes, particularly the image of patriarchal masculinity as a form of stoic invulnerability, manifestly fly in the face of 'nature.' Male humans are animals, and animals are not invul-nerable. The action of testosterone might make male animals more inclined to engage in risky behaviour, but it does nothing to protect them from being harmed by such actions. Nor does testosterone protect males from loss, grief, depression, need, dependence, or any of the manifold human experiences and emotions that patriarchal masculinity codes as 'weakness.' 'Patriarchal masculinity' turns centrally on this denial of human vulnerability, which is impossible to incarnate, and is centrally implicated, for example, in the higher suicide rates of men.

The function of patriarchal invulnerability is that it reinforces male dominance, most obviously by encoding tough-guy machismo, but more profoundly, by making it difficult for men to negotiate the vulnerability of their needs in an ethical way. 'Tough guys' take what they want and expect to get their own way. And they are acculturated to it by being raised in a society where, from boyhood, they get used to women bending the world around them, picking up after them, washing their socks, and giving them what they want. Conversely, girls are frequently punished for asserting their needs or opinions and expecting them to be met or listened to. There is no specifically masculine equivalent of the tendency to malign 'spoilt' or 'demanding' girls as a 'Princess' or 'Little Madam.' There is no reason on earth why male humans should be 'naturally' over-entitled, and female humans 'naturally' inclined to entirely subordinate their needs to serving the needs of males. And there would be little need for the panoply of discipline and shame brought down on women when they fail to fulfil their sweet, compliant service function, if women came equipped as 'natural' support humans simply by dint of being female.

This matrix of entitlement and service constitutes what I think of as the 'deep structure of gender,' and it is by no means all natural. By contrast, much of what is taken to be the substance of gender, by both conservative and queer accounts, is relatively thin or superficial, especially insofar as it focuses on the performance of aesthetic masculinity or femininity. We are by now all familiar with arguing with the same old entitled mansplaining dude who thinks he's queer because he's wearing black nail polish. This theoretical superficiality, along with the tendency to focus on *gender as a property of the individual*, rather than on the structural power it supports and maintains, allies queer and trans-ideological thinking more closely with conservative accounts than with feminism. Like conservative accounts, trans ideology also, fundamentally, accepts the equations male = masculine and female = feminine, but has simply reversed the direction of causality. Where conservatism thinks males should be masculine, and females should be feminine, trans ideology thinks masculine people should be male, feminine people should be female, and that people who are kind of both, which most people are, are neither male nor female and so *don't have a sex at all*. All this does is reify the 'boxes,' shorn of any grasp of their social and political functions, or why they even exist at all, other than a gratuitously naïve, and fundamentally quiescent, belief that they arise directly from people's innate natural gender, and that the only injustice these boxes represent is that some male people don't get to hang out in the 'woman' box and vice versa. There is nothing, we're told, inherently harmful about male entitlement or machismo or dominance, or women being made passive, pretty, and complaint. It's 'natural.' And any female person who doesn't repudiate 'being a woman' must be a-okay with it.

So much for 'smash the patriarchy.'

I think I'll stick to smashing boxes.

WHO ARE THE GENDER ESSENTIALISTS HERE?

Twitter

24 MARCH 2022

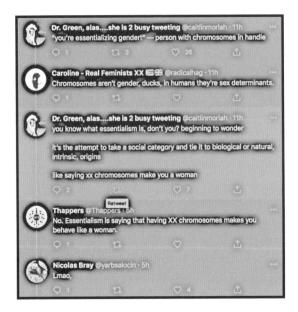

This exchange is a great demonstration of how trans rights activists have arrived at the conclusion that we are the essentialists here.

And it's a great demonstration of how that relies on them interpreting our words exclusively through their own ideological lens, even while the very core of what we're about is the rejection of that ideological lens.

1. Once upon a time 'gender essentialism' meant 'thinking women naturally behave in a 'feminine way' because they're female,' or 'thinking sex naturally determines gendered behaviour.'

As we constantly point out, trans ideology is gender essentialist, but it's a weird reverse kind of gender essentialism. Where the trad-conservative type of essentialism thinks 'women do x,' trans ideology thinks 'people who do x are women.'

2. The core of this conflict is, of course, about whether 'woman' is a sex-based or gender-based concept.

The TRAs are completely committed to the idea that 'woman' is a gendered or social concept.

They therefore read the claim that 'women are female' not as we mean it—as an assertion that 'woman' is a sex-based concept—but as a claim that the social role of 'woman' can only be occupied be female people.

(Note again, the reverse causality. It's not 'only female people can do the woman-gendered stuff' but 'the people doing the woman-gendered stuff must be women/female people.')

That's what they think we believe, which is why they think we are against gender non-conformity.

Their concept of gender non-conformity isn't our 'humans of any sex should be allowed to behave in any way without labelling or policing and we should as far as possible get rid of gendered roles.'

Their concept of gender non-conformity has no thought of getting rid of the social roles. Indeed, their concept reinforces these roles. Rather, their concept is 'people of any sex should be allowed to perform any gendered role, and in fact, their identity should be defined by it.'

As we've often noted, this leaves the structure of gender intact, and removes any critique of the nature and function of those roles, and the way they developed to uphold sex-based exploitation.

The only injustice in the system is that male people don't get to do the 'woman role' and female people don't get to do the 'man role,' and people who identify with neither/both don't get to do the special 'not/both man/woman' role.

This is laid out in this piece from our old friends at *Everyday Feminism:*

> The problem is not that the gender binary exists, but rather that gender is assigned non-consensually, and that anyone who steps outside of the culturally-defined boundaries are marginalized and experience systemic oppression and violence.
>
> The problem isn't femininity or masculinity. It is *compulsory* femininity and masculinity tied to a value system that devalues all things feminine.
>
> Denying the existence of cis privilege, the analyses put forth by TERFs oversimplifies the lived experiences of women in a society that devalues those experiences.

What gets entirely lost here, of course, is that gender functions to exploit and oppress female people, and the entire concept of oppression-as-double-bind—that is, that women get screwed by this system whether they comply or resist.[1]

And indeed, the fact of gender as oppression and double bind gets entirely written over with the facile concept of 'cis privilege,' that is, 'you are lucky enough to identify with your "woman role" and therefore you are privileged and the oppressor.'

That rewrites female people's oppression as a privilege. That takes some fucking gall.

As does the fact, that as this exchange shows, they *refuse* to understand, no matter how many times we say it, that when we say 'woman' we mean it *as a sex concept.*

And they will be the most condescending obnoxious pious assholes while doing so.

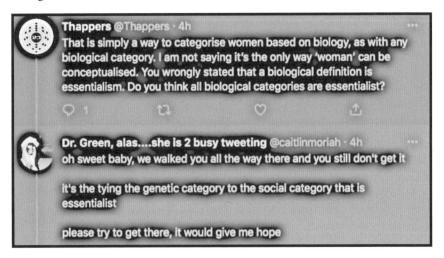

Thappers @Thappers · 4h
That is simply a way to categorise women based on biology, as with any biological category. I am not saying it's the only way 'woman' can be conceptualised. You wrongly stated that a biological definition is essentialism. Do you think all biological categories are essentialist?

Dr. Green, alas....she is 2 busy tweeting @caitlinmoriah · 4h
oh sweet baby, we walked you all the way there and you still don't get it

it's the tying the genetic category to the social category that is essentialist

please try to get there, it would give me hope

Of course, when read through their lens, this means that by accepting and asserting the word 'woman' for ourselves, we are accepting—indeed, *identifying with*—the woman role.

Which is precisely the opposite of what we're doing.

---

[1] Laura Kacere, 'Why the Feminist Movement Must Be Trans Inclusive,' *Everyday Feminism*, 24 February 2014.

It's the most insane circular suffocating example of narcissistic thinking you could imagine.

Viz:

"We have dictated that the word 'woman' is redefined to mean gender role.

Even though the fundament of this conflict is that you reject this redefinition of the word 'woman,' we will point blank refuse to even remotely grasp your assertion.

Furthermore, we will then interpret all your words and arguments through the lens of the definition you have explicitly rejected (while piously patronizing you).

We will hence produce a massive pile of gibberish, which we will claim are your views, even though by interpreting everything you say through our definitions, we will have erased and/or actually reversed the meaning of what you are saying.

And we will then call you names for believing things that bear no relation to your actual views, and which are entirely an artefact of our own narcissism, lack of good faith, and othering, and then we will slap ourselves on the back for what marvellous people we are."

It's fucking wild.

FEMALE CLASS POLITICS
Speech for the Women's Equality Party
23 SEPTEMBER 2020

Author's Note: This is the text of a speech I gave to the Women's Equality Party Assembly, looking into how their policy objectives should respond to issues raised by the gender debate. The question the WEP asked me to consider was about the inclusion of trans women in women's political representation.

To lay out my thoughts about women's political representation, I want to first outline my socialist and radical feminist analysis of women's politics. What I most want to underline is that from my perspective, feminism is a form of materialist class politics, not a form of identity politics. That is, my analysis of the position of women is rooted in understanding that female people have a particular type of body and reproductive capacity and are subject to a system of power on the basis of being female. This power structure exists because of the historical development of a hierarchical system to extract the reproductive and socially reproductive labour of female people, otherwise known as patriarchy. Consequently, women have a range of shared material political interests. Most obviously, these pertain to issues around reproductive and sexual autonomy, and the violences women are subjected to by male power's effort to control their bodies as a sexual and reproductive resource. This then extends to how women's labour is devalued, invisibilized, and appropriated by the intertwined structures of patriarchy and capitalism. This includes women's disproportionate poverty, the wage gap, maternity cover and child-care, the undervaluing and feminization of all forms of care labour, the concentration of women in low-paid and low status occupations, and the ways all these issues disproportionately impact working class and racialized women. Lastly, this leads to the demand for a fundamental structural transformation in order to challenge extractive relations, undertake a just accounting of women's labour, and do away with the symbolic representations and psychological conditioning that undermines women's humanity by positioning them as a sexual, reproductive, domestic, and emotional resource for males. The fundamental structure of patriarchal gender is then a matter of socializing women into the role of a service-class orientated to male needs, and socializing males into a mode of dominance and entitlement. Feminist politics that reinforces female socialization and de-centers the needs and interests of female people is thus antithetical to challenging gender in its deepest sense.

On the question of why women's political representation matters, let's focus on two key areas. The first involves the symbolic importance of women's representation, the way women's representation provides role models and opens possibilities for other women, and the fact that *representational justice* or equality is an important value in and of itself. With respect to the inclusion of trans women in women's representation, this immediately forces a confrontation with the bitterly contested ontological question of 'what is a woman?' As should be apparent from what I've just said, my answer to this question is informed by materialist class analysis. That is, women are a sex class. This matters not only because it frames women's class interests, but because the alternative interpretation, from our perspective, relies on essentializing gender, which we consider to be the mechanism of the oppression of women as a sex class. At the heart of this conflict is the fundamental question of the definition of women being changed from a sex class to a gender class. Given that we think that gender is *how* women are oppressed on the basis of sex, we consider it regressive for women to be recognized in public life as instantiations of gender, and to be redefined on the basis of an identification with gender that not only bears little relation to our experience as female human beings, but diminishes the way patriarchal gender profoundly harms our humanity.

I think it's worth briefly thinking about this under the rubric of 'Diversity and Inclusion.' The aim of inclusion is actually structurally contradictory to the aim of diversity. If everyone is included inside one category, then many salient differences between groups get lost, and we undermine diversity. Much present identity politics is focused on a possibly over-stated emphasis on difference, while conversely, the relation of women and trans women is being subsumed under the sole political directive of 'inclusion,' which is undermining the recognition of important political and social differences. What we should be aiming towards is a model that honours both similarity and difference. We need to recognize that female people and people who identify as women are not identical, and stop trying to erase this difference in a way which many women feel is overwriting their political existence and interests. This will allow us to stand in solidarity with each other, in areas where our political interests are aligned.

This leads to the second area where representation matters: the expression of women's political interests. This is not simple, because under patriarchy women have the most fractured class consciousness of any oppressed group, and it is far from evident that women in positions of political authority are in the business of representing women's interests. I would hope, however, that this is less true of the political consciousness of women inside a party set up by and for women. The question then is to what extent women and trans women share political interests. My claim here would be that trans women who respect the difference between trans women and women, and understand why women resist being redefined on the basis of gender, can stand in real and meaningful solidarity with women, although our interests still do not completely coincide. However, at present, given the effort to erase differences, redefine women by gender, and demand access to all sex-based spaces with no gatekeeping, the interests of women and those aligned with the present trans rights project, are, in fact, diametrically opposed. This was evident in Munroe Bergdorf's much criticized injunction that women shouldn't centre reproductive issues at the Women's March because it was "exclusionary." It is also starkly illustrated by how often advocates of present trans rights discourse diminish the impact of male violence on women's lives—as Judith Butler did recently[1]—and the extent to which being raised in a society that sexualizes women from their early teens necessitates that female people have sex-based spaces to preserve their dignity and humanity, as well as their safety. This is a source of great regret, as opposition to male violence is one of the places where women and trans women's interests should most closely align. On the basis of all these factors I would argue that—especially under current circumstances—it is *not* appropriate for trans women to represent women politically, and I hope in time we can move towards a place where we can stand in close solidarity with each other.

---

[1] Alona Ferber, 'Judith Butler on the Culture Wars, J. K. Rowling and Living in 'Anti-Intellectual Times," *New Statesman*, 22 September 2020.

GAY RIGHTS AND TRANS RIGHTS: A COMPARE AND CONTRAST

janeclarejones.com

SEPTEMBER 2018

So, Momentum made a video huh?[1]

To be honest, it's kind of a classic of its genre. Once more with feeling, everyone: *Trans rights are just like gay rights.* Anyone who thinks otherwise is some nasty backwards morally bankrupt fuddy-duddy asshole who is going to look back on their objections to the current trans rights agenda with an enormous eggy faceful of shame. Remember people, we're just telling you this for your own good. YOU DON'T WANT TO GO GETTING CAUGHT ON THE WRONG SIDE OF HISTORY DO YOU NOW????

This parallel between gay and trans rights has been leveraged for all it's worth by the trans rights movement. Owen Jones[2] has trotted out this talking point endlessly to justify his point-blank refusal to listen to anything any-one—particularly female anyones—have to say on the matter. It's embedded in the way trans rights are now the centre of activity for many LGBTQI+ or-ganizations, and has come, most notably, to dominate Stonewall's campaign agenda. And it's present, perhaps most potently, in the way any questions about the current trans rights project are immediately dismissed as bigotry and 'transphobia'—a thought-terminating cliche that lifts the notion of *dis-crimination-as-phobia* straight from gay rights discourse.

This strategy has been incredibly effective. One of the reasons the trans rights movement has soared from obscurity to wall-to-wall dominance is because—if you glance at it running from twenty paces—it does look exact-ly like the gay rights movement. And right now the whole world is basically going to shit and a lot of people are too up-to-their-eyes in grind, precarity, sugar, and anxiety to do anything *but* look at it running from twenty pac-es. People just want to be told what the good, right-thinking progressive position is and then get on with the business of trying to get on with their business. Fair enough. But there's a *massive* problem with all this. And that's

---

[1] Sienna Rogers, 'Momentum Enter Trans Rights Debate with New Video,' *Labour List*, 6 Septem-ber 2018.

[2] Owen Jones, 'Anti-Trans Zealots, Know This: History Will Judge You,' *The Guardian*, 15 Decem-ber 2017.

67

because the parallel between gay rights and trans rights is as superficial and insubstantial as that glossy soundbite-stuffed Momentum video.

What I want to do here is think through why the concept of 'discrimination-as-phobia' worked for the gay rights movement, and why, despite superficial similarities, it doesn't accurately capture what is at stake in the trans rights debate, and actually serves as a tool of political propaganda and obfuscation. That is, I'm going to argue that accusations of 'homophobia' were a politically powerful and basically on-the-money part of gay rights discourse, while the use of 'transphobia' is an inaccurate parallel that grossly distorts public perceptions of the issues involved in the trans rights debate, and is doing so in the service of actually preventing that debate from taking place.

So, to get down to it: the concept of 'homophobia' relies on the idea that gay people are discriminated against on the basis of *moral disgust*.[3] And inside that are two more interwoven ideas. First, that moral disgust is not a legitimate basis for telling people what not to do (correct)—especially not when your disgust-feels are causing serious harm to other people (also correct). And even more especially given that moral disgust is a nasty, vicious emotion that tends to shade very easily into violence (and I mean that in the old-fashioned sense of 'literal violence'). Second, that, because discrimination against homosexuality was entirely mediated by moral disgust, there was, in fact, no *legitimate* basis for that discrimination, and all objections were, effectively, moral disgust in drag. That is, the success of gay rights was substantially down to disseminating the idea that that were no good reasons for anyone to object to their agenda, and that everyone objecting was just a nasty evil bigot whose ideas shouldn't be given any weight as part of democratic political debate.

This structure has basically been transferred wholesale to the concept of 'transphobia.' And it's doing important work for the trans rights movement in several ways. First, the idea of the visceral virulence of moral disgust has been taken and amplified to the hundredth power. Our response to things that disgust us is to try and eradicate them, and I think this resonance of the 'phobia' designation is doing a lot to undergird trans activists' claims that any objection to their demands amounts to a 'denial of their existence,' or an effort to 'exclude' them bordering on intent to exterminate.[4] (It's also a key element of the endlessly recycled claim that a bunch of mostly left-wing

---

[3] Cf. Martha Nussbaum, *Hiding from Humanity: Disgust, Shame, and the Law* (Princeton: Princeton University Press, 2006).
[4] Jane Clare Jones, "'You Are Killing Me': On Hate Speech and Feminist Silencing,' *Trouble and Strife*, 17 May 2015.

feminist women would blend seamlessly into the Westboro Baptist Church or some such foolishness.)

Second—and we'll deal with this in detail because it's crucial—the use of the concept of 'homophobia' to dismiss objections to gay rights carried a ton of weight because the basis for a legitimate moral or political objection would be that something causes a harm, and in the case of gay rights *there is a complete dearth of convincing arguments as to why homosexuality is a harm.* Homosexuality doesn't harm homosexuals, and it doesn't harm anyone else—but repressing homosexuality causes harms.[5] This is precisely where the 'homophobia-transphobia' parallel completely falls apart. Because in the case of the trans rights agenda there are actually a load of potential harms we might reasonably worry about. (See 'What Is at Stake,' p. 36). Indeed, there is a kind of dull thudding irony to the fact that the very week Momentum decide to remind us that we're all scaremongering bigots on the wrong side of history it also became public knowledge that the rapist Karen White had been sent to a women's jail and sexually assaulted female inmates. (Who could have predicted it?)[6]

The key thing to understand about trans rights activism is that, unlike gay rights activism, it is not just a movement seeking to ensure that trans people are not discriminated against. It is, rather, a movement committed to *a fundamental reconceptualization of the very idea of what makes someone a man or a woman.* In theory, this equally affects both men and women, but in practice, almost all the social pressure is coming from trans women towards the idea of 'woman' and the rights of women. And that's because, when it comes down to it, this whole thing is being driven by male people who want something female people have, and that something, is, in fact, our very existence. Moreover, it turns out—who knew?—that male people have the inclination and social power to exert extreme coercive pressure on female people, and to court the sympathy and support of other males when they do so. (It's almost as if sex is a thing and that it has something to do with power after all, mmm?)

The central thought of the present form of trans rights activism is that whether someone is a man or a woman has nothing to do with sex—the material fact of which they try, endlessly, to undermine—and is determined instead by someone's 'gender identity,' some kind of internal gender essence or subjective sense of one's own gender that many of us simply don't recognize as a description of our own experience as men or women. This ideological

---

[5] I guess maybe it harms people who don't get to project their disgust-feels onto other people (yup, not sorry) and it maybe harms the model of the exclusively heterosexual patriarchal family (boohoo).

[6] 'Trans inmate jailed afor Wakefield prison sex offences,' *BBC News Online*, 11 October 2018.

manoeuvre is embedded inside the phrase 'Trans Women Are Women,' which looks, on the face of it, like a reasonable plea for trans women to be given the respect most people want to give them, but is actually used in political argument to deny all distinction between the existence and interests of male-born people living as women and the existence and interests of female people. It is under the rubric of 'Trans Women Are Women' that Karen White ended up in a female jail, because there's no possible difference between Karen White and any other woman, right? That is, there are, in fact, reasons to be concerned about the impact of this definitional change.

Calling people 'homophobic' was used by the gay rights movement to dismiss all objections to their political agenda as illegitimate moral disgust. Calling people 'transphobic' is playing on the same trope—and it's doing a hell of a lot of work to shut down all concerns about trans rights by painting them as sketchy hate speech beyond the pale of legitimate democratic discourse.[7] This is a *massive* distortion of what is going on here, because there is a far from insignificant number of very legitimate questions about the potential harms of restructuring our core ideas of sex and gender. This manoeuvre is, however, an absolutely central plank of the trans rights movement's political strategy, because—as those of you who've been out there trying to argue this know well—trans activists actually have no substantive answers to our questions and concerns. At all.

A few weeks ago, for example, I spent three hours 'arguing' with people from that great bastion of intersectional right thinking *Everyday Feminism* about what we do about the fact that under fundamentalist self-ID procedures it will become *de facto* impossible to stop any man entering women's space. I was called a transphobe and a racist and a bigot (of course); there was attempted emotional blackmail ('you come onto my TL talking about rape when I'm a survivor, you evil heartless witch'/'well, in that case don't use your considerably larger platform to RT the testimony of other survivors so you can mock and dismiss them'); and I was told that I was insinuating the trans woman I was talking to had a dick (I wasn't—wouldn't—and they couldn't show I had). It was a litany of name-calling, deflection, and emotional manipulation. There was not one attempt to sincerely address the problem at hand with something approximating thought (unless you count 'my rapist had brown eyes so should we try and ban brown-eyed people?' a thought), and not one acknowledgement that women might have a reasonable interest in this or could be motivated by anything other than pure baseless spite. And

---

[7] This state of affairs has significantly improved since June 2021, when gender-critical views were protected under the Equality Act as an outcome of *Forstater vs. CGD Europe*. (www.gov.uk/employment-appeal-tribunal-decisions/maya-forstater-v-cgd-europe-and-others-ukeat-slash-0105-slash-20-slash-joj.)

this, apparently, is how we're making public policy that will affect at least half the population now.

The way that the accusation of 'transphobia' is being used to control and close down the debate around trans rights is also inherent in what we might call the 'overreach' of the definition of transphobia being put to work here. As I've said, 'homophobia' identifies—correctly, I think—the fact that the discrimination against homosexuals, and especially gay men, was coming from moral disgust, and specifically, moral disgust about people's sexual practices.[8] If 'transphobia' is an analogue of 'homophobia'—and to ground the claim that it's an illegitimate basis for political argument it *needs* to be— then it should, also, refer to a form of moral disgust, and, moreover, as in the case of violence against gay people, there should be an obvious causal link between that moral disgust, the discrimination you're trying to combat, and the arguments people are using against you.

None of this stacks up with how 'transphobia' is being used politically. If there is moral disgust aimed at trans people—which there's no reason to dispute—then it would, one imagine, inhere in responses to people who are visibly transgressing patriarchal conventions by exhibiting gender expression in conflict with their natal sex. The people we'd expect to display such disgust would then be the kind of people who, say, find femininity in men distressing, i.e. patriarchally invested people, and particularly, patriarchally invested men. And indeed, the vast majority of literal violence suffered by trans people is, unsurprisingly, directed at trans women by non-trans men.[9] However, it isn't at all evident that the kind of concerns feminist have about the impact of self-ID on women and women's rights falls easily under the banner of 'moral disgust.' And yet, accusations of 'transphobia' flow, overwhelmingly, from trans activists towards the speech of feminist women

---

[8] It's not clear to me that the discrimination directed at gay men is of the same type as that directed at lesbians. The moral disgust aimed at gay men derives, at base, from the patriarchal injunction against the penetrability of men. I wrote my PhD on the 'metaphysics of penetration,' so, I'll try not to go off on a tangent that will take over this whole essay, but the basic point is this: patriarchal male subjectivity is grounded in the idea of invulnerability and impenetrability, and hence, being fucked is to be dehumanized by being 'made-woman' and/or 'made-object.' (Hence all those irritating 'Don't bend over' quips straight men make around gay men.) That is, the visceral—and violent—form of homophobia directed against male homosexuals is, basically, a variant of patriarchal sexual misogyny most viciously exhibited by straight men. By contrast, the aversion to lesbianism (when it's not being eroticized for the straight male gaze) is, I think, a lot more to do with men's outrage about women not being sexually available to them and, often, not being very interested in them at all.

[9] Briefly, the vast majority of murders of trans women are committed by men against trans women, and principally against black trans women, many of whom are in the sex trade. If you look carefully at the lists of names produced every Trans Day of Remembrance, you will notice that a lot of them sound Brazilian. That's because the highest global rate of murders against

who are pretty much the last people on earth who'd be morally disgusted by someone transgressing patriarchal gender conventions,[10] and whose speech has no obvious bearing on the kind of patriarchal violence directed at trans women.[11] That is, accusations of transphobia are being directed against the group of people—women who have theoretical and political objections to the trans rights agenda—who are actually least likely to experience moral disgust over trans people's gender expression, and this is being done for purely *political* reasons.

> **TRANSPHOBIA**
>
> The fear or dislike of someone based on the fact they are trans, including denying their gender identity or refusing to accept it. Transphobia may be targeted at people who are, or who are perceived to be, trans.

From Stonewall's 'List of LGBTQ+ Terms'

The politics of this becomes apparent when we look at the definition of 'transphobia' being circulated by trans advocacy organizations like Stonewall. The Stonewall definition of 'transphobia' is "fear or dislike of someone based on the fact they are trans, *including the denial/refusal to accept their gender identity*" (my emphasis). That is, 'transphobia' is being politically leveraged to denote, *not* a form of illegitimate moral disgust, but any refusal to understand someone as the gender they identify as, and, given that trans ideology believes that gender identity determines whether someone is a man or

---

trans people is against black Brazilian trans women in the sex trade. Given the high rates of violence against people of colour and prostitutes, this somewhat confounds the claim that this violence can be specifically attributed to 'transphobia.' Cf. Debbie Hayton, 'Martyrs of the New Religion,' *The Critic*, 20 November 2021; Wilfred Reilly, 'Are We in the Midst of a Transgender Murder Epidemic?' *Quillette*, 7 December 2019. It's notable these are both from the right-leaning/libertarianish press. Most 'progressives' will not publicly interrogate the claims about the exceptional vulnerability of the trans population for love, decency, nor money.

[10] As someone who openly identifies as 'Princesexual,' I find femininity in men the very opposite of disgusting. (And, while we're here, can you *please* not trans all the feminine men? There's precious few enough to go round as it is.) It is my firm belief that visceral aversion to gender non-conformity in men is not a common reaction, and indeed, would be incoherent, for most gender-critical women. It is true, however, that many women react negatively to what they perceive as males acting out stereotypes or caricatures of women, and this is expressed, for example, in some feminists' aversion to drag. There is a fine line between mocking people's appearance—which I would in no way condone—and pointing out that there is something offensive about, say, Pips Bunce turning up at an investment bank in a lacy hot-fuchsia dress that no female person would wear to work if they wanted to be taken remotely seriously.

[11] Jane Clare Jones, "'You Are Killing Me': On Hate Speech and Feminist Silencing,' *Trouble and Strife*, 17 May 2015.

a woman, this definition seeks to mandate the view that trans women are women, and inscribe as hate speech the view that trans women are male people who identify as women. That is, this definition of 'transphobia' seeks to enforce compliance with transgender ideology.

As I've already suggested, there's nothing minor about this. Trans rights politics is asking us to believe that human sexual difference is not a thing, that men are women because they say they are, and is demanding a thoroughgoing social and political transformation on that basis—a transformation that amounts to the legal and political erasure of sex. That is, trans ideology is mandating nothing short of a fundamental rewriting of how we understand the world,[12] one that runs entirely counter to the everyday perceptions of everyone who hasn't been indoctrinated by trans ideology (and even those that have will sometimes inadvertently let it slip that, lo, they do in fact perceive sex). Let me just state something really fucking obvious that apparently needs to be stated: *You cannot mandate how people perceive the world.* That is totalitarian as all living fuck. You cannot demand people perceive the world in line with your ideology and that perceiving something that ALL humans perceive is actually the same as being a genocidal racist. (And all you 'sex was invented by colonialism' philosophical-sophisticates-cum-idiots, it may surprise you to learn that that sounds racist af to everyone who hasn't marinated their brains in Tumblrized queer theory for eight years. And let's not even get started on the anachronism involved.)

What we have here then is a politically driven ideology that:

1. Refuses to engage in any meaningful debate about any of the implications of the changes it is forcing through and attempts to shut down every question or objection by screaming 'phobia' and 'hate speech' and 'genocide.'

2. Attempts to legislate people's basic perceptions of the world and recast the very fact of that perception as a form of illegitimate moral disgust overlaid with resonances of intent to harm or even eradicate.

It should be pretty evident that any political program based on attempting to reframe such a fundamental aspect of human perception is only going

---

[12] This move actually turns on a slippage between the two meanings of 'to discriminate.' Trans ideology is wedded to the notion that the negative treatment or value attributed to trans people (i.e. discrimination in the political sense) resides in the very act of making a distinction between male and female people (i.e. discrimination in the perceptual sense). The idea that we can recognize difference perceptually and not attribute hierarchical value is entirely incomprehensible to them. (See 'A Note on 'Smashing the Binary,'' p. 133).

to succeed by using totalitarian methods: by relentlessly drilling its axioms into public consciousness and by making people who reject them pay a high social price. The phrase 'Orwellian' is madly overused, but it documents the methods of trans activism almost to the letter. We have the profligate re-writing of history—including the trans-ing of the gender-non-conforming dead (um, I thought it was self-ID?), the trans-ing of the drag queens who started the Stonewall riot (even though they didn't, because that was a black lesbian called Stormé DeLarverie), and the absurd suggestion that literature or history about people cross-dressing for social, political, or economic rea-sons harms trans people because past cross-dressers were actually just ex-pressing their 'authentic selves' (you fucking bigot, Shakespeare). It's only slight hyperbole to say that right now a lot of us feel like we're stuck in Room IOI except O'Brien looks like Riley Dennis and the '2+2=5' is 'Sex does not exist' and the rats are a bunch of trans activists threatening us with baby-blue-and-pink baseball bats (and in case you want to wilfully misinterpret me, I'm *not* saying trans people are vermin, I'm using the exact reference of the thing that scares Winston shitless and is used to coerce him). We could go on pointing out the parallels all day, but seriously people, when you start projecting 'Repeat after Us: Trans Women Are Women' onto the side of gov-ernment buildings, you really should ask yourself whether you're getting a touch Ministry of Truth-y.[13]

To make the point plain. Some aspects of gay rights politics did involve the use of non-peaceful protest. As also did parts of the women's rights and black civil-rights movement. What none of these movements involved was the demand that people change their fundamental perceptual systems—as opposed to value judgements about things they perceived—and the at-tempt to enforce that perception using our culture's most lucid analysis of 'this-is-what-totalitarianism-looks-like.' (Clue: *Nineteen Eighty-Four* was never supposed to be a 'how-to' guide). The great sickening irony of all of this of course—as many gay men are now waking up to—is that the abolition of sex implies the abolition of sexual orientation. Trans ideology's conviction that the truth of our 'authentic selves' and whether we are men or women is based only and exclusively on 'gender identity' necessitates the effort to deny that we fuck people's bodies (at least in good part) on the basis of the *sex of those bodies*, and that sexual attraction is *sexual*, in both senses of the word. That is, the gay rights movement has wedded itself to an ideology that can-not actually recognize that *homosexuality is a thing*. Given the social and phys-ical power imbalances, this doesn't necessarily involve a clear and present danger to gay men (although it poses a real ideological threat, and for those

---

[13] 'Dazed Projected Statements Onto Parliament About the State of the UK,' *dazeddigital.com*, II July 2018.

of you who have seen it and are pitching in, I hope you know we see and value you). For lesbians, this is a first-order existential threat. Not only are lesbians being erased along with the class of women in general, but their right to be exclusively attracted to female-bodied people is being consistently challenged by some of the most rapey, entitled misogynist bullying I have seen in my entire life. To amend a famous slogan: Lesbians don't do dick. Get over it.

How the LGBTQ+ institutions—and public policy more widely—came to be colonized by a totalitarian political ideology that is hostile to the interests of women and is, in its fundaments, hostile to the very existence of homosexuals, is a million-dollar question. I strongly suspect that 'millions of dollars' is not just a turn of phrase here—and I hope, over time, we will come to better understand the deluge of cash and the corporate plutocratic interests that must be implicated in such a startling takeover of gay and lesbian politics. Right now, women, feminists, lesbians, gay and straight men, intersex people, concerned parents, and many non-ideologue trans people are fighting tooth and nail to stop the roll-back of rights we thought had already been secured. Time's arrow is not pointing forwards. Right side of history, my arse.

ON TRYING TO HAMMER IN NAILS WITH A FISH

Twitter

5 MAY 2021

I am so bored of teenage-esque solipsists who think the fact human concepts are created by humans (duh) means we just make them up willy-nilly.

If concepts for material phenomena don't help you interact with the world reliably the world tells you about it pretty fucking fast.

None of you people actually live in the world as if our concepts for material phenomena—and our perception of objects, because that's what those concepts allow—were just totally random wibble-wobble.

If they were, you'd never be able to cross the damn street.

And what you are demanding is that we replace a set of categorizations that we have been using pretty much since we worked out sounds for 'tree' and 'sun' and 'water' and 'fire' and have been using to reliably interact with the world for millennia, and manage a whole load of of social processes, and now medical processes, and replace it with a concept that *has no fucking content whatsoever other than someone's feelings about a bunch of gender stereotypes and doesn't allow us to meaningfully interact with anything or do shit other than validate people's feelings.*

You're basically telling me I can give you my hammer and you'll replace it with a fish and I can still use it to hit nails.

Idiots. High on some faux-sophisticate idea that makes their brains fall clean out:

> I never said we came up with these categories "Willy nilly" like you strawmanned my position... I'm stating we use real-world phenomena to determine those categories... just what defines said categories was defined by humans. We decided that the category of female is broadly defined by 'x' characteristics... catch up. @TheBraveScott1

Right, so it turns out that 'male' and 'female' are categorizations that allow us to interact reliably with the world. We did not just 'decide' that a certain set of properties distinguished males from females.

First, we distinguished the male and female types of ourselves and other animals by pairs, based on patterns observed between genitals, secondary-sex characteristics, and reproductive function. Man/woman, cow/bull, ram/ewe, etc... Turns out they knew about that by the time they wrote down a story about putting animals in an ark.

Then we abstracted the concepts of 'male' and 'female' relating to reproductive functions of animals, i.e. the one that gets pregnant and the one that inseminates and understood that was the same mechanism across animal types.

Then we abstracted the concept of 'sex' pertaining to 'differing reproductive functions' from that. And we did anatomy and observed that the differences we had perceived were related to different internal reproductive organs.

Later, we were able to do basic experiments on genetic inheritance, and as our technology improved, on sex-cell division, DNA replication, embryonic reproductive development, and so on. All of which told us that the very first distinction we observed between types of animals (and then plants) corresponds to a mechanism of anisogamous fertilization that, it turns out, is used by all organisms that do sexual reproduction.

This mechanism is probably *billions* of years old. And not one single thing in the millennia long history of our developing understanding of sex differences has undermined our first basic perceptual classification. In fact, everything we have learned since has confirmed it.

Until males decided that they wanted to be female.

CATEGORIES ARE FUZZY

Twitter

9 AUGUST 2020

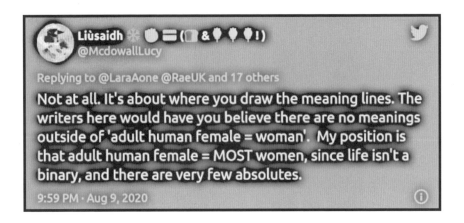

This conversation is a good example of where clever people make stupid mistakes about language.

Most categories have fuzzy edges. That doesn't mean that the category doesn't function meaningfully to pick out something in the world, and it doesn't mean that things that are not in the category are in the category.

Some mugs, like the ones for Irish coffee, are made of glass. That doesn't mean that the difference between mugs and glasses completely breaks down, and we can't tell whether a wine glass is a mug or not. And it doesn't mean a mug could identify into the class of glasses… or that the difference between mugs and glasses is in some sense entirely arbitrary…

Some things differ in matters of degree from things to which they are closely related. A big stream becomes a river. A big hill becomes a mountain. There is no line where a big stream definitively becomes a small river. That doesn't mean the concepts of 'stream' and 'river' are meaningless. And it doesn't mean the Thames as it flows through the middle of London is a stream.

This is what they are doing with the intersex argument. They are trying to present sex as a quantitative difference of degree between two points, with the implication that the difference is arbitrary, and that people can move along it as they choose.

Even were sex a matter of degree, this would be nonsense. There is a good deal of liminality between 'day' and 'night.' But night is not day, and if we all decided it was and we didn't need to put the lights on, that would be really fucking stupid.

Moreover, while some secondary-sex characteristics might differ by degree, sex, in terms of reproductive capacity is actually a difference in kind, not a difference of degree. As this diagram makes comically evident.

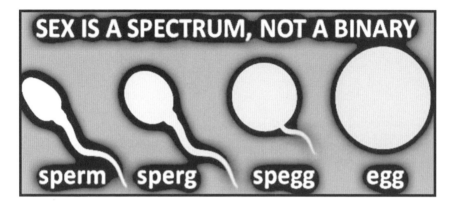

So, this is all a lot of bad thinking and smoke and mirrors.

Human categorization is usually fuzzy. Even in cases where it's fuzzy, that doesn't mean that things clearly outside of the category are in it. And the categorization of sex is actually, for all the obfuscation, one of the least fuzzy.

Egg-making humans are not sperm-making humans, and there is not a continuum between the two. You can argue that the word 'woman' doesn't mean 'adult human female' till you are blue in the face.

Adult female humans will still exist as a meaningful class and we'd like a word, please, thank you very much.

POSTSTRUCTURALISM, BUTLER, AND BODIES

janeclarejones.com

JULY 2018

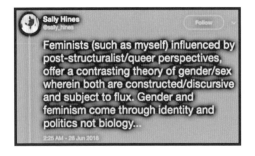

There's a ton of discussion out there at the moment about poststructural/postmodern feminism and its responsibility for undermining a) the material basis of the analysis of patriarchy, and b) 'woman' as a political category. And claims about this are being made on all sides. This is a thorny thicket of thickety thorns. We have a whole lot of philosophy, starting roughly with early deconstruction (starting in the late '60s), and running up to queer theory (from the early '90s onwards). We have the dissemination of deconstruction in the '80s and '90s, and how that fed into popular ideas of 'postmodernism.' And then we have how that idea of 'postmodernism' is interacting with ideas coming from queer theory, and how all of that is informing popular discourse.

The rough sketch ends up looking something like this: Early poststructuralism/deconstruction argued that everything was 'discursive' or 'textual' and didn't believe in material reality. Postmodernism is all about the 'play' of signifiers and how everything is 'constructed' through discourse. Then Butler comes along and invents queer theory by arguing, in essence, that bodies are discursively constructed, and we end up where we are now, and it's probably all Jacques Derrida's fault.

I have a bunch of dogs in this fight. I am a poststructural feminist. I am also, unreservedly, a second-waver, a radical socialist feminist, and I'm committed to the material analysis of patriarchy, because without a material analysis of patriarchy we can't, fundamentally, explain *anything*. I don't think these two positions are inconsistent with each other, and so I get a little troubled when 'poststructuralism' is used to mean 'discursively-constructed' and then to mean 'biology doesn't exist' and then to mean 'women don't exist' because in the bit of poststructuralism where I hang out (the bit that descends from Derrida through second-wave deconstructive French feminism), the *whole point* is understanding that patriarchy works by erasing women, and by erasing and appropriating the material (and maternal) reality of women's bodies.

So, I want to do a little parsing of intellectual history and try to think through what's going on here, and how these currents intersect with where we are now. There is a load of important and useful stuff in poststructural feminism that is in danger of being lost if we confuse poststructuralism simply with 'discourse all the way down'-type queer theory. There's no necessary reason why you should be interested in any of this, and it's probably going to get a little academic/technical in places, but if you are interested in it, I hope this might be helpful.

PART ONE: POSTMODERNISM, DECONSTRUCTION, AND 'DISCURSIVE CONSTITUTION'

One of the things that's going on here (and here I'm going to come off like a philosophy snob, and, um, *awkward shuffle*), is that deconstruction was largely disseminated in the Anglo-American university through English literature departments—because Anglo-American 'analytic' philosophy has tended to write off French philosophy as not really philosophy at all. (When I was at uni, the English department decided to give Derrida an honorary degree, and the Philosophy department more or less threatened to stand outside with placards reading 'JACQUES DERRIDA IS A BOUNDER, A CHARLATAN AND A CAD'.) In the late 1960s, Derrida published the three texts which made his name—*Of Grammatology, Writing and Difference*, and *Speech and Phenomena*—all of which used an analysis of language and meaning to advance his philosophical position. His work spoke particularly to people who were in the business of thinking about language and texts, and was taken up enthusiastically by people working in English—and across the humanities—particularly through the '80s. How this work was received is its own complicated story, but, to do a little violence to the history, it can more or less be captured, I think, by one famous phrase: 'there is nothing outside the text.'

This little string of words—which has become something of an axiom — crops up on page 167 of the English translation of *Of Grammatology*, and has often been taken by both advocates and critics as an expression of what, in philosophy, we would call 'linguistic idealism,' or the idea that everything is language, and that, therefore, material reality is entirely 'discursively constituted.' This idea—accompanied by other Derridean ideas about how meaning arises through the 'play' of signs—then coalesced with other parts of poststructural theory—supplied by Lyotard, Baudrillard, and Foucault—to form the philosophical underpinnings of cultural postmodernism, which was principally an aesthetic phenomenon arising from the proliferation and repetition of images and signs in a globalized, technologically advanced capitalist society. To make a complicated concept simple, there's an interesting phenomenon about signs: when repeated over and over, they start to lose their meaning. (If you don't know what I'm talking about, try saying your name fifty times and at some point it will cease to mean 'you' and it's *weird*.) The cultural sensibility of the late '80s and '90s (hey there, Gen Xers), was all about the alienation, *ennui*, and general sense of inauthenticity that arises from being bombarded with images and signs, repeated *ad infinitum*, and broken up and bricolaged together in various more or less random sequences. We mostly dealt with it by being mad-ironic about everything and wearing lots of kitschy clothes (hey there, hipsters), and watching Quentin Tarantino and David Lynch films on a never-ending loop. Good times.

Anyway, back to Derrida. The point I want to make—and it's been made, but it needs to keep being made—is that when Derrida writes "there is nothing outside the text" he doesn't mean there is *nothing outside the text*. And what I mean by that is that when Derrida says 'text' he doesn't, fundamentally, mean *text-as-in-language*. This is where the issue of the dissemination of philosophy through English literature becomes pertinent. Because, from my perspective, deconstruction is not fundamentally a theory of language. Derrida was using language or signs to make an ontological point: a point about the structure of reality. And that point wasn't 'reality is entirely made of language,' it was 'everything that exists exists in networks of relation to other things.' The point he was making by talking about signs—and he could just as well have been talking, as he did later, about subjects, or political states, or works of art, or pretty much anything—is that meaning arises through relational context, but that Western philosophy, and Western theories of subjectivity, are obsessed with ignoring and erasing that. We like to think that human subjects are self-sufficient, in-dependent, self-identical, invulnerable, that we are not affected by or dependent on the world around us, and that we owe no particular ethical or political debt to anyone. Which is bullshit. (Specifically, it's neoliberal-capitalist-patriarchal bullshit.)

So, when I—or anyone I know who works in French feminism—reads 'text' in Derrida, we don't read 'language,' we read 'relation.' Or, if we want to be technical about it, what I read is 'spatial and temporal relation.' So, 'there is nothing outside the text'—a better translation of the French is 'there is no outside-text'—becomes 'nothing exists which is completely separable from its spatial and temporal relations.' Which is true. Unlike 'nothing exists which is not language,' which is manifestly untrue. (Here we might also note that this change in meaning when you read Derrida in the context of the philosophical tradition he's working in is a pretty good demonstration of his point about the way that meaning is contextually determined). So, that's the first point. The deconstructive strand of poststructuralism is not a form of linguistic idealism and doesn't support the claim that material reality is entirely 'discursively constituted.' It is rather, an ontological claim about the necessity of what I'd call 'fundamental constitutive relation,' and—when it comes to poststructural socialist feminism—it's specifically aimed at critiquing the way patriarchy and capitalism is invested in pretending we are not relational beings. (Jordan Peterson is not completely off his head when he says postmodernism is a form of 'cultural Marxism,' and if you quote me on that I will be cross.)

PART TWO: DECONSTRUCTIVE FEMINISM AND THE BODY

The second point that follows from all of this is that it is philosophically incoherent to think that deconstruction is anti-materialist. As is relatively well known, one of the other main deconstructive ideas is the critique of binary hierarchies. This argument goes like this: The construction of patriarchal Western subjectivity functions through a network of metaphysical oppositions: Masculine/Feminine, Father/Mother, Rational/Emotional, Mind/Body, Immaterial/Material, Civilized/Primitive, Home/Foreign, Universal/Particular, One/Many, Eternal/Mutable, Immortal/Mortal, Sky/Earth, etc., etc., etc. The construction of meaning and subjectivity has traditionally focused on privileging one half of the binary—the masculine, and everything metaphysically associated with it, like the mind, rationality, and civilization—and devaluing/erasing the feminine half of the binary. And here the point about the necessity of relation becomes important. Because the argument is that all the binaries are interdependent, and, hence, privileging one half both misrepresents reality and has terrible political and social consequences, because the act of privileging one half is implicated in the oppression and othering of groups—especially women and people of colour—who are associated with the devalued half.

What I take from the poststructural analysis of binary hierarchy is that the erasure of the feminine, the maternal, the material, and the body is an axiomatic gesture of Western thought. A few years after Derrida's central texts were published, Luce Irigaray went on to call this elevation of mind over body "the foundational act of metaphysics."[1] This gesture enables the patriarchal male subject to construct himself as invulnerable, sovereign, and absolute, by disavowing his debt to—and dependency on—material reality in general and the bodies of women in particular. (See 'The Deep Structure of Gender,' p. 93.) This model fits neatly with the second-wave feminist analysis of gender. Patriarchy is a system which functions by erasing—and

---

[1] Luce Irigaray, *An Ethics of Sexual Difference* (Ithaca, NY: Cornell University Press, 1993), p. 27.

simultaneously appropriating—the bodies and labour of women. That is, at base, *why it exists.* Western philosophical thought—and the gendered structures it props up—facilitates that appropriation by withholding recognition from women's reproductive and domestic labour, and denying men's dependency on that labour, even while it creates and supports their existence.[2] And the fact that many men know they're doing this—and are still going to be dependent on us (and our wombs and breasts and vaginas) no matter how much they deny it—is not accidentally related to why they're often so controlling and violent towards us.

So, to recap: Deconstruction is a theory that stipulates that privileging one pole of a binary hierarchy is a) metaphysically unsupportable, and b) politically dodgy. It's therefore a) philosophically incoherent to think that deconstruction is anti-materialist or that you can use it to support your anti-materialism, and b) given that 'materiality' is historically associated with the oppressed/erased/appropriated feminine pole of the binary, anti-materialism is politically sketchy af.

PART THREE: ALL THAT TROUBLE WITH GENDER

The first claim I'm going to make, just to set the cat among the pigeons from the get-go, is that Butler is not a feminist, or rather, that what she's doing in *Gender Trouble* is not feminist philosophy—it's queer theory, and the reason why queer theory and feminist philosophy are different things is because they have a different set of political concerns. When I say she's not a feminist, I don't mean 'she doesn't identify as a feminist,' or 'she's not concerned about women's oppression in general terms.' What I'm saying is that women's oppression is *not* what she's concerned with in *Gender Trouble*, that she makes a move that creates *massive* problems for how to articulate and explain women's oppression, and it's less than evident how much she really cares about that. (And I REALLY want lefty dudebro types to stop throwing her in my face every time I make a political claim about the oppression of women because *Butler. Is. Not. A. Fucking. Feminist.*)

So, to try and back this up: The last time I read *Gender Trouble* I came across this passage at the start of the original preface that pretty much blew my mind:

I read Beauvoir who explained that to be a woman within the terms of masculinist culture is to be a source of mystery and unknowability for men, and this seemed confirmed somehow when I read Sartre for whom all desire, problematically assumed

---

[2] The same is true of the labour and subjectivity of peoples of colour, and also of the relationship between 'man' and the natural world.

*to be heterosexual and masculine, was defined as **trouble***. *For that masculine sub-ject of desire, trouble became a scandal with the sudden intrusion, the unanticipated agency, of a female 'other' who inexplicably returns the glance, reverses the gaze, and contests the place and authority of the masculine position. The radical dependency of the masculine subject on the feminine 'Other' suddenly exposes his autonomy as illusory. **That particular dialectical reversal of power, however, couldn't quite hold my attention.*** (My emphasis [!!!!!].)[3]

To break this down: what Butler is describing in this passage is one way of summarizing the essential insight of French feminist thought. Here it's framed in terms of the way patriarchal masculinity denies its dependence on the feminine through denying the expression of women's subjectivity in the gaze... but, as we just saw above, we can also frame it through the mas-culine dependence on the materiality of women's bodies. The central point is this: the Western patriarchal subject is invested in denying its depend-ence on women and is therefore invested in erasing and othering women, refusing to recognize both their personhood and their reproductive labour, and responds to all assertions of women's psychic and material existence as a threat to its 'illusory' autonomy, invulnerability, sovereignty, or mastery. And what we have next is Judith Butler—the great poststructural 'femi-nist'—summarizing poststructural French feminism's central thought about how the oppression of women works, and then telling us, basically, that *she's just not interested.*

   And she's not interested—either intellectually or politically. Philosophy, when it comes down to it, is an entirely motivated business. (All that bullshit about rational disinterest is just another patriarchal ruse.) What we work on is what matters to us, and what matters to us, more often than not, is what hurts us. We work on our wounds, on the places where we have bashed into the world or the world has bashed into us and we came away bleeding and tried to stem the flow of blood by imagining how things could be otherwise. When I say Judith Butler is not a feminist, what I mean is that her wound is not a wound of being oppressed *as a member of the female sex class*—or at least, that's not how she experiences it. Her wound is a wound of being oppressed as a gender-non-conforming lesbian, which she experiences not as a mat-ter of being female, but rather, as arising through what she calls 'the het-erosexual matrix.' As she goes on to say immediately following the passage above, what she is interested in is the way "power appeared to operate in the production of that very binary frame for thinking about gender," or "that bi-nary relation between 'men' and 'women,' and the internal stability of those

---

[3] Judith Butler, *Gender Trouble: Feminism and the Subversion of Identity* (London and New York: Rout-ledge Classics, 1990), p. xxix-xxx.

terms." That is, Butler's solution for dealing with her particular wound of homosexual gender non-conformity is to try and trouble the distinction between 'men' and 'woman' at a fundamental ontological level. (And for those of us who think we need the difference between men and women to describe *how* and *why* men oppress women, that is, *seriously*, trouble.)[4]

To understand how she does this we need more than just a flattened reading of deconstruction as an assertion of linguistic idealism, although deconstruction will play its part. What I want to point to here is that, while Butler had, of course, inherited her fair share of deconstruction, her fundamental method in *Gender Trouble* owes a lot more to Foucault than it does to Derrida. In basic terms, what this is about is anti-normativity. Queer theory as an intellectual movement more or less hinges on the idea of anti-normativity— which makes the uniformity of much of the present performance of queerness kind of hilarious and also sad-making. Foucault famously outlined an analysis of the 'micro-politics of power,' which was principally interested not in how power negatively oppresses or represses people, but the way in which power operates through social norms in order to positively 'produce' subjects. And there's a lot of good and useful stuff in there, about how legal, medical and educational norms and practices mould us into certain kinds of subjects—and how certain kinds of identities ('the homosexual,' 'the criminal,' 'the mad-man') not only describe, but *produce* people in line with those identities—in a way that Butler calls 'performativity.'

So far so good. Now the problems. The first main problem is that there is a tendency among Foucauldians to get completely carried away with the idea of normativity (BAD) and to decide that *all* norms (BAD) are simply socially constructed[5] algorithms designed to regulate and discipline human subjects. (It's never quite clear *in whose interests*, because power in Foucault is a diffuse

---

[4] I want to say here, I care about Judith Butler's wound, just as I care about everyone's wounds. Everyone has the right to address their own wounds, and the political interests that they feel follow from that—and we need to be careful about how we deploy the discourse of 'exclusion' when we are dealing with people who are just trying to deal with their own particular shit. The issue with Butler is not, fundamentally, that her interests are not feminist interests. That's fine, in principle. The problem with Butler is that in articulating a solution to deal with her own wound she does something that makes it near impossible for other women to articulate theirs. What that creates is a situation that feels like a zero-sum game in which two groups of people who both have very legitimate reasons for hurting end up playing their wounds off against each other. It's no surprise that in a situation like that things would get extremely ugly extremely fast, and lots of people would wind up getting very hurt. And, seriously, can we please try and work out how to make it stop???? PLEASE.

[5] Here we also run into the issue that 'constructed' is generally taken to mean something like 'not-real,' 'arbitrary,' or 'could-just-as-well-be-done-any-other-way-and-is-only-done-like-this-because-*insert-dubious-political-motive*.' And indeed, that is often what 'constructed' means.

business that circulates and reproduces itself, not necessarily for anyone's particular benefit—*HUGE problem.*) This is where the idea of 'discursive constitution' really ramps up. Because there is—at least in the early, most influential Foucauldian texts—no recognition that some of our social norms are there for good material reasons—because, actually, some things are just harmful to people. There is a completely horrifying passage in the first volume of the *History of Sexuality* in which Foucault tells a story about a man with learning difficulties who sexually abuses a young girl, and all he cares about is how these terrible, puritan sexual norms about not abusing young girls are deployed to support the evil disciplinary treatment of this poor, hapless man who was just, he claims, engaging in "inconsequential bucolic pleasures." (Fuck you, Michel.)[6]

I could go on a long rant here about how this aspect of Foucault's thinking has spawned a whole sub-industry of Foucauldian feminists spouting the most inane, rage-inducing drivel about how the problem with feminists talking about rape is that it creates 'rapists' and 'victims' and how rape would all just be not-very-harmful-at-all if only we stopped thinking it was harmful but I once wrote thirty-odd pages on it and spent three weeks wanting to smash things and feeling like I was being gaslit by people who are supposed to be on my side and so I won't go there today.[7] I'll just say: NAME THE FUCKING PROBLEM. The basic point is this: some things are norms because, as well as culture and language and discourse, or whatever we want to put in the box marked 'ideas' or 'immaterial,' there are also things like nature and biology and basic human needs—which are both biological and psychic—and whatever else we want to put in the box labelled 'material.' And some of

---

We could take, say, the way women's bodily comportment is policed so that women occupy less space as an axiomatic example of how a Foucauldian micro-politics of power moulds bodies in a manner certainly informed by dubious political motives. That said, many constructed things are not constructed 'arbitrarily,' and the reason for that is basic human needs and materiality. The best example of this is something that is, literally, constructed: *houses*. We can't build houses just any old way we want. They have to serve a certain function—providing shelter—and to do that, there are certain requirements they have to meet: some kind of wall/roof arrangement (which can be circular like an igloo or a dome tent but still performs a wall/roof function), and some way to get in and out. And there are certain things we can make houses out of—wood, concrete, baked mud, ice—and certain things we *can't* make houses out of, like candy floss, unfrozen water, mercury, or anything that rots too quickly. Then there are lots of possible variations on the basic parameters, informed by the climate and materials available in a particular place, the form of life of the people using the dwelling, and cultural and artistic traditions. But all this variation happens within basic parameters, also known as *norms*. And there is absolutely nothing 'arbitrary' about those norms, and nor are they informed by dubious political motives.

[6] Michel Foucault, *The History of Sexuality Volume I* (New York: Pantheon Books, 1978), p. 31.

[7] Jane Clare Jones, 'Queer Theory, Foucauldian Feminism and the Erasure of Rape,' *janeclarejones. com*, 30 August 2018.

our norms—eat vegetables, try to exercise, don't sexually abuse children—
are norms because they have something to do with promoting well-being or
avoiding harm, and might well promote well-being or cause harm (somewhat) irrespective of whatever we happen to think or say about them, and
will continue promoting well-being or causing harm even if people stipulate
that we should not talk about them because talking about them is actually
making them happen. (Because, yeah, that whole not-talking-about-rape-
thing has always worked out fabulously for women.)

This, basically, is where Butler's... let's just call it 'assault' on the normativity of the "binary relation between 'men' and 'women'" is coming from
(*Gender Trouble*, p. xxx). In crude terms, the thought is that 'sex' is just another
bad disciplinary form of discursive normativity. (Which is about as credible
as saying that the idea there's a problem with oil slicks in the sea is just a bad
disciplinary form of normativity. Go tell that to the poor puffins.) Now, of
course, had she just said 'gender,' we'd have had no problem with it, but as we
know—and as has become multiply apparent in the way this has come down
the pipes—Butler is seriously invested in troubling the sex/gender distinction. Here we return to deconstruction, and it's where things get pretty technical, but I think it's worth following because Butler deploys deconstructive
logic to try and break down the sex/gender distinction, and her argument is
subtle but—more importantly—wrong.

It goes something like this: The determination of any identity—be it 'sex'
or 'woman'—is formed in opposition to its other—in this case, 'gender' or
'man.' (True, or at least, that's how it works inside a patriarchy. We'll come
back to this.) 'Sex/Gender' is a binary pair that roughly corresponds to the
pair 'Nature/Culture,' or 'Material/Discursive,' and it would be an axiom of
deconstruction that we can't neatly separate these from each other and that
there's something wrong with pretending we can because such acts of separation are associated with acts of erasure and exclusion which, as we saw
above, are politically sketchy. Okay...

Now we get to the place where she makes the move I want to question. In
the part of the tradition I work in, we tend to think of deconstructive and
feminist thinking as 'both/and' thinking, which we contrast with patriarchal
'either/or' thinking. A useful way to think about this is as a difference between thinking of concepts (or conceptual poles) as bounded solids which
'can't occupy the same space at the same time' and hence have to exclude
each other ('either/or'), rather than thinking in terms of fluids or gases[8] or
something that can mix or interpenetrate with another thing while still being itself ('both/and'). So, the way I would think about the relation between

---

[8] To take an example: air consists of nitrogen, oxygen, and carbon dioxide (plus some other
stuff). The constituent parts are all mixed together, and we can't separate them from each other

sex and gender—or nature and culture—is as interpenetrating, or interact-ing phenomenon, which nonetheless, cannot be collapsed into each other, and are not identical. We can't draw a perfect line between 'sex' and 'gender,' just as we can't neatly separate 'bodies' from 'minds,' but that does not mean they are the same thing. They would be, in a Derridean phrase I'm fond of, "heterogeneous but indissociable."

But—(ta-dah!)—this isn't at all where Butler goes with it. Rather, Butler never steps outside of a patriarchal 'either/or' way of thinking the relation *between* 'two things that are different but inseparable'. A thinking that—as all the talk of 'lines of demarcation' will soon show us—understands relation according to a 'model of solids.' (That's Bergson's phrase.) For sex to have its own reality that is non-discursive, she suggests, it must be possible to draw a line between 'sex/nature/unconstructed' and 'gender/culture/constructed.' As she argues in *Bodies That Matter*,[9] the "moderate critic might concede that some part of 'sex' is constructed, but some other is certainly not, and then, of course, find... herself... under some obligation to draw the line between what is and is not constructed" (p. 11).

This is the bit I dispute. There is no obligation to draw a line here, either precisely around 'sex' or precisely around 'woman,' in order for these to be meaningful terms that do work in the world. Thinking that we have to draw lines around concepts for those concepts to be meaningful is exactly the same old essentialist, spatializing, phallic rubbish that we should be criti-quing. As Wittgenstein once usefully suggested, we do not have to be able to point at the line on the floor where 'here' becomes 'there' in order to use these words with sense.[10] Because essences and clear delineations and phallic oppositions are not the only—or most important—way that concepts work. (If essences and clear delineations and phallic oppositions are actually how concepts work at all.)[11]

---

and still get air. But, at the same time, the constituent parts are all still what they are, and none of them are 'excluding' or 'absorbing' or otherwise 'erasing' each other. They're all just being themselves mixed together and, in the process, producing the phenomena we call air. Essen-tially, the move I'm interested in is that Butler argues that because we can't neatly separate 'sex' from 'gender' or 'material' from 'discursive' (and separating them would be 'exclusionary') then these concepts can be collapsed into each other. And that's wrong.

[9] Judith Butler, *Bodies That Matter: On the Discursive Limits of 'Sex'* (London and New York: Rout-ledge, 1993).

[10] "One might say that the concept 'game' is a concept with blurred edges.—'But is a blurred con-cept a concept at all?'...Frege compares a concept to an area and says that an area with vague boundaries cannot be called an area at all. This presumably means that we cannot do anything with it.—But is it senseless to say: 'Stand roughly there'?" *Philosophical Investigations*, §71.

[11] Okay, here it's worth thinking about the moves that are being made against 'woman' and, re-latedly, 'female biology' in popular discourse at the moment. The strategy basically comes down

Effectively, what Butler is doing here is taking the way metaphysical binaries have traditionally worked as systems of exclusionary opposition—*either* nature *or* culture, *either* discourse *or* materiality—and then *naturalizing* it. (Kind of ironic, really. And what's doubly ironic is that in doing this, her thinking of the relation between sex and gender is precisely the opposite of 'fluidity' or 'flux.') We could only grant reality to 'sex' by drawing a "line of demarcation" between the 'unconstructed' and 'constructed,' and such a "delimitation… marks a boundary that includes and excludes… What will and will not be included within the boundaries of 'sex' will be set by a more or less tacit operation of exclusion" (*Bodies That Matter*, p. 11). To my mind, this is only true if we think that the phallic system of binary hierarchy, and the way it constructs the poles in exclusionary opposition to each other, is the only way meaning or existence arises. And I think that is a really patriarchal assumption. What this comes down to is that Butler is conflating the idea of 'difference' and the idea of 'exclusion'—the current political resonance of that should be clear—and suggesting that 'difference' is *entirely* constructed through 'exclusion.' This amounts to a refusal to think the possibility of difference—and of relations between things that are different—in any way *other* than the way that is currently mandated by exclusionary patriarchal logic. And that requires *missing the whole point* of French poststructural feminism. 'Difference' is not phallic-opposition, and it is not exclusion. 'Woman' is *not* just 'not-man.' Just as 'man' is not just 'not-woman.' Women have their own existence outside the grid of patriarchal oppositions. And so does sex. And nature. And materiality.

---

to claiming that woman has no essence or definition. (Because, hahaha, that wouldn't be anything like what patriarchy has been saying since year dot.) Anyway, this is either expressed by claiming that a) you cannot identify the essential defining characteristic that makes someone a woman, because there are always exceptions to every characteristic you pick (e.g. there will be women who do not menstruate, or have a uterus, or are not capable of bearing children) so women lack an essence, and b) you cannot draw a neat boundary around the concept of woman, which is where the use of intersex people comes into play to support the claim that 'sex is a spectrum,' thus 'woman' lacks a definition. (It's worth noting that intersex people are *not* happy about this because they are a vulnerable group with their own political interests and they're being instrumentalized in somebody else's political fight, which is fucking dehumanizing.)

The main thing to say about this is that *the whole point of poststructuralism is to critique this theory of meaning*. Here things get a little complex, but the basic point is this: If you try to destabilize a concept by pointing to its lack of essence or definition, you are still depending on a Platonic essentialist account of how meaning works. It's just a form of reverse-Platonism. And I would argue that poststructuralism shouldn't be about reversing Platonism, it should be about *binning* Platonism. This is actually where all the stuff about the poststructuralist destruction of meaning comes from. Because if you try to destroy Platonism while everyone still assumes that the Platonic account of meaning is the only way meaning *could* work, then what everyone hears is 'there is no meaning.' Yet, weirdly, there is.

What Butler does with the fact that we couldn't define 'sex' without an 'operation of exclusion' is to refuse to grant sex its own reality and refuse the concept of 'woman' reality as well. (How anyone got away with convincing a ton of people that undermining woman as a political category was a totally rad feminist move will never cease to fry my brains, even though the answer as to why it's been taken up so enthusiastically—patriarchy—is less mysterious.) If we can't neatly define sex, but sex and gender are indissociable, what that then means for Butler is that gender *subsumes* sex—viz. "If gender consists of the social meanings that sex assumes, then sex does not *accrue* social meanings... but rather, *is replaced* by the social meanings it takes on; sex is relinquished... and gender emerges... as the term which absorbs and displaces 'sex'" (*Bodies That Matter*, p. 5). If you're going to make this move, you could equally well argue that sex 'absorbs and displaces' gender—but, oh yeah, that really *would* be conservative. Either way, denying reality to either pole of a binary, claiming one pole 'absorbs' the other,[12] or arguing that because you can't perfectly disentangle two things they're actually one thing, is not any kind of deconstructive thinking worth its name.

The last thing I want to point at is why Butler makes this eminently patriarchal move of thinking that the reality of things must be locked inside this grid of exclusionary binary opposition. To me this looks like a bit of a weird Foucauldian/Derridean mish-mash. She takes the Foucauldian account of the way power produces subjects ("juridical systems of power *produce* the subjects they subsequently come to represent" (*Gender Trouble*, p. 2)), and the Derridean idea that patriarchal subjectivity functions through a logic of hierarchization and exclusion of its other, and then fuses them together and totalizes them, so you get the claim that all "subjects *are invariably produced* through certain exclusionary practices" (*Bodies that Matter*, p. 3) that "constitute the contemporary field of power" such that "there is *no position outside this field*" (p. 7; my emphasis). This is, from a French feminist—well, from *any* feminist—perspective, a catastrophe. It is, at base, a claim (and here I suspect Butler's Hegelian/Lacanian roots are showing) that the being of *all things*—subjects, signs, political groups, political states, whatever—can *only ever and exclusively* be produced through hierarchical operations of exclusion, erasure, and othering. Which is to say that all subjects are basically patriarchal (or conversely, no subjects are patriarchal), and that hence—and this is all where is all starts to feel sickeningly familiar—that 'woman' as a political category is produced by *exactly the same* exclusionary operation of power as is 'man.' To momentarily put this in the language of race—which I know has been decreed verboten but no one has yet given me an adequate explanation

---

[12] How the hell can 'exclusion' be bad but 'absorbing' things okay?

as to why—this would be equivalent to a claim of reverse racism, or that white people have been constructed as the 'other' of black people in exactly the same way as black people have been constructed as the 'other' of white people.[13] And as we know, that's nonsense. Because power. Which doesn't just circulate indiscriminately after all.

What Butler has done by generalizing Foucault's account of productive power to suggest that patriarchal mechanisms of hierarchical exclusion equally inform the creation of *all* subjects is to destroy the analysis of patriarchy as a hierarchy of power that works by othering women. And that's, y'know, not very feminist. (See 'Judith Butler: How to Disappear Patriarchy in Three Easy Steps,' p. 166.) In a 1998 interview she gave with some post-structural feminists who work in the same tradition as me, she wondered aloud whether the "symbolic order" of our culture is actually "primarily or paradigmatically masculine?"[14]

To which I'd say, yeah Judith, yeah, it is.

---

[13] To be clear, the claim that white women's experience of oppression isn't the same as black people's experience of oppression, and that white women shouldn't make analogies that appropriate black people's experience of oppression in order to illustrate their own, seems evidently right to me. At the level of the individual, we are all situated in our specific ways. However, what no one has adequately explained is why we can't draw analogies between how gender and race function as binary hierarchies. The racist-capitalist-patriarchal mechanisms of binary hierarchy and exclusion which have constructed both 'woman' and 'black' as the 'other' of the white, male subject, function according to the same fundamental logic, and the mechanisms of appropriation, colonization, and violence that follow from that logic have played themselves out in the history of both groups of peoples. (Although again, how that is experienced at the level of the individual will differ, and especially for women of colour, because intersectionality.) If we can't talk about the co-implication of gender and race when we are analyzing the binary logic of the system, we lose an incredibly important aspect of how we understand structures of oppression. And that's ground I don't want to give unless someone can explain why I should in a way that makes sense. Given the complete failure of anyone to give an adequate account of this with respect to the Dolezal-issue (and to be clear, as far as I'm concerned, if black people say no, then black people say no), I'm sceptical that anyone has a good argument about why these things are different at the level of metaphysical and political hierarchy other than 'because reasons or else.'

[14] Pheng Cheah, Elizabeth Grosz, 'The Future of Sexual Difference: An Interview with Judith Butler and Drucilla Cornell,' *Diacritics*, 28(1), 1998, p. 27.

THE DEEP STRUCTURE OF GENDER

Excerpt of talk given at Cambridge Radfems

NOVEMBER 2019

Poststructural feminism has many roots, but one of the central threads running through its intellectual antecedents is that the nature of human being can only be understood by foregrounding the relation *between* self and other, or self and world. According to this analysis, the dominant Western conception of the subject—which runs from Plato through Descartes to the modern liberal, and indeed, neo-liberal subject—is based on what we might think of as a sovereigntist lie. We are inclined to think ourselves as autonomous, independent, sovereign selves; pure Platonic minds; rational, disembodied *cogitos*; the atomic utility-maximizers of neo-classical economics. But what is necessarily, and I would say, deliberately, concealed by these dreams of independent sovereign selves is the degree to which human life—to which all life, in fact—can only arise, and can only be maintained, in networks of dependency, vulnerability, and relation.

To poststructural thinkers of a masculinist bent—and yes, I'm looking at you, Lacan—this impossibility of the sovereign self is a tragedy. The subject is fractured, its idealized self-identity irremediably split by relation, and we are each consigned to an endless, impossible quest to regain our lost omnipotence. Irigaray will be the first thinker to decisively challenge this story, to re-read the history of philosophy as an exercise in patriarchal fantasy, to question why we should assume that subjects must be absolutely sovereign, and to unpack how this fantasy produces the masculine erasure and appropriation of women. But Irigaray was not the first woman to apply such philosophical tools to examining how the sovereigntist subject produces the patriarchal projection of 'Woman.' That honour goes to Simone de Beauvoir's historic, and monumental, *The Second Sex*.

Beauvoir—along with Sartre, Merleau-Ponty, Jacques Lacan, and basically anyone who thought they were anyone in Parisian intellectual circles— attended a series of lectures given by the Russian philosopher Alexandre Kojève in the '30s on the subject of Hegel's *Phenomenology of Spirit*.[1] Kojève gave

---

[1] Alexandre Kojève, *Introduction to the Reading of Hegel* (Ithaca, NY: Cornell University Press, 1969/1980).

a reading of the centrality of Hegel's Master-Slave dialectic to the development of human subjectivity which would have an indelible effect on the next 50 years of French philosophy. In Kojève's Hegelian telling, self-consciousness requires an encounter with another consciousness, and this encounter is necessarily animated by 'fundamental hostility,' because each subject is striving for a kind of narcissistic sovereign omnipotence, and wants to force the other to recognize him in precisely the terms he dictates. (Hello, pronoun protocols!) The subjects then embark on a fight to the death to extract recognition from the other in exactly their own terms ('I Am Who I Say I Am'), which is only resolved when one party loses their nerve and allows themselves to be subjugated. Whereupon the shiny new Master discovers that recognition extracted by violent domination doesn't actually count as authentic recognition and he still feels completely alone and unvalidated. So, let that be a lesson to us all.

Trans activist protest outside the feminist conference FiLiA, Portsmouth, October 2021

There are serious reasons to trouble this assumption that intersubjectivity can only be understood in terms of fundamental hostility. Any woman who has mothered a child will tell you that the dyadic dance through which human consciousness arises consists of far more than just a rage-filled struggle to impose our sovereign omnipotence on the other. However, for Beauvoir, the drive to sovereign omnipotence is a kind of ineluctable nature, which leads to man positing 'Woman' as the 'Other.' As she writes in the Introduction of *The Second Sex*,[2] "the category of Other is as original as consciousness itself," for if, "following Hegel, a fundamental hostility to any other consciousness is found in consciousness... the subject posits itself only in opposition; it asserts itself as the essential and sets up the other as inessential,

---

[2] Simone de Beauvoir, *The Second Sex*, translated by C. Borde and S. Malovany-Chevallier (London: Vintage, 2011).

as the object." On the basis of the thought that "each consciousness seeks to posit itself alone as sovereign subject," and that this drive structures patriarchal subjectivity, we hence arrive at the famous declaration that "He is the Subject; he is the Absolute. She is the Other" (pp. 6-7).

While we may want to question Beauvoir's assumption about the necessity of this fundamental hostility, her analysis of a sovereigntist subjectivity that renders 'Woman' an objectified Other was a historic contribution to the thinking of patriarchal gender. What is so important about this analysis is that it established that 'Woman,' in Western culture, has never been thought in her own terms, but is, rather, fashioned by the negating projections of the male subject. Beauvoir was the first person to really grasp the thought of the universal—or default—male subject, and to understand how 'Woman' is produced by a mechanism of inversion *of* that male subject *by* that male subject. As she writes, "Humanity is male" while "Woman is the negative," and man defines Woman, "not in herself, but in relation to himself."[3] She notes, as many feminists have done since, that Aristotle defined the female *as* female by virtue of a "certain lack of qualities," or as "suffering from natural defectiveness," and that Thomas Aquinas considered femaleness to reside in being an "incomplete man" (p. 5). This understanding of how the patriarchal imagination centres the male subject as human and thus produces 'Woman' as an inverted absence is central to all deep-thinking of the structure of patriarchal gender, running right through second-wave feminist analysis, up to its recent empirical demonstration in Caroline Criado Perez's *Invisible Women*.

Irigaray then adds to—and complicates—Beauvoir's analysis of patriarchal gender. From poststructuralism, Irigaray takes the thought of how the sovereign subject constructs itself inside a web of conceptual binary hierarchies. The world is divided into binary pairs, and the male subject apportions to himself mind, reason, culture, ideas, immateriality, identity, eternity, and changelessness—all qualities which would allow him to transcend the limiting confines of a vulnerable embodied existence. By projection, 'Woman' is then made the repository of body, emotion, nature, matter, difference, process, and change: all those embodied, animal attributes the invulnerable

---

[3] It's worth noting here that the definition of 'being female' given in Andrea Long Chu's *Females* (London: Verso, 2019) is a frankly staggering demonstration of the patriarchal tendency to define 'Woman' by negation, viz. "femaleness is a universal sex defined by self-negation," or "any psychic operation in which the self is sacrificed to make room for the desires of another" (p. 11). There's a lot to say about the wrongness here, but it's usefully illustrative, and I have an almost grudging respect for the explicitness of Chu's misogyny. Chu might claim this passage constitutes a "wildly tendentious definition" (p. 12), but this is not remotely true. It is a simple articulation of the core of the patriarchal construction of 'Woman.'

sovereign self wants nothing to do with. This mechanism produces the hierarchy of value and activity that, in a significant sense, *is* the deep conceptual infrastructure of patriarchal gender. The sovereign male subject will instantiate the values of the properly human, while the female will be left with all the dirty, fleshy work—just as 'nature' has intended. Challenging this hierarchy—both in thought and in terms of our social organization—is one of the central tasks of feminist analysis. And, for all the snazzy sounding talk about 'smashing binaries,' erasing the existence of female people is definitely *not* the way to go about it. (See 'A Note on 'Smashing the Binary,'' p. 113.)

What Irigaray takes from poststructuralism is an analysis of how the patriarchal construction of the default, sovereign male subject depends on disavowing the material vulnerability of his own existence and projecting it onto women. However, unlike Beauvoir, she is not content to understand this projection of 'Woman as Other' simply in terms of the inevitable sovereign drive of all human consciousness. Rather, to her mind, this drive is fundamentally impelled by the male subject's inability to reckon with the vulnerability of material and maternal dependence. It is here that she innovatively critiques Lacanian psychoanalysis, and then re-reads Western philosophy as an idealist fantasy that rests on, and constantly repeats, the 'murder of the mother.'[4]

Lacan's famous theory of the 'mirror stage' of child development was also greatly influenced by Kojève's reading of Hegel. According to Lacan, the mirror stage is an archetypal moment in the development of the sense of self, through which a child comes to perceive himself as a coherent whole by identifying with his reflection in a mirror. (The child in Lacan's account is, of course, male.) This feat of triumphant self-integration lends the child the thrusting "impressiveness of statues."[5] It is this process that "constitutes the ego" with the "attributes of permanence, identity, and substantiality."[6] The basis of Irigaray's critique of Lacan was to notice that this mythical developmental moment doesn't actually involve a mirror. Children are not formed in relation to an impassive reflecting object, but in relation to an active reflecting *person*. That is, this mirror-thing is actually a mother-person. And crucial things are concealed by turning mothers into mirrors. Firstly, the dependency of all human beings on the material and psychic *labour* of women. And secondly, that all human beings develop in an interactive dyad *between* two subjects, and not simply by narcissistically projecting ourselves onto

---

[4] Jane Clare Jones, 'Luce Irigaray: The Murder of the Mother,' *New Statesman*, 14 May 2014.

[5] Jacques Lacan, 'Some Reflections on the Ego,' *International Journal of Psychoanalysis*, 34, 1953, p. 15.

[6] Jacques Lacan, 'Aggressivity in Psychoanalysis,' in *Écrits: A Selection*, translated by Alan Sheridan (London: Routledge, 1977), p. 17.

mute reflecting surfaces. Mothers, it turns out, are actually people.

Irigaray took the insight that patriarchal subjectivity functions by eliding intersubjective and material dependence and turned it back on the history of philosophy, meticulously examining all the places where the male philosopher had, in Beauvoir's words, made himself 'Absolute,' and uncovering the hidden traces of the mirror/mother. The reflecting surface of the mirror is an extremely powerful metaphor for conceptualizing the deep structure of patriarchal gender and understanding women's gender role within that structure. It is not for nothing that Virginia Woolf noted, 90 years ago, that "[w]omen have served all these centuries as looking glasses possessing the magic and delicious power of reflecting the figure of man at twice its natural size."[7]

The first point I want to make here is that the patriarchal role of 'woman-as-mirror' is fundamentally about service. As Woolf indicates—in a manner both Beauvoir and Irigaray would surely endorse—a central part of that service is reflecting back to men their chosen image of themselves, and responding to men as those men want to be responded to. To be a good mirror, women must not exhibit too much subjectivity, or introject too much personality, into this relation—because a surface that bears too much of its own image will do a bad job of reflecting what is demanded of it. It is here the patriarchal imagination posits the ideal 'Woman' as 'passivity,' and we encounter the many ways patriarchal femininity functions to constrain female subjectivity, restrict expressions of agency, and turn women into pliable, ever-smiling surfaces. This notion of ideal female passivity is evidently a patriarchal projection. Because the truth is that there's nothing remotely passive about servicing the needs of men, and a woman who refused to perform the metric ton of work it requires would soon cease to seem 'ideal.' But this is labour the patriarchal mind refuses to see. When men think of women as 'passivity,' what they mean is that we should make good mirrors. That we should reflect back to them what they want and attend to their needs without introjecting our own. What they mean is that we should be pretty, pleasant, eager-to-please, and compliant.

This image of the narcissistic male subject, expecting reflective service from his female Other, captures the basic structure of relations between the sexes *inside* the matrix of patriarchal gender. As feminists have documented, female service to men involves not only attending to egos but many other forms of emotional and mental service, as well as domestic, reproductive, and sexual service. From the perspective of what I'd call the 'psycho-ontology of gender,' all these forms of service, including those of material reproductive

---

[7] Virginia Woolf, *A Room of One's Own* (London: Grafton, 1977), p. 41.

labour, are performed as acts of one-way mirroring, and all serve the function of supporting the masculine ego's narcissistic self-conception. The material-being, needs, subjectivity, and labour of woman never enter the relational equation on equal terms. As Irigaray demonstrates in 'Plato's Hystera'[8]—her epic unpacking of Plato's famous analogy of the cave—the narcissistic ideal of sovereign patriarchal subjectivity involves the attempt to elide all recognition of the material bodies his existence depends on. The male subject will cut himself free from the mess and materiality of the underground womb and ascend into the sky to commune with the Forms, free and finally unencumbered. But this immaterial ideal is an impossibility. There is no human being, no self-consciousness, no conceptualization, no identity, without the interrelation of self and other, idea and matter, mother and child, male and female. When the patriarchal subject constructs himself as an invulnerable sovereign ideal, he creates, inexorably, the erasure, and appropriation, of the existence of women.

---

[8] Luce Irigaray, 'Plato's Hystera,' in *Speculum of the Other Woman* (Ithaca, NY: Cornell University Press, 1985), pp. 241-364.

II - MISTAKES LIBERAL FEMINISTS MAKE

THREE MISTAKES LIBERAL FEMINISTS MAKE

Twitter

27 JANUARY 2020

The women supporting this are using a fundamentally liberal concept of feminism, which has a number of assumptions that incline them to think that politically erasing sex is a good idea.

To codify:

1. BIOLOGICAL DETERMINISM

Patriarchy is a *historical* structure which has oppressed women *on the basis* of their biology.

Some people—who can't distinguish nature from history or necessity from contingency—then conclude that if we recognize the material basis of women's oppression, we are saying the oppression is *necessary* or *determined*. We're not. Because women's oppression arises from the *interaction* of nature and history. We can change the bit that is historical.

Biology is not destiny.

But it is biology.

2. DENIGRATION OF THE FEMALE

Because patriarchy has used women's biology in order to explain, naturalize, and justify the oppression of women, liberal feminists have tended to think that we must therefore deny the biological difference between males and females.

This is understandable, especially given that 'Woman' has been denied humanity by associating her with the body, with the natural, with the earth, etc.

It seems then that to claim humanity, women must deny these associations.

The insight of difference and radical feminism is that this move is fundamentally an acceptance of the patriarchal claim that maleness—understood as mind, reason, etc.—*is* the definition of humanity, and women are only human insofar as they are the same as men.

It is, fundamentally, a form of internalized misogyny that cannot conceive femaleness and humanity as compatible concepts. That is, which hasn't moved past the patriarchal construction of 'Woman.'

3. EQUALITY = SAMENESS

Thus, a certain camp of feminists ends up believing that liberation or equality of women depends on pretending that women are identical to men.

Again, this is readily understandable. If patriarchy has used women's difference as justification for our subjugation, it would seem to follow that liberation depends on denying that difference.

However, again, this repeats the error of staying inside the patriarchal frame, and leads to the situation we have now, where women engage in the public world, as designed by men on the basis of men's needs and assumptions, while continuing to do most of the work in a relatively unreconstructed domestic sphere.

Women's liberation demands that we change our social organization fundamentally so that it is based on a just accounting of the value of their reproductive labour, in a manner that also supports women's full participation in public life.

The denial of sex, while superficially compelling if you are stuck inside patriarchal logic, will simply repeat the refusal to grant adequate recognition and value to women's labours.

And that is why this version of feminism is the one that has been most widely disseminated.

And why it has offered no resistance to trans ideology.

#DifferenceNotEqualityFeminism

SEX-BASED OPPRESSION AND BIOLOGICAL DETERMINISM

Twitter

8 AUGUST 2020

Right. Once more for the people at the back.

Women are oppressed *by* gender *on the basis of sex.*

When we say that female oppression is 'sex-based,' we mean 'female people are oppressed on the basis of sex,' NOT 'female oppression arises necessarily and ineluctably because of sex.' Female people are oppressed by a cultural mechanism and power hierarchy that feminists called, once-upon-a-time, 'gender.' Gender is a social system, we think it harms female people (and children, and men, and the planet) and we want it dismantled.

Gender, however, is applied to people *on the basis of their sex*. It arose historically, because the development of private property, agriculture, and class-based social relations turned female people into a valuable reproductive (and sexual) resource.

That is, women's bodies are not accidentally related to the structure of gender, and the application of gender to women is, fundamentally, derived from male desire to control and appropriate their bodies.

You cannot understand male dominance and its replication through the gendered power structure if you forget that the structure is about male control of resources, and that this applies also to the patriarchal exploitation of the land, the bodies of other exploited peoples (both people of colour and working-class people), and the mechanisms of colonial appropriation.

The sexed nature of female bodies is, hence, a necessary condition to explain the structure of male dominance (aka 'patriarchy'), and the other systems of exploitation it patterns.

But the sexed nature of female bodies is *not a sufficient condition* to explain patriarchy, because patriarchy arises out of the interaction of nature—given material limits and processes—and culture—the way we organize our societies.

The task of feminism is to think about how these cultural aspects of the power structure might be *otherwise*, and how we could change our culture so that social organization between the sexes and the organization of the crucial processes of reproduction and reproductive labour are more equitable and don't lead to the exploitation of women or limit their self-actualization as human beings.

Pretending that the exploitation of women's reproductive labour has nothing to do with women's reproductive capacities won't get us there. Female people are going to carry on having the babies and pretending otherwise will do nothing to address the social inequality that arises through the lack of recognition and appropriation of women's reproductive labour, or the system of enculturated male entitlement and female service that propagates that system.

If you don't understand the relation of nature and culture, the difference between necessary and sufficient conditions, or the difference between biology existing and biological determinism, that's *your* problem, not ours.

WOMEN ARE NOT A GENDER

Twitter

22 MARCH 2022

The claim that thinking 'women are female' is 'gender essentialism' only makes sense if you believe that 'woman' is a gender word and not simply a sex-class designation.

This reinvention of 'woman' as only a gender word, rather than a sex word, is singularly the creation of academic feminism—mostly third-wave academic feminism (there are some instances in second-wave feminism, but it was not the majority interpretation). It is especially the creation of Judith Butler, exemplified by her misreading of Beauvoir's famous line: 'one is not born but becomes woman.'[1] What Butler misses is that, for Beauvoir, 'Woman' designates the *projection of the patriarchal idea of women.* Beauvoir doesn't confuse the empirical existence of female people—'women'—with the patriarchal projection of 'Woman'[2] and, moreover, *The Second Sex* is a *critique* of the patriarchal projection, not a treatise on 'how women should be redefined as a projection.'

So, anyway, off went academic feminism getting confused and deciding that all references to 'women' denoted the patriarchal projection, while the empirical existence of female people got lost, somehow. This has a lot to do with the way academic feminists got completely freaked out and confused about biological determinism, and decided that the relationship between the existence of female people and the gendered projection could only be either 'determinist' or completely 'arbitrary,' and that seeing as it isn't and can't be

---

[1] Judith Butler, 'Sex and Gender in Simone de Beauvoir's Second Sex,' *Yale French Studies*, 72, 1986, pp. 35-49.

[2] In 1976, Beauvoir was interviewed by the feminist philosopher Susan J. Brison in Paris. Brison asked Beauvoir: "If one doesn't want to define woman negatively in relation to man—woman as an inferior man, a failed man—how can one define her positively?" Beauvoir replied: "A positive definition of 'woman'? Woman is a human being with a certain physiology, but that physiology in no way makes her inferior, nor does it justify her exploitation." *The Cambridge Companion to Simone de Beauvoir*, edited by Claudia Card (Cambridge: Cambridge University Press, 2003), pp. 190-191.

determinist it must then be 'arbitrary' and then deciding that the best way to demonstrate how arbitrary it is was to recognize male people as women.

While all this bonkers confusion was happening in universities, most women were getting on with their lives. The basic common-sense feminist understanding that women are female and that gender refers to the system of oppressive social norms still rang true to many of these women, and they still managed to grasp what academic feminism somehow forgot: that the system of norms applied to women is neither determinist nor arbitrary, but is applied on the basis of their sex to facilitate their exploitation and control.

How academic feminism made such a series of stupid mistakes is almost beyond my comprehension. But I think it has a lot to do with the increasing separation between the women's movement and the academy. Many ostensibly feminist academics lost touch with the materiality of women's actual lives. Feminist thinking became increasingly abstracted, and bowed to pressure from a patriarchal institution to produce a version of 'feminism' that isn't actually any kind of threat to male power.

I will never cease to be kind of amazed—not to mention disgusted—that as academic feminism has been forced to come back into contact with the women's movement and with women who didn't get the memo that academics had decided women are not female—and that anyone who disagrees is some kind of simplistic Nazi dinosaur—they have generally acted with unrelenting sneering superiority.

The only people who think women are a gender are academics, trans ideologues (how these two strands end up intersecting is another whole story), and the kids who have been raised on Tumblr.

The rest of the world has been, and largely continues, going about their day using the natural language meaning of the word.

Acting like this has all been settled, coming along and sneering at people who didn't get your abstruse academic memo (which is based on a bunch of intellectual errors, anyway), talking down to people, accusing them of 'gender essentialism' when *you're the one* who has completely fucked up the meaning of the term, and then calling them all the names under the sun to try and get them to comply with your nonsense is the very definition of elitism.

THE RADICAL NOTION THAT WOMEN ARE PEOPLE

janeclarejones.com

SEPTEMBER 2019

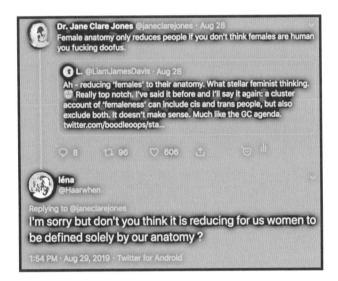

So, after a summer recess spent trying to forget that the world is going to hell in a handcart, this week's 'Back to Twitter' experience has involved a lot of feminists being berated for 'reducing women to their genitals/biology/anatomy/whatever.' This woke-approved soundbite has been around for an AGE, and my usual reaction to it is a long, slow, disbelieving blink. (It's always slightly staggering when some wokebro comes along to pronounce on your 'unstellar feminism' based on his complete inability to grasp the relation between 'biology' and 'destiny.')

Anyway, I'm not about to write a thousand-odd words to clarify this for the benefit of the TRAs (it's pretty clear the TRAs are not interested in *anything* being clarified), or even for their male accomplices (who evidently have no intention of relinquishing their shiny new get-out-of-misogyny-free cards). I do, however, care about the many young women who are buying this bullshit, and I especially care about the degree to which they are buying this bullshit because of uninterrogated, internalized assumptions about the horror of being female. (Women? Being raised to devalue their femaleness? In a patriarchy? Nah, mate.)

The first thing to note about the way this seductive soundbite works is that it relies on a slippage in meaning between 'defined by' and 'reduced to,' which plays on an inability to think *both* the 'female' and the 'human' bit contained in the proposition 'women = adult human female.' Let's for a moment take out the 'human' bit of the meaning of woman, and just think about the meaning of 'female.' Female *is* a biological classification. It is 'being the member of the reproductive sex class that produces large immobile gametes,'[1] a classification that exists reliably across the vast majority of living species, and is accompanied by a range of secondary-sex characteristics. Anyway, I have mostly resisted getting involved in the conversation about what 'woman' means because I find it all basically irrelevant to the current debate. ('Female people exist. Existence precedes essence. Next.' As far as I'm concerned.) To wit: What I'm interested in is defending the political rights of female people, and no matter how many times TRAs insist on telling us sex is unfathomably 'complex,' it really isn't. Female animals make big gametes. That's just *what female means.*

The idea that there is something 'reductive' about 'defining' female animals as female makes absolutely no sense. What must be meant, therefore, is that there is something damaging, or harmful, or morally bad about 'defining' female humans by—or 'reducing' women to—their reproductive function. Which of course there is. When we say women are adult human *females* we are defining 'being female' in terms of a reproductive function, because that's what female means. We are *not*, however, 'defining' the entirety of the existence of adult *human* females in terms of that function. What is conveyed by this second sense of 'defined by' is actually something more like '*reducing* or *limiting* the entire existence of human females to their reproductive function,' which would make us um, Thomas Aquinas. ('Yes, Judy, I know you think we're all mad Catholics.')

Now I don't think trans activists believe half the shit they throw at the 'let's undermine the existence of women' wall, but let's take them at their word for the moment. What is going on when they accuse us of 'defining' women by or 'reducing' women to our reproductive function has a lot to do with their own inability to think sex independently of gender. This is the sense in which they are, in fact, entirely in hock to a conservative patriarchal metaphysics of gender—which they then project onto us, before merrily accusing *us* of being the anti-feminists. If feminists insist that women are female, then, they suppose, we *must* mean that women are thereby yoked to all the patriarchal bullshit about how female people should or should not behave, and we *must mean* that the lives of women are to be valued solely in terms of their reproductive function. But since we don't share their inability to distinguish between sex and gender, we mean nothing of the sort.

---

[1] Emma Hilton, Twitter thread on how to recognize female animals: "She makes large gametes." 27 May 2019. (www.twitter.com/FondOfBeetles/status/1133120326844506112?s=20.)

It's worth noting that this abject failure to understand the difference and relation between sex and gender is a manifestation of a more general problem that permeates trans activist discourse (and, maddeningly, also the minds of the third-wave feminists who support them). That is, the abject failure to adequately think the difference and relation between nature and culture, or between biology and history. This one comes up over and over. We see it especially in discussions around the origins of patriarchy, or whenever we try to get TRAs to produce an even barely passable account of why women are oppressed. When we make the claim that women are oppressed because of their biology, we are obviously *not* claiming that the patriarchal system of gender that positions women as a reproductive and sexual resource arose *inevitably* on the basis of that biology. (Shulamith Firestone was wrong on this one.) Patriarchy is a socio-historical construct. Feminists are not biological determinists. But socio-historical constructs do not arise willy-nilly with no relation to material constraints. (As I say when I get exasperated, try building a house out of candy floss and tell me how 'arbitrary' social constructs are.)

Turning women into a resource in a manner that abnegates their humanity and freedom was not a necessary outcome of female biology. To explain that outcome you'd need to examine why a certain form of masculinity is so. damn. committed. to denying its vulnerability by exploiting and appropriating everything it's materially dependent on. But for persons to be converted into materially appropriable resources, they have to have *some* quality that makes them valuable as such. In the case of women, that's our reproductive and sexual use to men—followed closely by our domestic and emotional service. That is, women's biology is a *necessary but not sufficient condition* of patriarchal domination and, therefore, any undoing of patriarchy will have to reckon with women's reproductive and sexual function and men's long-inculcated entitlement to it. Beauvoir was right that biology is not destiny. But delivering on that promise demands that we challenge the entire socio-historic edifice that has constrained women's destiny *in order to* appropriate their biology, and we won't get there by playing make-believe with unicorns and piles of glitter.

The thing that really concerns me here, however, is why this little soundbite is so seductive to young women. To return to our proposition about women being 'adult human females,' what this comes down to is an inability to think the *being-together* of femaleness and humanness. This is not at all surprising. Patriarchy has constructed the being of women as a kind of maternal-bovine non-being, a life made up of self-abnegating sexual-reproductive service, while dispensing all the exciting, creative, self-actualizing, human-like activity to the penis people. (Note: I am *not* saying this is what maternity is, I am saying this is what 'woman-as-mother' is in the patriarchal imaginary.) Given that we're all raised inside the patriarchal imagination, it's easy to see why girls and young women decide they rather fancy the 'human-box,' and then further conclude that the way to do this is to renounce their femaleness. Pretty much every feminist I know has walked this way. Pretty much all of us were, at some point or other, the kind of woman who considered it an unerring compliment to be told that we were 'one of the boys.' Pretty much all of us believed that—unlike those other silly girls—we were never going to be constrained by either the yoke of femininity or the obdurateness of embodiment. Until we got pregnant. Or were sexually assaulted. Or discovered that no matter how rational and male-identified we were, the penis people were still never going to take us seriously. Because we were women.

At some point in there, it occurred to us that in trying to divest ourselves (impossibly) of our femaleness, we were simply agreeing that women were lesser humans. It occurred to us that all the patriarchal devaluation about what female people are and what female people can do, all the images, too, of motherhood as bovine-passivity rather than an active and creative endeavour, were just so much masculinist hogwash held in place by the enormous edifice of binary hierarchy our adversaries seem so certain they're smashing. There is no challenge to patriarchal gender in colluding with its devaluation of femaleness. There is no challenge to patriarchal metaphysics in recoiling from the body, in thinking that because it is the historic and ongoing site of our appropriation, freedom depends on dissolving into an immaterial masculinist mind. And there is no path to liberation for human females in thinking our humanity can only be won by renouncing our femaleness.

The task of feminism is to assert, and to fight for, the humanity of female people.

It is the radical notion that women are people.

Not the radical notion that if women are people, they cannot be female.

DIFFERENCE VS. EQUALITY FEMINISM

Twitter

17 APRIL 2021

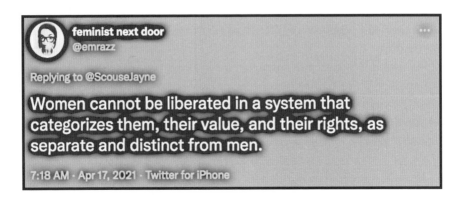

This is a perfect illustration of the conceptual mistake made by liberal/ equality feminism, viz. the inability to think difference free from hierarchy of value.

If you think difference equals hierarchy, then you will think you must abolish difference to create equality, with equality being conceptualized as 'sameness.'

Within this frame, the demand to abolish the recognition of the material and political specificity of women will be read as liberation, and the women objecting to that erasure will hence be positioned as 'conservative.'

What this forgets, of course, is that there is a whole tradition of 'difference feminism,' which develops out of the thought originally articulated by Beauvoir: that patriarchy functions by positing 'Woman as Other.'

Difference feminism would argue that our entire culture is structured by ideas of the human that are based on men's thinking, experience, and systems of value, or what we could call the 'male default.'

A very useful, concrete, illustration of this thought is given by Caroline Criado Perez in *Invisible Women*, which looks at what happens when you design the world around the male default, and never bother to pay any attention to the specificity of women's lives, experience, or bodies.

Difference feminism therefore comes to a completely different conclusion about how women should be liberated than equality feminism.

Equality feminism thinks justice—understood flatly as equality-as-sameness—will come about as the result of denying any difference between women and men. Difference feminism thinks that we already live in a culture built on denying the difference between women and men because it structures everything around the male default.

Difference feminism argues that justice—understood not as equality, but as meeting the specificity of people's needs/'equity'—requires recognizing difference, and structuring the world so that the specificity of different needs are met.

A good concrete illustration of this are issues that arise from women's reproductive role. If you treat women as men in the context of reproduction, and in relation to the workplace, you are being unjust, because the specificity of women's needs are *different*.

Women therefore need sex-based rights and protections around pregnancy and maternity. Indeed, in British law, they have them. (This is where I lapse into ranting about American feminists looking down their noses at British feminists over the trans issue when they haven't even sorted out proper maternity rights for American women.)

Which is all to say, thinking women's liberation can be found in equality and sameness is massively inadequate and does not produce justice for women. It leaves the entire patriarchal structure intact, and allows for women's freedom only insofar as we can be accommodated by a world designed around the needs of men. Moreover, it allows for our liberation only insofar as we can be assimilated to a model of the human structured by men's assumptions, priorities, and values. That is, in the final analysis, it grants women humanity only insofar as we are *like* men.

Difference feminism, by contrast, demands that the entire structure of the male default and its values, assumptions, and hierarchies be junked, and we start from the premise that there are *two types of humans*. Two types of humans who are both *equally* human, and who share many of the same characteristics, but who are also, in some significant ways, different. This calls for attention to the specificity of women's material, political and lived experiences, and the rejection of the patriarchal denigration, erasure, and appropriation of those experiences.

What equality feminists never seem to understand is that in demanding equality-as-sameness-as-being-like-men, what they are fundamentally doing is colluding with the patriarchal hierarchy of value that thinks men *are* the default human and women are the 'Other'.

And whether women haved internalized this view has a lot to do, I think, with where they come down on the trans issue.

It's what makes all the talk of 'reducing women to their biology' compelling to some women, because they are still basically operating inside a patriarchal frame that cannot conceive that *female people in all their material specificity are as human as men*, and therefore thinks women's freedom will be won by renouncing their femaleness, and by abolishing women.

<Ends>

A NOTE ON 'SMASHING THE BINARY'

janeclarejones.com

OCTOBER 2018

> *"All western culture rests on the murder of the mother."*
> *Luce Irigaray*

Trans ideology is what we might call a 'scavenger' or 'magpie' discourse. My sense is basically that it's reverse engineered: it's a set of central claims fashioned to achieve political objectives, which have then been backfilled with whatever bits and bats of argument were needed to appeal to the woke, give succour to misogynists, and create the general impression that it makes some kind of sense. Although the entire discourse is not academic—we have no complete academic genealogy for its development—many of these bits and bats do come from the academy. And one of the most important of these—particularly, I think, with respect to why many academics have been so mystifyingly receptive to this pile of incoherent wiffle—is the idea that trans ideology is doing the venerable, emancipatory work of 'smashing the binary.'

What I want to do here is think through what 'smashing the binary' *would* or *should* mean in its original context, and to lay out the fundamental conceptual mistake in how it's being thought in trans ideology. My claim—surprise!—is that this conceptual mistake is so dramatic that when trans ideologues and their allies wheel out some vague-ish claim that they're leading us to liberation by 'undoing' or 'challenging' binaries, they are, in fact, repeating *exactly* the problem that the original critique of binaries was trying to address. What this comes down to is that people don't understand the distinction between 'a binary' and 'a difference.' And in some sense this whole stupid clusterfuck rests on that confusion.

So, first off, 'binaries and why they are bad.' As I laid out in my essay on 'Poststructuralism, Butler, and Bodies' (p. 80), the critique of binaries descends from Derrida through the deconstructive strand of poststructuralism, and is central to French poststructural feminism. The central idea is that Western thought is structured around a series of conceptual *oppositions*, and that these oppositions are *gendered*.

They look something like this:

Masculine (Father)	Feminine (Mother)
Mind	Body
Reason/Rational	Emotion/Irrational
Idea/Immaterial	Matter/Material
Universal/One	Particular/Many
Independent/Self-sufficient	Dependent/Relational/Contextual
Eternal/Static/Immortal	Mutable/Process/Mortal
Civilized/Human/Culture	Primitive/Animal/Nature
White	Black
Absolute/Pure/Immune	Corrupted/Polluted/Infected
Impenetrable/Inviolate/Invulnerable	Penetrable/Violable/Vulnerable

There are several things to note about these binaries. The first is that they are *hierarchical*: the masculine term is privileged over the feminine term (e.g. it's better to be mind than body, immaterial than material, and so on). The second is that they are defined by conceptual *opposition*—and this is where the concept of 'othering' comes in. The inferior terms of the binary are understood only as negations of the superior term. They're defined by their deficiencies (non-men, anyone?). The significance of this is that the binaries arise through a process in which some people *are defined in opposition to the one who defines*, a process by which the white male subject defines his others—women and black and brown peoples—as an inferior negation of himself. This conceptual mechanism is historically interwoven with violence and exploitation aimed at people on the 'wrong' side of the binary. Ergo, binaries are bad.

Now we get the conceptual clanger made by intersectional feminists and adherents to trans ideology. The whole point of binaries is that they are *conceptual discursive oppositions* laid on top of *empirical differences*. The effect of layering a binary on top of a difference is that it effectively *denies being to*, or *erases*, the inferior pole of the binary, because the inferior term in defined *only* as a negative mirror-image of the superior term, and is not granted reality, or given worth, *in itself*. The remedy for this, according to French feminist thought—that is, the way you 'deconstruct binaries' according to the intellectual tradition that thought hardest about it—is to insist on the reality of *both sides of a difference*, and to reject the way they are hierarchically constructed in discourse. So, according to French feminism, what you do is to spend a lot of time thinking through what women *are*, and what women's lived experience *tells us* in order to challenge the construction of 'Woman' as simply 'the Other of man.'

And this is where it goes completely, utterly off the rails for the woke. Instead of granting reality to both sides of the difference, and working to move our discursive structures away from the way our culture codes those differences, trans ideology has decided to try and *abolish the difference itself.* What is so interesting—and distressing—about all of this is that this 'not grasping that a difference-exists-that-is-not-a-binary' is an effect of the patriarchal conceit that underpins the whole binary structure in the first place: the inability of the patriarchal subject to relate to anything that differs from itself in *without imposing its own projections onto it.* What informs this inability to grant reality to a difference is good old-fashioned patriarchal narcissism. This is an impoverished way of relating to anything that differs from oneself only through an inverting mirror. A way of relating that cannot conceive that there could be *any other way* of relating across difference.

For the well-meaning woke, it seems like this is all opaque. They get that binaries are bad, but think that to abolish binaries we must deny the *difference* that underpins them. This is a colossal failure of imagination rooted in the way the patriarchal structure of hierarchy, othering, and domination makes itself look so natural that many people cannot imagine that there can be differences that we don't turn *into hierarchies.* If you can't imagine difference without hierarchy, you will find yourself arguing that, if we want men and women to relate equally to each other, we must pretend that they don't really exist as two distinct types of humans.

This is evidently absurd, both because the difference between males and females is not made by discourse, and the way that difference is hierarchically coded in discourse *is not determined by the difference*, and to think that it is is to mistake patriarchal hierarchy for reality. Set aside the well-meaning woke for the moment. For the people driving this discourse, the *whole point* of trying to abolish sexual difference is to allow female people to be easily appropriated by male people. When you refuse to recognize sexual difference, what actually occurs is a re-doubling of the erasure of women effected by binary hierarchy itself and of the appropriation that erasure has always allowed—because if there's nothing there in the first place, how on earth could anyone be appropriating it? One thing this debate has made screamingly, terrifyingly evident to me is the rightness of the French feminist assertion that—within the binary conceptual structure of Western thought—women do not actually exist. If we did, our existence would never have been so easily handed over by nearly everyone concerned, and the appropriation we are resisting would never have been so easily caricatured as an act of illegitimate hatred.

Which is all to say, well-meaning woke, you've been played. And as for the rest of you misogynists....

JUDITH BUTLER: HOW TO DISAPPEAR PATRIARCHY IN THREE EASY STEPS

janeclarejones.com

JANUARY 2019

TRIGGER WARNING: Fucking Pissed Off.

So, as many of you are aware, the high priestess of genderology decided to descend from her exalted academic plinth and relay her thoughts[1] on the on-going internecine shitshow that she, probably more than anyone else, has helped to inspire. Except of course that, with her usual intellectual integrity, the thoughts she decided to relay about said shitshow totally ignored what is really going on, in favour of pretending that this is a conflict between the wibbly-wobbly-gender-and-sex-is-fluid-rah-rah-liberation crowd and, basically, um, the Pope. Despite being entirely predictable, it's staggeringly disingenuous. As Judy should know, this is a conflict over the fault line in feminism that she, probably more than anyone else, created—a fault line between those of us who think patriarchy is a system of sex-based male dominance enacted through cultural mechanisms (also known as 'gender') and those who think that patriarchy is...like, seriously, what the fuck do they even think it is...? Some kind of free-floating cultural system that has nothing to do with actual bodies and their appropriation and domination? A randomly generated set of signs and signifying practices that shape our subjectivity? A thought that leads, in practice, to staking feminism's whole liberation project on the epic transcendent power of some spectacularly superficial idea of gender-fucking.

Look, I'm a feminist and a Prince-fan. I like superficial gender-fucking as much as the next woman. (I actually think Prince's gender-fucking wasn't merely superficial, but that's another story...) BUT superficial gender-

---

[1] Judith Butler, 'The Backlash Against 'Gender Ideology' Must Stop,' *New Statesman*, 21 January 2019.

fucking has fuck-all effect on the fundamental patterns of male dominance. Gender-fucking, in practice, encourages male people to think they're 'smashing the patriarchy' because they dare to pair some nail varnish with their beards. Never mind that they act like exactly the same entitled, narcissistic, dependency-denying, mind-over-matter, female-erasing assholes they've always been. If gender isn't just a penchant for gold lamé pocketbooks and lace and is actually something to do with the psychic, material, ontological, and economic structures that underpin male dominance, then, lo, it turns out *you still need an analysis of male dominance* if you're going to actually do a bloody thing about it. And I'm sorry, Judy, I know you were traumatized by Dworkin and MacKinnon trying to ban porn, but having an analysis of male dominance doesn't actually make me, y'know, the fucking Pope.

Yesterday, I spent the day studiously ignoring the misogynists over on The Boyce of Reason's *YouTube* channel screaming all the things misogynists scream when women point—no matter how calmly, while smiling—at male violence and say we really want it to stop. (If anyone wants to do a statistical analysis I'd be interested in the relative proportions of a) NAMALT (Not All Men Are Like That), b) You're incapable of reason, c) Stop emasculating us, d) You're unfuckable, e) She was asking for it, and f) 'We hunted the mammoth.') Meanwhile, Emily the Nazi Hunter was posing with semi-automatic machine guns and wheeling off a point-by-point plan for 'God's Own Avenging Angel's TERF Apocalypse' to a soundtrack of intersectionalibfems excitedly chanting 'Big Dick Energy.' (For ripping the thorough piss out of it, I salute you all.) And, with the sound of men being emasculated by a Gilette razor ad still ringing in my ears, everywhere else I looked, that posturing smug Donkey Kong meme spilled like dick-waving poison out of that damn Twitch thread in which a bunch of glitter-spattered Gamergaters sat around screaming 'FUCK YOU EAT SHIT' at Graham Linehan in support of the great progressive cause of Susie Green medicalizing gender-non-conforming kids with absolutely no oversight.

This week there's a conference going on at Brighton University, in which a load of 'critical thinkers' will sit around and think very *critically*. Judith Butler is doing the star turn. I was supposed to go with a friend, and put on my polite academic face, and listen while she is lauded by room full of people, many of them male, who cannot get over how fucking psyched they are that 'feminism' no longer asks them to even acknowledge, let alone challenge, male dominance. I cannot and will not do it. At this moment the thought makes me rage. And so what I want to do, instead, is to sit here and try to channel my rage into an excavation of how, and why, Judith Butler performed the magical and much-rewarded feat of making patriarchy—and the critique of patriarchy—vanish from feminism.

STEP ONE: THE ERASURE OF SEX

If Butler had a shred of honesty in her, she'd at least have the intellectual decency to acknowledge that the root of this conflict is the effort by trans activists to mandate the political, social, and legal erasure of sex. Trans ideology has thrown all manner of arguments at the task of making male and female people disappear. And a number of those arguments came from Judith Butler:

1. The instrumentalization of intersex conditions (this is principally derived from Anne-Fausto Sterling, but a version of it turns up in *Gender Trouble*, and Butler trotted it out again in the *New Statesman*).

2. The denial of the sex/gender distinction (also in *Gender Trouble* and *Bodies That Matter*, see 'Poststructuralism, Butler, and Bodies,' p. 80). Which then leads to...

3. The idea that because all concepts are human constructions (duh), then everything they name is likewise constructed. As we saw in her NS piece, Butler is *very* fond of making some kind of claim that the determination of sex is historical or cultural, and then moving seamlessly to running sex and gender together as if they are exactly the same kind of cultural phenomenon, which they're fucking not. 'Mountains' are not the same kind of thing as 'justice,' and not remotely the same kind of thing as 'telling male people they mustn't be a sissy.' Sorry.

4. 'Colonialism invented the gender binary.' Just fucking no.[2]

5. 'Intersectionality means there's not one experience of being a woman because different people's experience of being a woman is differently affected by different axes of oppression, and feminism used to exclude black women and that was bad and now it should include male people too because that's

---

[2] The most noted academic source of the 'colonialism invented the gender binary' argument is Maria Lugones's 2007 essay 'Heterosexualism and the Colonial/Modern Gender System' (*Hypatia*, 22(1)), which basically blends Fausto-Sterling's intersex arguments, Butler's account of how the heterosexual 'gender binary' constructs sex, and some decent ethnography on pre-colonial kinship and gender structures that is completely mangled by being read through Butler. For a more detailed discussion of the development and critique of this argument please see my essay 'The History of Sex: Sex Denial and Gender Identity Ideology,' forthcoming in *Sex and Gender: A Contemporary Reader*, edited by Alice Sullivan and Selina Todd (London: Routledge).

just like including black women.' Where to fucking start? (See 'Unreasonable Ideas,' p. 213.)

6. 'Women can only exist if there is a magic essence of womanhood and since women are all different there is no magic essence of womanhood, and feminism has always been against essentialism so it's feminist to think that women don't exist even though you must also believe that trans women are women because they possess the magic essence of womanhood, which is also what makes you a woman.' For fuck's sake. Read some Heidegger. Existence precedes essence. Nothing exists because of essences, and anyway, the only thing that everyone wants to abolish because it doesn't have a fucking essence is women.

I've written elsewhere about how a sexual difference reading of Western thought would posit that we live in a culture in which female people, as actually existing human beings, have, in representational terms, never existed.[3] The whole cultural system is a hall of mirrors, an endless series of male projections *onto* women, in which women's role is to reflect, grant recognition, and serve as an emotional, sexual, and reproductive *resource*. I always used to read this claim of Irigaray's as a metaphor of the structure of patriarchal male narcissism. Having now seen how easy it was to convince the whole world and his aunt that erasing female people is the path of true liberation, and the total inability of most people to even grasp what we're screaming about—let alone consider whether we have a point—I think 'metaphor' is really underselling it. The point is this: *gender*, as a hierarchical system of male power, has *always* depended on refusing to recognize that *there exists a class of human persons who have all the attributes of full human personhood and are female*. To wit: 'Feminism is the radical notion that women are people.' WE ARE STILL NOT REMOTELY CLOSE TO GETTING THIS.

Anyway, for all you friendly neighbourhood male-dominance-deniers out there, this is all remarkably helpful. If you don't recognize that female people exist and that male people exist, then you can't recognize that there is a cultural power structure in which male people are the default humans, and female people are defined, appropriated, and erased by the cultural projections—and the acts of domination those projections impel and licence— that flow from male people towards female people. If you can't recognize that male and female people exist, then you can't recognize that all these cultural tropes that we call gender have anything to do with a power relation

[3] See 'The Deep Structure of Gender,' p. 93, 'The Radical Notion that Women Are People,' p. 106, and 'A Note on 'Smashing the Binary,'' p. 113.

between male and female people, with the prioritization of the needs of male people and with the positing of women as a resource in a way that seriously fucks with their humanity. That is, if you don't recognize that male and female people exist, there *can* be no male dominance, there *can* be no female oppression, there can, in short, be no fucking patriarchy. And there can't be any female resistance to patriarchy either. Stunning work, Judith. Let's make you the boss of feminism. Back-slaps all round.

STEP TWO: POWER JUST GOES ABOUT CIRCULATING

As if pretending male and female people don't exist wasn't enough, Butler has another trick up her sleeve. This comes in the form of the Foucauldian account of power, which I discussed in more detail in 'Poststructuralism, Butler, and Bodies' (p. 80). The basis of the feminist analysis of patriarchy is that power functions as a hierarchy, and that it functions through the simultaneous acts of appropriation and refusal of recognition—because you can't be accused of appropriating something if it isn't even there can you? But Foucault—and Butler—have different ideas about power: power is not a hierarchy, it doesn't work in anyone's particular interests, and it doesn't have any underlying pattern or stable structure. Rather, power is something diffused throughout society that sculpts and structures subjectivity (more on this in a moment). Foucault himself famously wrote three volumes of the *History of Sexuality* without ever stopping to consider whether there might be something resembling a stable pattern about the way in which *male* desire (or entitlement) impacted men's relations to other people's bodies. Butler has *never* considered it (although she has denied it plenty).

STEP THREE: DESCRIBING IS PRESCRIBING

The first two steps erase the material basis of sex differences and deny the possibility that any stable power hierarchy exists. (Poof goes the patriarchy!) Having cleaned up that irksome mess, we're ready for the third step, which also stems from Foucault—and is repeated *ad infinitum* by Foucauldian and queer feminists—and which strikes at the very core of second-wave feminist analysis. It follows from the half-reasonable claim that social norms function to *produce* subjects, and morphs seamlessly into the claim that descriptions of social phenomena become normative, and hence produce the things they describe. When coupled with the belief that there is no basis for an account of 'the kind of things that are harmful to humans' (and certainly not one that says anything as gauche as 'domination is harmful to humans'), you end up with a critique that has no moral calculus other than 'norms are BAD.' (Oh, hai there queer theory, towering over the academy, not being normative in the slightest.)

What this leads to, then, as I documented with respect to Butlerian accounts of rape,[4] is that critiques of domination come to be seen as the sites that *produce*, rather than critique, harms. And when that happens, a funny thing happens to feminism. Instead of spending its time critiquing male power and the damage it does to women, it then spends almost all its time *critiquing feminism for harming women by describing the structures that cause harm*. (Super handy, guys, and I'm sure nothing to do with the irresistible rise of porn-bro 'feminists' like Noah frickin Berlatsky.) Butlerian accounts of rape are all about how rape prosecutions are terrible because they 'reinforce the gender binary,' and consciousness-raising about rape is terrible because it 'creates' victims, and describing acts of mass rape is terrible because it 'undermines women's agency.' This is also how we get to one of the greatest male-violence erasing ruses of them all: the idea that men pose no inherent danger to women in prostitution, that prostitution is in no way positioned within an matrix of male sexual entitlement and economic power, and that 'sex-work activism' should be aimed squarely at calling feminists names for enforcing 'whorephobia,' which is where the 'sex-work-is-work' crowd places the entire blame for the harms of prostitution.

This, as with all third-wave feminism, is just so much male-pandering bullshit. For reasons I can't quite fathom, I spent a good deal of time trying to work out how the modern-day intersectional catechism was in any way coherent—until I realized that the only thing that held it all together was that it all benefitted men. Pole dancing. Porn. Prostitution. Attacks on 'carceral feminism.' Trans activism. Individual empowerment over class analysis. *Denying the existence of female people*. So, what the fuck is going on here? Why are women so eager to buy this self-annihilating male-appeasing bullshit in liberation drag, and what has any of that got to do with Judith Butler?

As trans activism is fond of reminding us, this is partly a 'generational' issue: the young people 'get it' and the old crones like us will be left where we belong, languishing on the wrong side of history. (Irigaray was right as usual... female genealogy is *crucial*.) If you say something like that to an old feminist hack like me, my response will be: 'You just haven't fallen off the patriarchy cliff yet, and when you do, we'll be here to catch you.' We get it. The fall is terrifying. If other women had not been there to catch *us*, maybe none of us would ever make it. But for some women, it seems, the fear of the abyss is too great to ever face. They never find out that after the fall, you learn, remarkably, to float.

---

[4] For further discussion of Foucauldian feminist account of rape please see my 'Queer Theory, Foucauldian Feminism, and the Erasure of Rape,' *janeclarejones.com*, 30 August 2018.

Last night, Sally Hines turned up on my Butler thread to snarkily ask why I was calling Judith Butler 'Judy.' (*Flat stare.*) By way of reply, I dug out the 1993 *Judy!*-fanzine,[5] full of sub-dom eroticization, and a lovely riff on the 'Lesbian Phallus' detailing Butler's awesome ability to make grad students cry—"Judy is the number one dominator... the Phallus masquerading as the Phallus." I followed a quote from the zine about how alienating Butler found lesbian feminism—all that celebrating women's music, UGH GROSS—and it took me to a 1992 *ArtForum* interview.[6] Here we find Butler distancing her-

---

[5] 'Judy!—the 1993 Judith Butler fanzine available online,' *progressivegeographies.com*, 27 February 2015.

[6] Liz Kotz, 'The Body You Want: An Interview with Judith Butler,' *ArtForum*, November 1992.

self from "naïve...liberationist forms of thinking" (reckon that must be us then) and expounding on how the "oppressor lives within as a mechanism of constant psychic subjection." It's not a great surprise that someone who deliberately removed the material planks of the analysis of male dominance should also insist that dominance is psychically *unavoidable*. (There's a lot of stuff in there about the importance of cross-gender identification, for which read: 'It's all good, ladies! Everyone can have (or not have) the phallus now!')

What we would say, what I would *always* say, is that this kind of phallic identification, this explaining away the possibility of the *otherwise*, this *refusal* to imagine there could be anything other than these mechanisms—now unsexed!—of power and subjection and dominance and submission, is, in essence, Stockholm Syndrome. The fall *is* terrifying. Anyone who has experienced abuse or has worked with people who have experienced abuse knows this. The mind recoils. It is easier to erase and efface and reify and excuse and normalize and explain away than to look squarely at it and see it for what it is. Butler's work is one big recoil from what she can't look at squarely, a revulsion that's particularly evident around male violence and above all around rape. (She never directly acknowledges rape,[7] none of her work deals with it, her intellectual mentor—Foucault—was an apologist, her most significant contribution was editing an essay[8] that said women need to 'change the rape script'—because if you just stop thinking of yourself as rapeable then you totally won't get raped.)

In the *ArtForum* interview, she flat out admits that she finds "feminism [as] a position which asserts the systematic domination of women by men" to be "very scary to me." Let that just sink in. Then, having recoiled from the recognition of patriarchy as male dominance, she goes on to outline that her opposition to 'fixed gender positions' is because that would mean "women's psyches are nothing but scenes of violation." (So, we'd better just cover that

---

[7] In September 2020, Butler was again dispatched to the UK press to have another crack at telling off gender-critical feminists. In this piece she claimed that women's fears about males entering their intimate spaces show "a domain of fantasy...at work." She dismissed any thinking that considers "the penis is the threat," or that male people might seek to enter women's space for dubious reasons, as "a rich fantasy...[that] does not describe a social reality." This is disturbingly redolent of Freud's refusal to accept the reality of the sexual abuse he uncovered among his female patients and decision to theorize it as a product of his own patients' fantasies of seduction. Women's fears of male sexual violence are not 'fantasies' Judith. And you have a serious problem dealing with the reality of male violence. See Alona Ferber, 'Judith Butler on the Culture Wars, J. K. Rowling and Living in 'Anti-Intellectual Times [LOL],'' *New Statesman*, 22 September 2020.

[8] Sharon Marcus, 'Fighting Bodies, Fighting Words: A Theory and Politics of Rape Prevention,' in *Feminists Theorise the Political*, edited by Judith Butler and Joan Wallach Scott (London and New York: Routledge, 1992).

> LK MacKinnon was even on the cover of the Sunday *Times Magazine*.
>
> JB And she was ABC's person of the week. It's very scary to me because it makes feminism into a position which asserts the systematic domination of women by men, distills both those categories into very fixed places of power, sees women as always in positions of relative powerlessness, as victims who then only get to claim power through recourse to the state—a very frightening prospect. The attack on the First Amendment is horrible for anyone who cares about the rise of censorship on the right, for anybody who cares about sodomy laws; it just strikes me as a very reactionary position. And this kind of procensorship feminism is implicitly based on a very antipsychoanalytic understanding of sexuality and subjectivity as well.

shit over, then, hadn't we?)[9] I was also reminded here of another of her interviews, in which she says she's "probably too frightened" to "engage" Irigaray's texts "that closely" because they strike her as the product of "a certain heterosexual trauma."[10] (They strike me as the product of a woman who has an unfathomable grasp of the structure of narcissistic male dominance and is fucking *done* with women being erased, but hey ho.) Which is all to say that the woman who has been elevated as the future of feminism—and welcomed with open arms by a bunch of men who never so much as *opened* as second-wave text—is a woman *who is too scared to even think about rape* and has a deep visceral aversion to women who are not.

How this all relates to the current clusterfuck should be obvious. So much of what is going on in this debate—both at the level of specific concerns and in its core psychic structure—is about boundaries and violation. (See 'TRAs,

---

[9] This dynamic also surfaced several times in the course of comments made by Professor Sally Hines on Twitter. Sally has claimed that "GC feminism...To be blunt, it's a movement of traumatised women." (Tweet now deleted, see www.twitter.com/janeclarejones/status/1314484905427062784.) In response to my interrogating her about her complicity with erasing the axis of women's oppression, she responded, "I'm sorry that you've been hurt in life but your trauma is not mine and you can't bully me into taking it on." (www.twitter.com/sally_hines/status/1066506455778508800.) I was finally moved to block Sally on Twitter after she went into a several hour tweet meltdown that consisted of pretty personal attacks (mostly about how I apparently think I am soooo cool, because that seems to be a primary currency for her), interspersed with variations of 'I AM NOT TRAUMATIZED. I WILL NOT ALLOW YOU TO BULLY ME INTO BEING TRAUMATIZED. I WILL NOT ACCEPT YOUR POLITICS OF TRAUMA.' This dynamic of denial—and hostility to women who will not collude with it—is, I think, central to what is going on between trans inclusive and gender-critical feminists. We will not allow them to erase male violence and male dominance, and they evidently find our refusal to collude with their denial psychically intolerable. I have a lot of sympathy for women's inability to look at things that are really incredibly hard to look at. But this refusal to grant witness to other women's experiences of male violence is a fundamental betrayal of feminism.

[10] Pheng Cheah, Elizabeth Grosz, 'The Future of Sexual Difference: An Interview with Judith Butler and Drucilla Cornell,' *Diacritics*, 28(1), 1998, pp. 19-42.

Rape-Logic, and the Economy of Entitlement,' p. 156.) One of the reasons it is so damn hard for us to get men to listen to us—and one reason they're all so eagerly jumping on the boundary-smashing bandwagon—is because, when we get down to it, this is about rape, and most men neither want to think about rape or about the way their narcissism and refusal to recognize our humanity is implicated in its mechanisms. This is not a question of whether trans women are more or less likely than any other group of males to pose a threat to women. It is simply *that* they are male, that male people pose a threat to women, and that male people posing a threat to women is not a symptom of *our* hysteria. (Our hysteria was only ever produced by what we could not name, which now, *under the banner of feminism*, we are being told, once again, *we must not name*.) But more than all this, more even than the spaces, and who does or does not enter them, more than the fact that women's boundaries are being piously derided as 'gate-keeping,' is the importance of the boundary set by our right to name ourselves, and our refusal to fulfil our historic role as the passive dumping ground of male projections.

I've been meaning to write, and will write soon—see 'Why Feminists Are Not Nazis,' p. 133—something on how the left's current obsession with 'inclusion' and 'openness' and 'smashing boundaries' and 'deterritorialization' makes sense *only* as a critique of the psychic structure of dominance—go tell it to Donald Trump and leave us the fuck alone. It is entirely, gratuitously, inappropriate when turned *against* the boundaries *of* the violated, of those who are raised in a society that leads them to understand—when they are grabbed or catcalled or made to feel like meat—that *that* is where they are positioned. It is no wonder that a woman who cannot even bear to *think* about this fact, who prefers to deny the power that frames it, who prefers to think it could all be rewritten by playing games with superficial scripts, would avert her eyes from the mess she has made and what this is all actually about. Women's psyches are far more than 'scenes of violation,' but there can be no feminism that refuses its reality, or that recoils from recognizing that 'smashing boundaries,' when used *against* women as a class, is the axiom of male power and that, at its heart, everything that is happening here is as it always was.

ON THE SOVEREIGN VIOLENCE OF WOMEN

janeclarejones.com

FEBRUARY 2015

Author's Note: This piece is addressed to the feminist academic Sara Ahmed, and was inspired—or rather I should say enraged—by this monumentally pious and dismissive tweet written in response to a piece by Rachel Hewitt explaining why female-only space had been vital to her healing-journey as a rape survivor.[1]

> **feministkilljoy** @SaraNAhmed · Feb 24
> I cannot articulate how sad I feel when the language of feminism becomes a screen for violence.

So it is when feminism is no longer directed towards a critique of patriarchy, or secured by the categories 'women' or 'gender,' that it is doing its most 'moving' work.

—Sara Ahmed[2]

So, it is extremely important that people think a little more critically about what they are saying when they are talking about essences, and I have probably been guilty or more guilty than anybody else in not thinking quite clearly enough. So, if someone were to ask me if the category woman is something without which we cannot do, I would say, absolutely, it is a category without which we cannot do.

—Judith Butler[3]

I am trying to understand—I have been trying to understand—how, having steeped ourselves in a similar tradition, we could come to such different conclusions.

[1] Rachel Hewitt, 'When I was raped, it was female-only spaces that helped me recover,' *New Statesman*, 24 February 2015.

[2] Sara Ahmed, *The Cultural Politics of Emotion* (Edinburgh: Edinburgh University Press, 2004), p. 176.

[3] Judith Butler, in Pheng Cheah, Elizabeth Grosz, 'The Future of Sexual Difference: An Interview with Judith Butler and Drucilla Cornell,' *Diacritics*, 28(1), 1998, p. 22.

You claim that certain women should not say certain things. That a woman who finds healing from male violence in the company of other women should be silent about the power of that healing. That she should not try to protect that space (or even raise questions about protecting that space). That she is wrong to be concerned that it will no longer be there for the women who come after her. Because that healing comes at the expense of others. Because that healing, therefore, is violence.

I understand something of the logic. I have spent my life thinking the resistance to sovereign violence, unpicking the way the impossible conceit of safety is used to appropriate and exclude. We see it everywhere. Indeed, it is everywhere. But when I first read the demand of unconditional hospitality and felt the ethical pull of openness resonate, I also thought, a moment later: what about a woman's need to say 'no'?

Unconditional hospitality is impossible. We know this. Without a home, without some degree of safety, there is no place from which to be hospitable. And more than that, people—*women*—in the grip of a profound trauma created and perpetuated by a system of power invested in the annihilation of their needs are the very last people from whom it is appropriate to demand unconditional openness. Women are the very last people who are capable—or should be capable—of answering this demand.

The system of power you are attributing to women is not theirs. Women are not guilty of exercising an excess of sovereign power. Sovereignty, in its fundamental denial of dependency and relation, in its incessant imperial expansion, is a structure of the patriarchal-colonial imaginary. Women suffer not from an excess of sovereign power, but from its deficiency. We are raised to say yes to the needs of more important others, are we not? And our political practice has been, and continues to be, about the affirming necessity and justice of our need to say 'no.'

You are arguing for the pre-eminent violence of women's 'no.' You do understand that. That in a society in which the emotional and physical and sexual and reproductive labour of women is appropriated day in, day out, with more or less explicit violence, the 'violence' you are most compelled to resist is that of a woman saying 'no.' The people whose needs you prioritize are those who show not a single shred of empathy for why, in this world, a woman might need to say 'no.' And what saddens you most—when a woman recounts how female-only space helped her recover from violence—is not the violence she suffered but the 'violence' you hear in her 'no.'

But what is feminism without this 'no'? What is a feminism that is concerned, above all, with the sovereign violence of women's 'no,' and with exerting pressure on women to surrender their 'no'? What is a feminism that denies the reality of women's lives in order to attribute to us a sovereignty which we do not possess? There is no way to read women's 'no' as an exercise in sovereign violence—analogous, as is so often claimed, to the exclusions performed by whiteness—without denying that the entire system of power bearing down on women is predicated on granting them no sovereignty at all. It makes sense only as a denial of the oppression of women *as women*, or as the denial of the existence of women at all. It makes sense, therefore, only as a form of anti-feminism.

This is what we are fighting about. We are fighting about who is the sovereign and who is the subjugated. We are fighting against the (ab)use of the critique of metaphysics to erase the political category of woman—while being told that our objection to that erasure—our 'no'—is an act of violence. We are fighting against the deployment of the discourse of intersectionality to deny that the oppression of women as women affects all women, and that all women exist under conditions of appropriation which render their 'no' a resistance to—rather than a performance of—sovereign violence. We are arguing about whether the fact that other oppressions intersect with, amplify, and modify certain women's oppression should be widely used in practice (often, we note, by left-wing men) to suggest that, actually, women (if they exist) are not really that oppressed as women at all (convenient, that).

We are fighting against a feminist discourse which positions women as the oppressor, and repeats the foundational patriarchal gesture of denying us the affirmation of our needs and an explanation of how and why we are wounded by this world. Feminism—the practice of love and understanding, passed between women—has saved many of us from lives blighted by the violence drilled into our bodies and souls by the needs of men. And so, above all, we are fighting to ensure that this healing is not denied to the women that come after us. That when their youthful confidence in (neo)liberal empowerment and the shock of the new—their absurdly Platonic belief in the possibility of neatly dismantling an age-old structure of material appropriation with pronouns—runs headlong into the implacable violence of domination, we, the dried-up, hate-spewing bigots they've been schooled to despise, will still be there for them. And for them, we will not give up.

III - WOMAN AS OTHER, OTHERING WOMEN

THE MOST MULTIPURPOSE BOGEYWOMAN IN HISTORY

Twitter

28 MARCH 2022

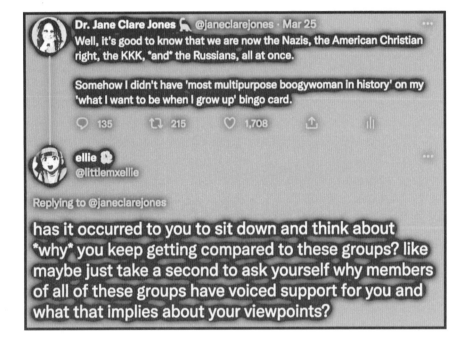

Yes, it has occurred to me. Everything occurs to me, and unlike people committed to trans ideology, I think *everything* through, and check my workings, all the time.

My core belief is that female people exist as a distinct class of humans, that we live in a society that oppresses women on the basis of sex, and that women need to be able to organize politically, and have resources and spaces on that basis.

I think gender is the mechanism of the oppression of women, and that defining women *by* gender is *extremely regressive.*

I think confusing female human beings with the patriarchal projection 'Woman' is a mistake made by both traditional and new-form gender conservatives.

And I think imposing definitions on female human beings against their consent and then attempting to enforce that using threats, or by shaming and demonizing them, is a pretty much axiomatic instance of patriarchal power.

Then I look at what right-wing authoritarian men think. I see that they agree with me that humans are sexed. I wonder why that might be, and I conclude that it's because humans *are* sexed. This isn't evidence of any great political alignment.

Then I look at the right wing's other views about gender. Hmmmm, is Vladimir Putin concerned about essentializing gender as a mechanism of the oppression of female people I wonder? I wonder if he is concerned that young lesbians might be being guided in a way that plays on their internalized homophobia. I wonder if he is worried about female people not being able to access female-only counselling for rape.

In fact, NO, I DON'T ASK MYSELF THIS BECAUSE IT IS FUCKING OBVIOUS HE IS COMING FROM A TOTALLY DIFFERENT PLACE AND THAT FEMINIST CONCERNS ABOUT REIFYING GENDER ARE NOT WHAT IS MOTIVATING A MAN LIKE PUTIN.

Also, I can see quite clearly that men like Putin have a geopolitical interest in getting Western society to consume itself with an insane conflict over whether male people are women and that he's no doubt laughing his ass off at us. Your local right-wingers are having a good laugh, too, because—although it fucks your narrative up and you'll never admit it—this is predominantly an intra-left conflict.

Like fucking seriously, how on earth do you expect people to genuinely believe, if they think about it for, like, five minutes, that radical feminism is actually exactly the same as what right-wing authoritarian men think?

And so, the question then becomes *not* 'why don't I realize that the 20 years I spent studying the structure of male domination was actually just me prepping to become an authoritarian right-wing man?' but 'why are these people so invested in trying to conflate feminist critiques of gender with right-wing authoritarianism?'

There are a lot of answers to that:

First, you can't actually deal with any of our concerns or questions, and so monstering and dismissing us is your best political tactic.

Were this not the case, were you actually in any way interested in being honest about this—at least one of you once would have actually listened to us, and been able to produce a decent recitation of our argument. But then you'd have to admit that our position is nothing like right-wing men's and that wouldn't do at all.

Second, although your entire movement is styled around alleged tolerance and a flattened view of the world that is basically structured by what we can understand as a 'xenophobic metaphor'—i.e. those people are all the same because they do hateful 'othering' and that is what is wrong with the world and we are against 'othering,' and the trans person is the ultimate symbol of the 'other' and if everyone accepts trans ideology then 'othering' will have been overcome and we will all be saved, and anyone who 'others' is the BADDIE and we don't 'other' and we are the GOODIES... you have just split the world into BADDIES and GOODIES again, and are REALLY REALLY COMMITTED to 'othering' people who 'other'—and you can try and wave that away by pointing at the paradox of tolerance—but the fact that you will not for *one second actually look at who we are and are SO fucking invested in us being the monsters* (it's convenient when the monster who is now the symbol for everything wrong in the world is actually just a middle-aged lefty woman you can go and shout out safe in the knowledge she won't actually do anything to hurt you even though you can whip yourself up pretending that she will, isn't it?)...this is all, y'know, an absolutely perfect exemplification of 'othering.'

Which is to say, you think you are good and pious because you do not 'other,' and we are bad and the same as bad right-wing men because we do 'other,' but the very fact that you WILL NOT SEE WHO WE REALLY ARE and NEED US TO BE THE MONSTERS is a performative contradiction the SIZE OF A FUCKING PLANET.

And I want you to go away and sit down and think about why you are so invested in a bunch of mostly middle-aged radical/socialist feminist women being Nazis/Vladimir Putin when it is obviously a) nuts, b) fucking dehumanizing, and c) political strategy to justify bullying us.

So that's what I think when I sit down and think about why you keep comparing us to THE BADDIES.

WHY FEMINISTS ARE NOT NAZIS

Paper delivered at Reading University

MAY 2019[1]

What I want to do today is bring our attention to the way this debate is being both explicitly and implicitly structured by what we might understand as 'metaphors of sovereignty,' or what I'm going to call 'the sovereign imaginary.' I'm using 'imaginary' here in the Lacanian, or more specifically, Irigarayan sense, to talk about the way discourse is underpinned by certain spatialized images that express certain ontological assumptions, and which structure our thinking about certain issues. And my claim is that a lot of what is happening in the present debate around trans inclusion is being determined by a particular imaginary, and that we can unpick some of the bad thinking going on here if we can unpack that a little.

First, I'm going to trace the structure of the sovereign imaginary for you, and explore the role it plays in this conversation, paying particular attention to how progressive antipathy to sovereignty is related to the moral imperative of 'inclusion,' and how this helps us understand the intuitive appeal of the *prima facie* implausible claim that a bunch of lefty feminist women are now indistinguishable from the Pope, conservative evangelicals, the alt-right, the Ku Klux Klan, and the Westboro Baptist Church.

Second, I want to explore why it is gratuitously inappropriate to suggest that female people's desire to be protected from males is an expression of the sovereign imaginary and should be legitimately censured by all decent people. As we'll see, as well as being the animating principle of right-wing nationalism and its nostalgia for primordial ethnic purity, the sovereign imaginary is *the fundamental ontological infrastructure of patriarchal masculinity*. Women's bodies are the territory on which male fantasies of purity and virginity and invasion and conquest are played out. And the meaning of those fantasies is evidently very different for the women whose bodies are marked by them than for the males who enact them, unless, of course, you've forgotten that women actually exist in their own right and have their own experiences of the world distinct from the projections of the masculine imagination.

---

[1] For those who would like to look at the slides that went with this talk, they are available at www.janeclarejones.com/2019/10/31/why-feminists-are-not-nazis.

THE SOVEREIGN IMAGINARY

As some of you know, my background is in French poststructural philosophy. As I've discussed elsewhere (see 'Poststructuralism, Butler, and Bodies,' p. 80), one theme of the present conversation among gender-critical people is the tendency to blame the erasure of materiality we see in trans ideology on 'postmodernism' or 'poststructuralism,' understood as a kind of 'discourse all the way down' idealism. However, to my mind, poststructuralism is an ontological project aimed at critiquing the metaphysical structure we're discussing here under the name of sovereignty. So my hope is that this talk will present an alternative reading of poststructuralism, and make a case for what is useful about it, when properly interpreted.

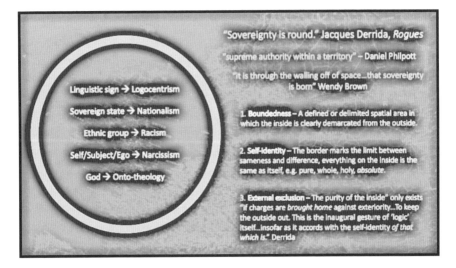

In my work, I've often examined this metaphysical structure using the concept of sovereignty because this points us towards the intertwining of power with the incision of space. Sovereignty is a territorial structure, and comes into existence only through the creation of demarcated borders. The imagery of sovereignty is of a space encircled by high, impregnable walls, because sovereignty is motivated by the drive to make oneself invulnerable.

The sovereign imaginary thus has several notable characteristics:

- *Boundedness*: A defined or delimited spatial area in which the inside is clearly demarcated from the outside.

- *Internal self-identity*: According to the ideal of the sovereign imaginary the area inside the border is marked by a perfect and pure homogeneity. It is a realm of absolute sameness. Which therefore also implies...

- *External exclusion*: In order for the inside to be perfectly self-same, everything outside, or 'other,' must be rigorously excluded. The crucial point to grasp here is that the sovereign imaginary is the fundamental figure of all purity logics, in which the purity of the inside can only be maintained by excluding anything 'other' or different that threatens to 'pollute' or 'contaminate' it. In this sense, the sovereign imaginary is structured by a kind of xenophobia, by a desire to exclude 'the foreign.'

Inside (Identity/Sameness/'Us')	Outside (Difference/'Them')
Same, Safe, Secure, Pure, Home-land, Virgin, Inviolate, Impregna-ble, Invulnerable, Whole, Holy	Different, Other, Bad, Foreign, Pol-luting, Contaminating, Dangerous, Threatening

I think it's evident how this kind of spatialized purity logic underpins the right-wing populism of both Trump and Brexit and fuels people's tendency to respond to economic insecurity by retreating into fantasies of absolute security promised by enclosing the homeland within impregnable borders. The President of the United States has never given a cogent account of why the Great Wall of Trump will 'Make America Great Again,' just as the Brex-iteers can't actually explain why keeping out immigrants will cure a malaise that is fundamentally caused by the global economic crisis. But the point is they don't actually need to provide a cogent account of anything because the power of their discourse relies entirely on the sovereign imaginary, and the networks of anxiety and invulnerability it mobilizes. What is at work in the present debate, I'd argue, is instinctive progressive antipathy to this hu-man tendency to deal with insecurity by xenophobically projecting it onto a 'scapegoated' other, as is manifestly the case with respect to Brexit and Trump. And this antipathy is then informing a number of crucial claims in this debate:

1. That all acts of 'exclusion' are always and only motivated by the projection of anxiety, fear, or hatred. That such fears are necessarily irrational, and that any reasons given for exclusion are only ever a pretext for the psycholog-ical benefits of projecting fear and/or hatred. This is where the claim that expression of women's political interests in this conflict are just a pretext for bigotry and transphobia gets all its traction from.

2. From this, it follows that there are never any legitimate grounds to ex-clude, that 'inclusion' is a universal moral good and 'exclusion' a universal moral harm. It's worth noting here that the moral opprobrium denoted by the word 'TERF' [Trans-Exclusionary Radical Feminist] inheres entirely in the word 'exclusionary.'

3. The progressive recognition that sovereigntist mechanisms are inherent in all forms of atavistic and ethnic nationalisms, as well as discourses of ethnic and racial purity or superiority, is providing the intuitive infrastructure of the claim that someone like me—a lefty radical eco-feminist—is, in fact, a white supremacist neo-Nazi.

4. And it's this association between gender-critical feminism and various iterations of right-wing ideology that lends credence to the claim that our speech is hate speech, that it is 'literal violence,' that by expressing our views we are harming trans people and inciting harm against trans people, and that, therefore, it is legitimate for our speech to be censured.

So, we're just going to look at a few examples of how this is playing out. I'm principally interested in discourse out there in the public square, rather than in a purely academic context, so all my examples here are from Twitter.

The first is from a human-rights activist from New Zealand. I was struck here that she could go through this thought process as if she was having an entirely original insight, given how rhetorically well-worn these associations are in trans activist discourse.

@zenpeacekeeper:
I've been thinking a lot this week about transphobia, and the way that fear can be created & exploited for the purpose of oppression. I recently went to the Museum of African American History and the Holocaust museum in DC. Both tell this story. I think the fear is very real for many people. In the same way that many Americans were genuinely afraid that desegregation would lead to white women being raped by black men, I think many cis-women are genuinely afraid of transwomen. That fear is built on a foundation of intentional misinformation driven by hatred, then spread through fear and ignorance. When we're afraid we lose our capacity to be rational and all we want is to be kept safe. We know this pattern. It lead to the Holocaust. And Apartheid.

Here are some more examples making evident the way the rejection of a sovereign logic of exclusion, boundedness, purity, and corruption is underpinning the moral opprobrium directed towards gender-critical women, and how frequently that is expressed through analogies between gender-critical feminism, racism and facism.

> @ajventer: And this has nothing to do with WOMEN'S boundaries. This has everything to do with bigottry [sic] and segregation. I don't respect TERF's boundaries anymore than I respect the boundaries of white people who think black people shouldn't be in THEIR spaces. Both are the SAME EVIL.
>
> @MorganeOgerBC to @janeclarejones: Going further, discriminating on the basis of any purity test for sex-segregated spaces requires the same discrimination for all other explicitly protected classes. Think for a moment what this means: It's the basis of pandering to supremacist purity ideals. Have you considered your text is an exact application of nationalist white supremacist arguments being used against refugees?
>
> @wallace_milner: I don't think people understand how insidious anti-trans (TERF) ideology is. The idea that lgbtq people are 'corrupting' the nature of womanhood is fascist. Not just far right. Not just conservative. Literally fascist.
>
> @jasonintrator (Jason Stanley): As someone who studies fascist movements, I have become very sensitive to hysteria focused on trans women. It's a kind of signal beacon for fascism, in my experience. The far-right globally likes to target Judith Butler.

WHY FEMINISTS ARE NOT NAZIS

Okay, so I actually have a lot of time for the critique of the sovereign imaginary. It was developed by French philosophers, many of them Jewish, in the aftermath of the Holocaust, and it is, indeed, an incredibly useful analytic for understanding the mechanics of ethnic fascism and racial supremacy. However, as I've intimated, my problem here is that applying this analytic to female people in a patriarchal culture is wildly inappropriate.

The main reason I, as a feminist philosopher, spent the best part of my training studying the structure of the sovereign imaginary is because, as well as illuminating the mechanics of ethno-fascism, the sovereign imaginary also supplies the fundamental ontological infrastructure of patriarchal masculinity. It's not an accident that along with 'the metaphysics of presence,' one of the philosophical epithets for this ontological infrastructure is 'phallocentrism.' The sovereign imaginary is the architecture of that impossible fantasy of narcissistic omnipotence, mastery, and impenetrable potency that psychoanalysis calls 'the phallus'—the figure of the phallic-ego, which, according to Lacan, is "symbolized in dreams by a fortress."[2]

So, to return to our sovereign circle as the representation of the bounded incision of space. First off, evidently, this conflict is about access to spaces, and we can include in this actual physical spaces, as well as virtual, social, and conceptual spaces. It's worth briefly noting here that the language we use to talk about the determination of meaning is also explicitly spatialized,

[2] Jacques Lacan, 'The Mirror Stage as Formative of the Function of the *I*,' in *Écrits: A Selection*, translated by Alan Sheridan (London: Routledge, 1977), p. 5.

we talk about *de-fining*, and *de-lineating* concepts. And it's worth further noting that while I am a great advocate of 'both/and thinking,'[3] we are talking here about access to spaces and that means that we *are* dealing with an 'either/or' choice: a single space cannot be provided on the basis of both sex and gender identity *at the same time*. That means that in this case, rights are actually a pie, and for the trans rights movement to insist that changing the basis of the allocation of spaces has no effect on female people is extremely disingenuous, at best.

Anyway, what I particularly want to highlight here is how the thinking of spaces, and the meaning of *entering* spaces, is gendered and sexualized in the sovereign imaginary. What this comes down to is that the sovereign imaginary thinks bodies as territory and territory as bodies. It thinks sexual penetration through metaphors of invasion and conquest, and territorial invasion through metaphors of rape. Indeed, this is not only a case of rhetoric or metaphor. Acts of invasion are almost always accompanied by rape. And the structure of the sovereign imaginary is at play in why that is the case.

a) *Women's sexual violation does not mean to feminist women what it means to patriarchal men*

What we're going to do now is take a detailed look at how this 'metaphysics of penetration' plays out in the sovereign imaginary, and in particular, in its most extreme ethno-fascist iterations.

The first thing to understand, returning to our idea of the phallic-ego as fortress, is that patriarchal masculinity is fundamentally structured by the imperative of invulnerability as impenetrability. As Catherine Keller writes in her study of the structure of the patriarchal imaginary, '[v]irility lies about all in impermeability.'[4] By contrast, women are constructed as penetrable, as either virgin or conquered territory. While we're here, it's worth noting that this is the basis of the traditional patriarchal horror of male homosexuality, which is driven by the fear of being 'made woman' through penetration.

---

[3] It's important to note that 'either/or' thinking is appropriate when thinking about actual physical spaces, or the distribution of actual physical resources. One of the features of solid material objects is that two objects 'cannot occupy the same space at the same time,' and hence, the occupation of spaces does proceed by exclusive logic, i.e. if a space for deaf children includes hearing children, it is not actually a 'deaf child's space.' Similarly, if a single-sex space includes people of the other sex, it is not a single-sex space. The relationship between non-physical things, or between poles in conceptual binaries, should not, however, be thought exclusively, and rather, should be thought through an interpenetrating 'both/and' logic. (See 'Poststructuralism, Butler, and Bodies,' p. 80.)

[4] Catherine Keller, *From a Broken Web: Separation, Sexism and Self* (Boston, MA: Beacon Press, 1988), p. 9.

This metaphoric infrastructure is what is at play in ethno-fascist invocations of foreign or racialized others as sexual threat, figured either, or both, as a threat to the body of the nation or group or, most often, as a threat to the bodies of women as ciphers for the body of the nation or group.

We see this, for instance, in Islamophobic claims that Europe is in the grip of a Muslim rape epidemic, a trope that recurs in the thought of the Norwegian ethno-fascist mass-murderer Anders Breivik and which I've written about previously.[5] We see it in the deployment of fears about black men raping white women, and the horrendous role such narratives played during slavery and segregation, and we see it in Trump's charge that Mexican immigrants are rapists and why, allegedly, "Women are [being] raped at levels that nobody has ever seen before."

Jason Stanley, who I cited on p. 137 criticizing the 'hysteria' about trans women, touches on this in his recent book, *How Fascism Works*. To create moral panic, Stanley argues, fascist propaganda represents the targeted group as:

Particular kinds of threats to the fascist nation—most important, and most typical, a threat to its purity... The basic threat that fascist propaganda uses to raise fear is that members of the targeted group will rape members of the chosen nation, thereby polluting its 'blood.' The threat of mass rape is simultaneously intended as a threat to the patriarchal norms of the fascist state, to the 'manhood' of the nation... it raises sexual anxiety, and an attendant need of the protection of the nation's manhood by the fascist authority.[6]

Clearly, Stanley understands here that fascist rhetoric functions by using the spectre of rape as a threat to the purity of the nation in its psycho-ontological interrelation with patriarchal manhood, but his understanding is a little blunt, because he doesn't fully grasp the structure of the sovereign imaginary, and how it plays out its interwoven sexual and territorial anxieties by *projecting them* onto the bodies of women. What Stanley is discussing here is what the rape of women belonging to 'other' men *means in the patriarchal imaginary*, what it *means between men* who are using women's bodies to signify territorial integrity or conquest. But what Stanley doesn't seem to notice, is that the actual experience of raped women has been completely invisibilized here and entirely subordinated to patriarchal signification. Because women don't experience rape as 'a threat to the nation's manhood.'

[5] Jane Clare Jones, 'Ander's Breivik's Chilling Anti-Feminism,' *The Guardian*, 27 July 2011.
[6] Jason Stanley, *How Fascism Works: The Politics of Us and Them* (New York: Random House, 2020), p. 126.

As this image makes almost comically apparent, what is going on in ethno-fascist invocations of rape is, to be blunt, masculine penetration anxiety. I'd also like to stop here for a moment and observe that images like this are kind of indicative of why I have such a huge problem with being lectured about how unimportant genitals are and being told that my concerns are 'creepy.' A vast swath of the psycho-ontological infrastructure of our culture is informed by the morphology of genitals and the resultant metaphysics of sex, and until we have taken phallocentrism apart in its deepest aspects, I reserve the right to think that genitals matter very much indeed.

Okay, so, finally, after a fair amount of backstory we get to the point. All this projected penetration anxiety about the other as rapist and the playing out of fantasies of absolute sovereign security on the bodies of women is *about men's symbolic systems* and has almost nothing to do with actual women's actual experience of sexual violation. The kind of men who whip up fears about the other-as-rapist are markedly unconcerned—indeed, are usually the first to flatly deny—the existence of any kind of 'epidemic' of rape that does not cross racialized lines, because, for them, the crime only signifies within the sovereign imaginary. Such men are frequently extreme misogynists, evaluate women on the basis of a stark hierarchy of sexual purity and pollution, and, as in the case of Breivik, will frequently link immigration-cum-rape to feminism's alleged emasculation of the nation and corruption of women's sexual morals. They are, moreover, wedded to a logic of phallic sexual dominance and, often, the heroism of conquest by force. It is no coincidence that the man obsessed with the Great Big Wall is also the infamous Pussy-Grabber-In-Chief.

All this is a million miles away from what rape means to women and why radical feminism is so centrally concerned with the devastation of women's lives by rape. There is nothing in male discourses about purity and pollution and conquest and invasion that expresses concern for the *actual harm caused to actual women by sexual trauma*, and the fact that we are damaged not by an invasion of *territory* but rather by a profound assault on our humanity and personhood. We are not just bits of land on which men play out their sovereigntist fantasies and battles: we are persons in our own right and assaults against our personhood mean what they mean to us. We are not worried, for example, about male people in rape-crisis centres because we trying to recreate the primordial tribal purity of women (as if that is a thing) and have, to that end, conjured a figment of invading contaminating males. We are worried about male-bodied people in rape-crisis centres because they are highly likely to be a source of trauma to women who have been sexually assaulted by males.

To assimilate women's concerns about policies that compromise their dignity, comfort, and sexual safety to ethno-fascist discourses structured by masculinist metaphysics is to deny that women have their own experience of the world apart from male symbolic projections, to unthinkingly position women as a male default, and hence, most fundamentally, to erase the specificity of women's own existence. It is to insist that women, and especially feminist women, understand and experience male violence in masculine symbolic terms, when our entire political project is precisely about challenging the assumptions of the phallic construction of our social world. To wit, what rape means to women is not the same as what rape means to racist patriarchal right-wing men, and it's actually absurd—and exhibits profound disregard for women's experience and repeats the patriarchal assimilation of women to the male default—to suggest otherwise.

b) *Women are not the dominant class*

Which brings me to my second point. It's no accident that in the previous examples of rhetoric positing the 'other as rapist,' the speakers are all white men using sovereign purity logic to construct non-white men as a threat. Indeed, being able to comfortably read an accusation that an 'other' constitutes a threat as an illegitimate instance of ethno-fascist logic depends, in good part, on the accuser being a member of a dominant class attempting to vilify a member of a minority class. Notably, according to left-wing political rubric, if a member of a minority class claims that a member of a dominant class is a threat to them or is trying to dominate them, lefties tend to believe them.

Well, usually.

By progressive political logic, then, the entire claim that it's ethno-fascist for feminist women to be concerned about giving trans women unilateral access to our spaces must rely on positing women unambiguously as the dominant class vis-à-vis trans women. Indeed, progressive political thinking accepts without hesitation the claim that minority classes have the right to exclude oppressor classes from their spaces and resources, in order to allow them to organize and congregate away from those who are perceived to be a source of harm.

Given that female people are an oppressed class, and that sex, along with race and class, is one of the three main axes of structural oppression, it is somewhat staggering that vast chunks of purportedly progressive people have been swayed by an analysis that only holds if we deny that women are oppressed *as* women, and that posits instead that we are a dominant and privileged class, and hence, that the protection of our spaces and resources is analogous to the exclusion of racial minorities by white supremacists.

One of the main ways this has been effected is by the creation of the 'cis/trans binary,' a device which functions to posit all non-trans people—hence 'cis' women—as the *de facto* oppressors of trans people. This strategy has been supplemented by a massive amount of rhetoric aimed at underlining the absolute vulnerability of trans people, while simultaneously hand-waving women's appeals to their own vulnerability and oppression as 'weaponization' or 'scaremongering.' The result of this is that spaces and resources allocated to female people to protect them from male people, or to compensate them for structural disadvantages incurred by living in a male-dominated society, have been recontextualized as egregious instances of exclusionary privilege which must rightly be taken away without due process or protest. And notably, the cis/trans binary underpinning this works according to exactly the kind of inside/outside, 'us vs. them' structure characteristic of sovereign purity logic, and posits 'cis' women, unequivocally, as the 'bad other'. The trans rights movement's claim that 'cis' is just an innocuous Latin prefix that merely distinguishes trans from non-trans people is another instance of extreme disingenuousness.

How we are to correctly understand the power relations between women and trans women is a complicated and difficult question. Trans women's position vis-à-vis women is not straightforward, because they are both and at the same time a vulnerable minority, and, with respect to women, members of the oppressor (male) sex class. This, to a great degree, is what underpins the conflict over the attempt to change the definition of 'woman' from one grounded in sex to one grounded in gender identity. Women, especially women with a developed awareness of male dominance, strongly object to the demand that we must not perceive, and must not name, male people as male. According to the doctrine of gender identity, what I have just said is, in itself, a heresy which constitutes an act of hatred. I would, however, strongly assert that it is simply a fact, that moreover, in a world of male dominance it is a highly pertinent fact, and that decreeing that women may not even utter this fact is an act of mass gaslighting. Which is all to say, women are not concerned about the presence of trans women in women's spaces because we are determined to mobilize sovereign logic against a demonized sexual minority or are obsessed with the purity of some mythical idea of 'womanhood.' We are concerned about the presence of trans women in women's spaces because trans women are male, and women are oppressed by male people.

If we emphasize trans women vulnerability vis-à-vis the larger class of males, what we have is a rights conflict over resources between two vulnerable groups who are both subject to patriarchal violence, and which should be adjudicated as such. If, on the other hand, we emphasize trans women's status as males vis-à-vis female people, what we have is members of the dominant class attempting to colonize the resources of the subjugated class. I think there's truth to both of these readings, but I'd like to underline here that the trans rights movement's present strategy of trying to aggressively coerce women's boundaries could not be a more effective method of making us incline towards the second interpretation. And what that means, effectively, is that what the trans rights movement likes to characterize as a dominant class scapegoating and violently excluding a vulnerable minority, we are experiencing as resistance to an act of coercive domination by our historic oppressor. And people wonder why this debate is so toxic.

c) *Inclusion is not a synonym of justice*

What the discussion in our previous point shows, then, is that the evaluation of a demand for access to spaces or resources is inflected by our understanding of the power relation between the two parties. A wealthy, largely white sovereign nation attempting to deny asylum or immigration status to refugees or migrants of colour by casting them as a sexual threat to the purity of the body politic is quite different from, say, efforts by Native Americans to resist further encroachment on tribal lands. The fact that advocates of trans ideology would, correctly I think, defend the right of queer, trans, and people of colour to their own spaces, and indeed, are adamant about the necessity of excluding gender-critical women from public discourse because it violates their notional 'safe space,' suggests that not even those who wield the charge of 'exclusion' as if it was an invariant mark of moral turpitude really think it is invariant. That means they agree that sometimes there are reasons why excluding people is morally justified.

This becomes even more readily apparent if we attempt to entirely dispense with thinking about this issue from within the infrastructure of the sovereign imaginary. To the trans woman who suggested in the *New York Times* that 'womanhood' was like a land she could immigrate to,[7] and that

---

[7] Jennifer Finney Boylan, 'Is Being Trans Like Being an Immigrant?' *The New York Times*, 3 April 2019.

anyone who would exclude her was essentially a Trumpian wall-builder, what I want to say is this: women are not, in fact, countries. And neither are changing rooms, or consciousness-raising classes, or rape-crisis centres. What we are talking about when we talk about women's boundaries is *not*—first and foremost—an incision of space but an expression of women's needs. We inscribe spaces and set them apart because doing so allows these spaces to fulfil certain functions and meet certain needs. When we express concern about the presence of male people in female people's spaces it is because including male people in those spaces will impact the way they meet female people's needs. And justice, I'd argue, is a matter of recognizing and adjudicating between people's needs, not applying some facile rubric of 'inclusion good'/'exclusion bad.'

What is actually going on here, when we strip away all the sovereign metaphors, is a standoff between two groups of people and their needs. Trans women want to be included in female people's spaces because it affirms their identity as women and gives them protection from the people who are actually a threat to them—namely, other male people. Female people are concerned about how we may be impacted or harmed by including people who are not female in female people's spaces. Given that trans women are male, that male people are socialized in a culture that inculcates male dominance, and that female people are oppressed by male people, we maintain that our concerns are not a confection of ethno-fascist scaremongering, that we have every right to raise them, and that full and open consideration should be given to the implications of changing all provision which has hitherto been provided to women on the basis of sex.

We maintain, furthermore, that what is actually going on under all this rhetorical sovereign window-dressing, and the reason why progressive people suddenly seem so confused about whether women are an oppressed class with rights to their own spaces and resources, is—when it comes down to it—the widespread and age-old intuition that male people's needs should be prioritized over female people's. Male people have a need and are in pain, and female people, as ever, are expected to bend and accommodate and give service to that need, even at their own expense, and those women who refuse to comply are hateful and unkind. Women who insist that they have their own needs will be persistently, violently, and, indeed, gleefully vilified.

Which is all to say, that what is going on here, actually, is just patriarchy as usual.

#NOTYOURSUPPORTHUMANS

Twitter

3 MARCH 2020

Stop. Emotionally. Blackmailing. Women. Into. Giving. You. Their. Political. Existence. You. Utter. Narcissists.

P.S.—If you really were female, nobody would give a shit anyway.

This is what has happened.

Under the guise of being 'nice' and 'diverse' and 'inclusive' our entire civic structure has allowed itself to be captured by a political ideology that considers female people asserting their own existence to be a violent threat.

We have not denied the existence of trans people.

All we have done is drawn a boundary and asserted that female people exist as a political class and that we should be allowed to maintain the rights given to us on that basis.

Drawing a boundary is not a threat.

The only context in which people would respond to other people drawing a boundary in this hyperbolic, manipulative, and aggressive manner is one undergirded by narcissistic entitlement.

The kind of narcissistic entitlement to women's *being*—our attention, our energy, our time, our spaces—propagated by patriarchal socialization.

This behaviour in response to us asserting our existence is precisely why we have long considered the trans rights movement to be the most condensed expression of patriarchal logic we've ever seen.

The fact that this society is so soaked in the tropes of male entitlement is in good part why nobody fucking stopped for a single moment to think whether changing the political definition of women because males wanted access to it might somehow concern women.

Newsflash: IT DOES.

Contrary to the views of the smiling pretty women telling us to 'be kind' outside Women's Liberation 2020, feminism is the practice of supporting women in their right to assert their own needs and interests.

This is not a threat.

This is not violence.

This is simply what should be accorded to all full human subjects in a just society.

We exist. We have our own needs. Your needs are not the same as ours. And we are not your support humans.

#NotYourSupportHumans

WOMAN AS OTHER

Twitter

13 JUNE 2020

> *One is not born, but rather becomes, woman. No biological, psychical or economic destiny defines the figure that the human female takes on in society.*[1]

The more I think about it, the clearer it becomes that Philip Pullman's tweet perfectly exemplifies exactly what is going on in this debate and—ironically—exactly what Beauvoir was actually saying about the position of woman as 'Other.'

Imagine turning up in a foreign culture, taking one of the founding texts of that culture, opening it randomly, picking one sentence out of it, and thinking you were equipped to interpret it knowing nothing about the people or the culture or their history or the *rest of the book* or EVEN THE NEXT DAMN SENTENCE.

Imagine taking that sentence—"One is not born, but rather becomes, woman"—and thinking you could tell the people who had been reading that book for the last 80 years, who had, in fact, built that entire culture on interpretations and elaborations of that book, what that sentence meant.

---

[1] Simone de Beauvoir, *The Second Sex*, translated by C. Borde and S. Malovany-Chevallier (London: Vintage, 2011), p. 293.

And imagine thinking you could tell them that what that sentence meant was not only that the culture they'd built on that book was bad and wrong, but that *they didn't even exist as a people at all.*

The fact that this keeps happening—that men think that this is how they can treat women's culture and women's thought, that they think they have the right to randomly appropriate bits of it without knowing a damn thing about it and use it to tell us that we are wrong and they are right—is precisely what Beauvoir was on about when she talked about the othering of women.

Our culture couldn't be an actual thing with its own existence that should be treated with respect and isn't just there to be taken apart at will and appropriated to meet the needs of male people.

Because we couldn't be actual people with our own existence who should be treated with respect rather than being taken apart at will and appropriated to meet the needs of male people.

And that is the whole damn point of the book.

As I've said before, Irigaray, who is probably the person in the direct tradition of Beauvoir who did the most to elaborate the idea of 'Woman as Other,' went so far as to say that in Western culture, women do not exist.

What she meant by that was that the patriarchal projection of 'Woman' was so totalizing that there was no recognition of the existence of actual female people in our culture at all.

Believe it or not, I used to think she was talking in dramatic metaphors.

Nope.

THE MALE POWER OF NAMING

Speech given at Oxford Feminist Union

OCTOBER 2021

Good evening. I'm very honoured to be here amongst these amazing women, and I'd like to give my thanks to the Oxford Feminist Union for organizing this event, and to say how happy it makes me to see feminists claiming their space and their right to speak about the existence and interests of women. Which brings me to what I'd like to talk about tonight. The theme of this evening's event is 'Words and Deeds,' and what I'd like to think through here is what is actually at stake in the struggle over the word 'woman,' and what that struggle tells us about the core mechanisms of patriarchal power.

So, to start us off, I'm going to read a sizeable quote from by the 1979 book *Pornography* by the incomparable Andrea Dworkin, and then I'm going to do some unpacking and think about how her observations relate to our present situation. This slightly abridged excerpt is from the opening chapter of the book, where Dworkin is outlining her analysis of the 'tenets of male-supremacist ideology':

> *Men have the power of naming, a great and sublime power. This power of naming enables men to define experience, to articulate boundaries and values, to designate to each thing its realm and qualities, to determine what can and cannot be expressed, to control perception itself. As Mary Daly, who first isolated this power, wrote in* **Beyond God the Father***: "it is necessary to grasp the fundamental fact that women have had the power of naming stolen from us."...Men have defined the parameters of every subject. All feminist arguments...are with or against assertions...implicit in the male system, which is made credible...by the power of men to name. No transcendence of the male system is possible as long as men have the power of naming... As Prometheus stole fire from the gods, so feminists will have to steal the power of naming from men...As with fire when it belonged to the gods, the power of naming appears magical...But this magic is illusion. The male power of naming is upheld by force...It is the naming by decree that is power over and against those who are forbidden to name their own experience.*

> *The male does not merely name women evil; he exterminates nine million women as witches because he has named women evil. He does not merely name women weak; he mutilates the female body...because he has named women weak...He names her ignorant, then forbids her education. He does not allow her to use her mind or body*

rigorously, then names her intuitive and emotional. He defines femininity and when she does not conform he names her deviant, sick, beats her up...If she wants him sexually he names her slut; if she does not want him he rapes her and says she does...He names her housewife, fit only for the house...He names her whatever suits him. He does what he wants and calls it what he likes. He actively maintains the power of naming through force and he justifies force through the power of naming. The world is his because he has named everything in it, including her...The fourth tenet of male supremacy is that men, because they are intellectually and creatively existent, name things authentically. Whatever contradicts or subverts male naming is defamed out of existence."[1]

What Dworkin identifies here is that a core mechanism of male power over women resides in men's power to name, or define, women on his own terms. In fact, in her discussion of the 'first tenet' of male supremacy, Dworkin makes it clear that "the power of men is first a metaphysical assertion of self, an *I am* that exists *a priori*...indifferent to denial or challenge," and we should definitely be thinking here about the trans activist assertion 'I am what I say I am,' and whether that assertion would fly if it was only female people making it. Male power resides first in men having unquestionable authority to name or define themselves and then unquestionable authority to name or define *women*. Or as Twitter user The Bewilderness has summed it up nicely in her "8th rule of misogyny": 'Men are whatever men say they are, and women are whatever men say they are.'

This defining of women is very much connected to Beauvoir's analysis of 'Woman as Other,' the thought that our society revolves around a male default subject, who gives to himself all the characteristics of the properly human while submerging female human beings under the patriarchal projection 'Woman.' As Dworkin makes clear, this act of projection is not benign. It has devastating effects on the material lives of actual female humans. 'Woman' is fashioned out of what Patricia Hill Collins has called 'controlling images,'[2] an assortment of denigrations and fantasies designed to discipline women into behaving in ways that benefit men. And so we are, by turns: Madonna, whore, virgin, Lolita, hysteric, nag, ball-breaker, domestic goddess, prick-tease, Medusa, siren, crone, feminazi, witch.

These projections have little, if anything, to do with the lives of actual

[1] Andrea Dworkin, *Pornography: Men Possessing Women* (London: Plume, 1981), pp. 17-18.
[2] See Patricia Hill Collins's chapter 'Mammies, Matriarchs, and Other Controlling Images,' in *Black Feminist Thought* (London and New York: Routledge, 2000). Collins is of course concerned here with the way 'controlling images' of black women function to objectify them and enable their exploitation. Her analysis is however situation inside an understanding of the 'othering' function of binary hierarchy which is consonant with my argument here.

embodied female humans, other than the role they play in bending women into shapes that serve male needs. As Dworkin says: "He names her whatever suits him." What is fundamentally at stake in this brutal game of naming, then, is whether actual female humans are seen to exist in their own right as beings with their own needs and interests, which may or may not be amenable to males. As Dworkin makes clear, citing Mary Daly's acute observation that women have had their power of naming stolen from them, male power forbids women from asserting their right to name and define their own experience, and our actual being must, at all times, be subjugated to the patriarchal projection of 'Woman,' which is to say, to serving male interests. This process of men naming women in terms that serve male needs is, I would argue, the very heart of patriarchal gender.

This is the sense in which Luce Irigaray has claimed that women do not actually exist in Western culture. As I've noted often before, while I was working on Irigaray as a postgrad, I used to take this claim about our non-existence as an accurate if somewhat overblown metaphor about how patriarchal gender works. But that was before I ran into trans activism. The fact that male people can convince a good chunk of society that they get to redefine women as whatever they say we are, and *a lot of people don't even grasp that we have a right to object*, let alone realize they are colluding with the core operation of male dominance, is pretty much the greatest demonstration in history of the truth of the claim that we live in a culture in which living breathing human women don't really exist at all.

As Dworkin points to here, this act of de-fining women is simultaneously an act of drawing, or erasing, boundaries. We are presently arguing about the boundaries of the concept of 'woman,' but more fundamentally, about the real material consequences of this, about the boundaries of women's single-sex spaces, or our right to set limits on who we organize with politically. Even more fundamentally, what we are actually expressing when we talk about 'boundaries' is women's assertion of our specific needs or interests, and the claim that those needs should be respected. A boundary is drawn when a woman says 'no,' or 'I don't like that,' or 'I don't want to.' When she refuses to abnegate herself and subjugate her own needs or desires to the needs and desires of the one who claims the power of naming over her. For all their claims to be 'smashing the gender binary,' what is so notable about trans rights activists is the entitled patriarchal fury they unleash whenever women will not comply with their demands. And their obdurate failure to grasp that it is us—in our refusal to just 'be kind' and move over —who are the real gender fuckers here.

What I particularly want to unpack a little more tonight, then, is how men's assertions that they are really women perfectly exemplifies the twin strands of the male power of naming and its devastating erasure of women.

Trans activism turns on redefining actual female humans as the patriarchal projection 'Woman' in law and public life, accompanied by the concerted effort to erase all language that links the concept of woman to the concept of female. By defining themselves *as us*, trans activism enacts the purest expression of the intertwining of men's authority to define themselves and their authority to define us in the process. And what is laid bare by this process, especially in the capacity to break the class of living breathing women into a dehumanized pile of body parts and functions, is that the core of the patriarchal power of naming is the erasure of women by subjugating them to any descriptions, and indeed, any *perceptions*, that suit male interests.

I am not claiming that *all* trans identification involves invoking harmful projections about what women are, nor that it *necessarily* entails erasing the reality of female people as a biological class, and breaking women into body parts. But the ideology of gender identity is fundamentally structured by this double gesture of redefinition and erasure, and often invokes such flagrant patriarchal stereotypes of women that it gives the lie to all the manipulative claims of powerlessness and vulnerability. What I am struck by when I see, say, a male member of my profession posting public pictures of himself in a French maid's outfit, or Pips Bunce decked out in frilly fuchsia lace no woman would dream of wearing to work at an investment bank, is a complacent assurance that men will be granted the power of defining what women are, no matter how caricatured, and that women will be denied the slightest authority to challenge them.

As I've suggested, this defining of women as the patriarchal projection 'Woman' has always been an act of erasure, a way of denying women's actual existence and needs, and turning us into a service class or resource for men to use and appropriate. Traditionally, the resource men are trying to appropriate is women's bodies, in both our sexual and reproductive capacities, and women's domestic and emotional labour. Trans activism is distinguished by the effort to appropriate the patriarchal *image* of 'Woman,' and to assert the absolute reality of this image over-against women's actual existence, by replacing a sex-based definition with a gender-identity-based definition and erasing any language that recognizes that women are female. What this does is make starkly manifest the erasure of the living breathing embodied reality of women always implicit in the patriarchal projection, while the generalized refusal to recognize we even have a legitimate interest in our own political definition, makes absolutely evident the extent to which our culture assumes that the power of naming belongs only to men.

What trans activism is demanding, fundamentally, is that women accede to the erasure of our existence implicit in the patriarchal projection 'Woman,' in order to allow that projection to be appropriated to meet male interests and gratify male desires. What this conflict makes evident is not only the core patriarchal power of naming, but that the power of naming enacts the complete subjugation of female people's reality to what male people want. In its barest terms, this is a straight up-down conflict between men's desire and women's existence, and it turns out that we live in a world in which many people simply and unthinkingly assume that male desire should win. Indeed, the prioritization of male desire inherent in the male power of naming is what makes it possible for men to name themselves women if that is what they want, and for many people to think that is in any way reasonable. The irony of this of course is that it proves precisely what trans activism is going to such mad and maddening lengths to deny. The truth of our claim that power in this society is structured and distributed by sex.

This dramatic unconcealment of what is at stake in the patriarchal power of naming is one of the main reasons, I think, why this conflict has brought so many women back to the second-wave analysis of male dominance. Or, to borrow a word from our political opponents, why so many women have been 'radicalized.' It's typical of trans activist hypocrisy that a bunch of people who style themselves anti-status-quo commie anarchists have adopted a term used by the counter-terrorist state apparatus to describe a bunch of non-compliant women, as if the women of Mumsnet have somehow been brainwashed by the evil terves into planning jihad. *Contra* this nonsense, what needs to be underlined here, is that people often become 'radicalized' when political circumstances make absolutely transparent some mechanism of domination that, hitherto, was operating just under the radar. And in a world which has long been saturated with the patriarchy pleasing faux-fun feminism that Julie Bindel is so good at unmasking, trans activism has, in a certain sense, done real feminism a favour.

What we are all living right now, day in and day out, is a direct encounter with the very core of patriarchal power as the male power to name us, and through that process, to erase and subjugate our existence to male needs. For all the stories about God speaking the world into being, or Adam claiming dominion over the animals by naming them, the male power of definition is not, as Dworkin notes, some kind of supernatural magic. It is, rather, held in place by force. And the direct encounter with this force is also what we are all living through right now. This system of enforcement has three moments. Its first moment is the complete denial that women have any right to define ourselves, any legitimate interest in our own definition, or any right to contest the definitions being imposed on us. This denial, and the power of this denial, is invoked every single time people dictate that there is no rights conflict here or insist that there is 'no debate' about whether women are to be redefined against their will.

Second, as Dworkin indicates, the entire structure of patriarchal projection will also be brought to bear on women who will not comply with those projections. As she wrote in *Pornography*: "whatever contradicts or subverts male naming is defamed out of existence." This is the absolute heart of the patriarchal power trans activism is wielding against women, and it's where we most clearly see how 'controlling images' of women work by forcing us in a double bind. Trans activism demands that we must accede to the self-abnegating image of ourselves, to the thought that, in Andrea Long Chu's bluntly misogynist terms, being female is "any psychic operation in which the self is sacrificed to make room for the desires of another."[3] However, if we refuse to comply with this "operation" in which "the self is hollowed out, at your own expense," then the entire panoply of demonizing projections will be leveraged against us. That a group of women calmly and clearly assembling facts and arguments to support the assertion of their own existence and their political interests can be so easily monstered as a frothing, spouting, spewing swarm of demonic Furies—or, if you prefer, as fascists, Nazis, white supremacists, and so on—is the purest exhibition of the patriarchal playbook at work in trans activism. As J. K. Rowling famously tweeted: "'Feminazi', 'TERF', 'bitch', 'witch'. Times change. Woman-hate is eternal."

The last moment of this patriarchal enforcement is the violence—and threats of violence— used to coerce women into accepting patriarchal projection. If we cannot be disciplined by being monstered, we will be disciplined by actual force. The demonization firstly functions to coerce us by trying to make us internalize the projections, by eroding our defiance with shame, but also to justify the violence being brought to bear against us. As Dworkin notes: "He actively maintains the power of naming through force and he justifies force through the power of naming." Here, aided by the catalogue of patriarchal monsters, women's boundaries, or assertion of our own interests, are effortlessly redefined as bigotry, prejudice, hatred, aggression, and 'weaponization.' And the extreme, often blatantly sexualized threats applied to coerce our boundaries are then, conversely, redefined as a just and justified act of self-defence. As many people have observed, what is happening here reveals how male violence functions as a structural, not accidental, feature of a male supremacist society, in order to coerce women's boundaries and force women to comply with their own self-abnegation to serve male ends.

In the baldest terms, this entire mechanism—males defining women in their own terms, demanding women erase their own existence to serve male needs, denying that women have any right to object, denying that women have any right to consent, monstering women for not consenting, and trying to coerce their consent by demonizing them and threatening them with

---

[3] Andrea Long Chu, *Females* (London: Verso, 2019), p. 11.

violence—all of this is the logic of a male supremacist rape culture writ large. To return to the subtitle of Dworkin's *Pornography*—'men possessing women'—what we have in trans activism is this entire mechanism of dominating rape logic being brought down on women, not in the service of men using women's bodies for their own pleasure, but in the service of enacting the fundamental erasure of women's embodied being that was always at the core of patriarchal projection, in order to please themselves by possessing that projection *as reality*. Far from being any kind of challenge to the mechanisms of patriarchal gender, trans activism is the greatest enactment of the coercive rape logic of a male supremacist society I have seen in my lifetime.

In this context it becomes apparent, I hope, why what might seem to some a trivial conflict over a word is, in fact, far far more than that. The definition of the woman as 'adult human female' defines our existence as a sex class, the boundaries of our spaces, our right to resources, our capacity to organize politically and to speak about our own oppression, the legitimacy of our political interests, and our capacity to reject the abnegating projection of 'Woman' as a compliant class of servile support humans constructed to meet male needs. When we struggle over this word—when we use our words to define the boundaries of our consent—we are, in and of itself, *doing* something that has very real, and very material, consequences for the lives of women. We are resisting the whole dominating rape logic of a male supremacist culture that would happily destroy the existence of living breathing female humans to take from us what it wants, for its own gratification.

It is imperative then that women come together now to draw and redraw the boundaries around our word, around our spaces, around our needs, around our very existence, again and again.

We must repeat:

We exist.

We are adult human females.

We are not your projections.

We refuse your right to name us.

We will defy your monstering and coercion.

No means no.

TRAS, RAPE-LOGIC, AND THE ECONOMY OF ENTITLEMENT

janeclarejones.com

JULY 2020

The last few weeks have been incredibly distressing.

When Joanne[1] Rowling released her essay,[2] there was a moment of collective, tearful hope. A woman with enough power had spoken our truth, with all the eloquence at her disposal, and, for a moment, I think we thought that they would have to hear.

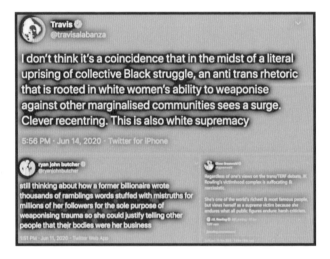

But now it seems that a woman's words—no matter how eloquent or precise—cannot be credited. Our pain, etched into our bodies, mimed over centuries and finally wrested into speech, will never be taken as intended: as evidence of our humanity, and an explanation of how that humanity is harmed by what is done to us. We are still, only ever, an object and repository, a resource for the needs and wants of others whose humanity matters more. Our pain, like our speech, like our politics, could never be *for* or *about* ourselves, because it has never registered—and this moment is nothing but

---

[1] I hope she's okay with this, but I'd like to ditch the J. K.. The occlusion of her sex is a symptom of—not a remedy for—male power.

[2] J. K. Rowling, 'J. K. Rowling Writes about Her Reasons for Speaking out on Sex and Gender Issues,' *jkowling.com*, 10 June 2020.

the concatenation of this denial—that we actually, in our own right, exist.

This argument is not, therefore, an appeal for empathy with the damage done to us by male power and projection, by the immemorial and immovable demand that we efface ourselves before the needs of more important others. We know our pain doesn't *count* in your economy, that it only registers on your balance books as a sly deceptive weapon or a vicious wilful harm to the interests of the only kind of people given credit. That you're so certain of the justness of your accounting, you never seem to notice that this one obvious fact gives the lie to the 'validity' of your catechism. If you really thought that trans women were women, their pain would be a nought to you as well.

I'm writing this for myself, and for all of us, I hope. The last few weeks have been more painful than I remember. After the torrent of cocks and the exhortations to choke,[3] the parade of denunciations and the trolling kids with porn, the media spin, the charges of 'weaponizing your trauma,' all polished off with tech-bro corporate might coming down on us like a ten-ton brick, it was the implacable, imperious requisition of Allison Bailey's words that finally broke me. Or rather, it was the attempt to justify that requisition by claiming that speaking the violent, often sexual, threats against us, was, in and of itself, an act of 'severe' discrimination *against the people threatening*

us.[4] On a quiet Wednesday afternoon, sitting at my desk, something happened I haven't felt for years. The back of my brain went metallic. I managed a few, incandescent tweets and then fell, quickly, into inarticulate rage. By Friday, on the phone, my 'discourse'

---

[3] Rebecca Reilly-Cooper, 'J. K. Rowling and the Trans Activists: A Story in Screenshots,' *Medium*, 9 June 2020.

[4] In June 2020 the barrister Allison Bailey launched a crowdfunder to sue her chambers and Stonewall following their harassing treatment of her due to her involvement with the LGB Alliance. Crowdjustice summarily suspended her page, claiming the text was discriminatory. One example given was a direct description of the contents of *terfisaslur.com*: "the same males who would have society regard them as women, were quick to brandish knives, axes, baseball bats and nooses, as they threatened with rape women who questioned the wisdom of replacing sex with gender." That is, Allison's crowdfunding page was censured for *describing* the violence directed *at us* by trans activists, and we were being told that we were *discriminating against the people threatening us*, by describing their threats. Allison Bailey's case was finally heard in April/May 2022. (www.twitter.com/BluskyeAllison/status/1278317988429561857?s=20.)

consisted mostly of a series of guttural, groaning sounds. I stuck needles[5] in my body, and the vice receded long enough to write and speak a poem, before tightening again. Rage passed into anger passed into despair passed into heavy, body-crushing sadness. Eventually the tears pooled in the centre of my heart and the bottom of my back so strongly I could cry them out. And then I started to see, and needed to try to speak, what was happening.

What we're witnessing is a violently enforced, three-tiered denial of our words, our right to name the reality of our experience, and the reality of the violence perpetrated against us because of our sex. Two tiers of this denial have long been evident. Now, in this battle between our discourse and their silencing, because we have fought so fucking long and hard for our words, our speech is, finally, beginning to be heard by some, the third tier is becoming ever more obvious. It was this that tipped me off the edge and, for a couple of weeks, stole most of my words. It looks, as my friend said last night when I explained it on the phone, like a near-perfect stitch up. It looks like this:

TIER ONE

We know this one well. This is the stealing of our language, a theft that sits at the very core of trans ideology. The redefinition of the word 'woman' as an amorphous meaningless gender class against our consent. The removal of all words that link the word 'woman' to the concept of 'female.' The imperious imposition of the essentialist bullshit label 'cis' ('IT'S LATIN!'). The dehumanizing conversion of female people into fragmented body parts and functions.[6] The command to call conspicuously male people 'women' even when engaged in conspicuously male behaviour, like, say, downloading child pornography or getting out their cocks at work.[7] This all amounts, we've said repeatedly, to the political erasure of sex. We have said, perhaps too abstractly, that we object to 'the erasure of the axis of our oppression.' What we mean is this: We object to male entitlement—to our bodies, to our time, to our attention, to our care, to our service, and now, above all, to our existence and the words that name it. We need to name the reality of sex: for medical reasons, and sporting reasons, but above all because women are oppressed by turning our bodies into resources and your idealist gender-bullshit can't explain

---

[5] For people who don't know me, the needles in question are acupuncture ones, not the ones attached to hypodermic syringes. This shit is hard work, but I'm not doing smack.

[6] Irischild, 'Menstruator and Other Words that Rhyme with Hate Her,' *irischild.blogspot.com*, 9 March 2018.

[7] Karen Finlay, 'Transgender Students' Officer Suspended for Allegedly Publishing Pictures of Male Genitalia; Faces No Additional Sanctions,' *womanarehuman.com*, 3 November 2019.

patriarchy *in the slightest*. But we need to name it most of all, because—as you never seem to grasp—gender is the system of entitlement that runs along the lines of sex. And the system that enforces that entitlement by means of threat or force. We need to name sex because we need to speak the violence males commit against us. Because our ability to speak at all depends on it. Which brings us to....

TIER TWO

In response to your demands—for our existence and its words—all we've said is 'no.' We haven't threatened, or intimidated, or besieged, or tried to cancel. We've explained, millions of times, why we're saying no, why we won't let you take our words, because we need them. But the economy of entitlement that belies all your claims to gender non-conformity will not respect our boundaries. The boundaries here are literal, around our spaces, around the de-lineation of our words, but they are, above all, figurative. They arise from the expression of our own subjectivity. The naming of our needs and interests. They arise when we say 'no,' and 'I don't want,' and 'you can't have.' In an ethical economy, among adults, it should be understood that the demand 'I want to take' never has right of force over 'I don't want to give.' You do not take from others what is not given freely, you don't coerce them into giving things they do not want to give. Doing so is an act of narcissistic domination. It subordinates an-other's needs and interests entirely to your own, and in so doing, annihilates their subjectivity. In its core, this is the logic, and the deep traumatic injury, of rape.

The narcissistic rage trans activists have unleashed on women to try to force us to be silent and comply is an exact exhibition of this logic. That so much of this coercive rage is sexualized, from the phallic pink-and-blue baseball bats to the desire to choke us on their cocks, is far from accidental. That people have been so easily convinced that gender lives inside a tube of eyeliner, while ignoring the sexual economy of entitlement being enacted in plain sight, is evidence of how far feminism has left to go. The women using argument and evidence to defend their 'no' are clearly monsters. A 'swarm' of uptight, cruel, castrating cunts who heartlessly refuse to meet a need so small it costs them nothing but their own existence. And everyone agrees. The litany of slurs and threats are warranted by the provocation of a 'no.' Just stop being such bitches. Just shut your fucking mouths and give us what we want you witches. Our desire or your existence. No contest cunts. 'Be Kind.'

TIER THREE

It is only inside this economy of entitlement that the indictment of 'weaponizing trauma' makes sense. Trauma is our explanation of why we need our words and the boundaries that they draw. (Although, let's be clear, people shouldn't have to give reasons to justify their boundaries, and the fact we feel the need to reveal our trauma to do just that shows how fucked this situation is already.) The claim that our trauma is a weapon, is then, at base, a claim that our boundary is an act of aggression. And this claim, relies, in turn, on the belief that the needs of, and harm done to, those who seek to transgress that boundary far outweighs the needs of, and the harm done to, those who will be violated. (This is precisely how the acronym that became the slur exerts its vilifying power—what distinguishes, we might ask, 'inclusion' from 'violation,' other than consent?) The people pressing, and supporting, this claim will ground it by appeal to the specific, and extreme, vulnerability of trans people. And while that appeal is not without foundation, the willingness to uncritically accept, and endlessly disseminate, empirically sketchy and appropriative statistics[8]—to accept then, in its fundament, the claim that the oppression of trans people neatly and completely overrides the oppression of women—is, in itself, a product of the economy of entitlement. The readiness of people, both male and female, to identify with and elevate the pain of males not being given what they say they need or want, over and against the females who tell them 'no,' is the psychic substance that greases the wheels and gears of the whole patriarchal shitshow. And it is the psychic

---

[8] Georgina Lee, 'Fact Check: How Many Trans People Are Murdered in the UK?' *channel4.com*, 23 November 2018.

substance that serves to justify, exculpate, and explain away any violence used to press male claims.

There is no logic, no quantity of need or pain, that justifies male people violating women's boundaries, that isn't rapey. What got to me about the response to Joanne Rowling's words—and by extension, the words of all of us who would defend our boundary—is how audaciously and easily left-wing journalists and politicians lined up to collude with rape logic, so immersed inside an economy of male entitlement and its narcissistic rage they likely have no fucking clue that that is what they're doing. Women's boundaries are not an act of aggression. Painting them as such is part of the economy

of entitlement used to justify taking what has not been given freely, and to justify both the violence that is that taking, and the violence often used to *enforce* that taking. (This is the difference between rape and aggravated rape. Rape is violence, rape is sometimes violence enforced by violence. One of the key feminist fights was the effort to make clear that it was not the enforcing violence alone that constituted the violation.) The indictment that we are 'weaponizing trauma' is hence, both, a contestation and delegitimization of the boundary that we have re-drawn in response to trans activists' requisition of our words and the spaces they inscribe (Tier 1), but is also then a *justification* of any force or threat of force brought to bear to press the claim against that boundary (Tier 2). Here, the accusation that women like Rowling are 'weaponizing trauma' acts as just another, subtler variation of the endless exculpations and woman-blaming bullshit used to justify the violences against us: 'She had it coming.' 'She made me do it.' 'She was asking for it.'

It is here too that the contours of Tier 3 emerge. It consists of the effort to justify and/or dismiss both the violence that is the violation of our boundaries

(Tier 1) *and*, in particular, the violence used to press the claim *against*, or en-force the violation of, our boundaries (Tier 2). This thought has always, in fact, been around. It often inheres in the classic patriarchal reversal under-pinned by the economy of entitlement. That is, because female people hav-ing boundaries is an act of intolerable *exclusion*—and is now, in fact, being recast as 'oppression'—then any violence used to press the claim against the boundary justifies itself as self-defence. It also turned up in another form just last night on Twitter, the wilfully circular 'the boundaries of bigots do not need to be respected,' which fails, of course, to recognize that 'bigot' in trans activist discourse means nothing but 'a woman whose boundaries stop me getting what I want,' viz., in fact, 'women's boundaries are bigotry.' Such is the power of the economy of entitlement that someone can seriously type 'I do not need to respect the boundaries of someone whose boundaries stop me getting what I want' and think that it will fly. Such is the power of the economy of entitlement that, in fact, it does.

Of course, the defenders of the faith won't accept a word of this. And to return to where we started, at Tier 1, they won't accept it because it's blasphe-my against the catechistic sanctity of the Trinity—'Trans Women Are Wom-en, Trans Men Are Men, Non-Binary Is Valid, Amen'—and its disavowal of the structuring of power along the lines of sex. (Remember, always, anyone who can actually *defend* their faith need not be so dogged with ex-communi-cating heretics.) Indeed, everything I have said here, because it relies on the sexual economy of entitlement, would be deemed to be hateful—although, as I've underlined, the transparent operation of that economy in this whole affair belies the truth of its own dogma. It is here that the denigration and dismiss-al of Jo Rowling's testimo-ny slips into the almost non sequitur of Owen Jones's reply. Jones's response here depends, *entirely*, on ostensi-bly reversing the balance of power between males and females, on denying that Jo Rowling speaks as a mem-ber of a class oppressed as female (this is the work of so much Tumblrized intersec-tional discourse about 'cis' women, 'rich' women, 'white' women, 'cishet' women,

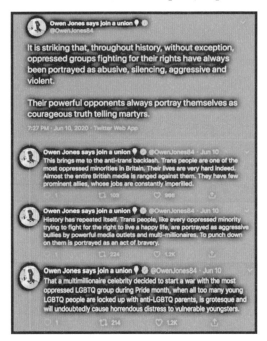

etc.), and denying that the vulnerability of trans people as trans does not magically negate the fact that the ones dictating that our boundaries are bigotry and can be rightfully overridden are still *male*. The epithets 'abusive,' 'silencing,' 'aggressive,' and 'violent,' when applied by females to the behaviour of males trying to coerce their boundaries, are not the sneaky gambit of a 'powerful' majority jealously hoarding their piles of privilege. It is how female people name, explain, and process the violence they experience *because* they're female, in a society governed by a sexual economy of entitlement.

Because OJ catechistically believes that trans-ness negates maleness, he can effectively make a claim that, without such catechistic cover, is something no self-respecting progressive should ever say, because it's incel-MRA-speak. That is, that women should not name male violence, and that in doing so, they are demonizing and discriminating against males. This is an effect of an argument that, as Owen never tires of reminding us, was used by the gay rights movement. It is true that the association of gay men with paedophilia as an excuse to refuse them rights was reprehensible (and just to underline, the general analogy with gay rights fails because gay rights did not involve violating the boundaries of another oppressed class, see 'Gay Rights and Trans Rights,' p. 67). It is not true, however, that no gay men are paedophiles, and that suspecting a gay man of being a paedophile is *a priori* an act of bigotry, if you have reason for your suspicion *beyond them being gay*. (Just as it's not *de facto* homophobia to think there might be a safeguarding issue if a gay man dresses in fetish gear and wanks in *the toilet of the national children's charity and then puts it on the Internet*.) Jones's claim in that case, effectively, was that gayness negates maleness (which it does not), and similarly here, that trans-ness should provide a negating shield of perfect immunity around males who identify as women, or non-binary, or maverique, or whatever, from any indictment of conspicuous male-pattern violence. (Cue Family Guy cartoon.)[9] A society that took the sexual abuse of women and children remotely seriously would understand that creating a sub-class of males who are *a priori* immune from being suspected or indicted of male-pattern violence is a safeguarding risk the size of a fucking planet.

It is this—the 'you're demonizing us as predators' stitch-up gambit—that leads directly to the moment where Allison's Bailey's description of the contents of *terfisaslur*[10] is summarily requisitioned as an act of 'severe' discrimination against trans people as a whole.[11] (Here we move from 'Not-AllMen'-MRA-logic to the equally dismissive 'NotAllTransWomen.') There is

---

[9] Family Guy, 'It's Okay I'm Transgender,' *YouTube*. (www.youtube.com/watch?v=59kf86v_Cpc.)
[10] *terfisaslur.com*.
[11] For more background on this case please see n. 4.

no way a decent person of progressive persuasion can look at the contents of *terfisaslur*, or the memes of gun-toting anime characters emblazoned with 'Shut The Fuck Up TERF,' or the phallic threats aimed at Jo Rowling, and conclude that these are not 'abusive,' 'silencing,' 'aggressive,' and 'violent.' It is an epic gaslighting piss-take to tell us to choke on cocks, threaten us with rape, soak t-shirts with our fake blood, emblazon signs with death threats, erect guillotines that bear our names, sketch our hanging bodies, and openly, gleefully, fantasize about the many other ways you want to kill us, and then turn around and say by *describing* this violence we are invalidating and demonizing you in an act of prejudicial malice.

The fact that much of this violence is enacted by males who are trans does not transubstanti-ate it into 'not violence' and it doesn't mean that people coercing female people's bound-aries with the kind of baseball-bat wielding rapey bullshit always used to coerce female boundaries are some-how, alchemically, 'not doing male-pattern vi-olence.' And your cat-

Exhibition by genderqueer art collective, The Degenderettes, San Francisco Public Library, April 2018

echism-that-we-don't-believe is no defence, not a get-out clause, not some kind of magic immunizing shield that will stop us naming what we see right before our eyes. We've often noted, sometimes caustically, sometimes rue-fully, that if people wanted to convince us that they were women, and *not a threat*, telling us to choke on cocks and hammering down the door with bats was probably not the way to go. We will keep our words, the boundaries that they draw, and the naming of the violence they allow, because the survival of our subjectivities and the possibility of our healing depends on it. And though we may be silenced sometimes by your animation of our trauma and your refusal of our power to name, all you will achieve, with your catechistic dictates, in the end, is demonstrating why we wouldn't let you take our words from the beginning.

We say again:

No means no.

MALE POWER

janeclarejones.com

JULY 2020

Now that the TechBro-mofos
Have tipped their hand,
Laid it down,
Said the quiet part out loud,
'SHUT THOSE WITCHES UP ALREADY'
There'll be no cyber-space or quarter given
To that pit of 'spewing' vipers
And their 'hateful' talk of boundaries,
Who refuse to bend
Or 'educate themselves'
By reading Holy scrolls
And transcriptions of The Law
Until they see the light and
Dutifully accept
Into their hearts
The godlike eminence of male desire
And its validity
Above all else.

Sixty-thousand women snuffed out
Of speech, while
The Struggle-Fuck goes on
Because our degradation makes them hard.
And who are we to judge?

A chorus of pearl-clutching prudes,
Uptight cunts
Fucking with their freedom
(Their dicks must go anywhere they please),
They will judge
The justice of your case
Like some virtualized
Extraordinary rendition

165

And find you guilty
Of 'severe' offence
For speaking of the pointed knives
And wire-encrusted baseball bats
They said they'd rape you with
If you did not comply
With their desire.

Our job, as always,
Is to serve their needs.
Their entitlement
To our flesh
Now so overweening
That, having laid the body
Of the earth to waste
With their fantasies of immortality and
Techno-domination,
They demand the very substance
Of our sex
Be placed
Under the dominion
Of their idea.
The power to name
The matter of the world
According to their will
(Or lust),
Like The Good Book
'In the beginning.'

And all we said was 'No,'

All we said was:
'The matter of our bodies
Matters,
And this form of your dominion
Is no different than it was before
And holds no space
For us
To actually exist
And incarnate
Beyond the dead-eyed dreams
Your minds have made of us.'

What happens when that flat
Reflecting surface
Of the mirror
Starts to speak? The insubordination
Is unbearable and
Must be punished.
They will say that we are 'throwing bricks,'
Although all I will remember
Is that night when,
Surrounded by a baying crowd
Transported in an ecstasy of
Seeing us all tarred and feathered,
We boarded up the windows
So we could breathe
Enough to talk.

They cannot still our tongues.
They will try to take us
One by one
And make a Philomela of us each
As a warning to the others.
They will hunt down Baronesses
And dispute their right to adjudicate
The words.
They will descend in legions
And fantasize
Of stopping up
Our mouths
And choking us to silence
With their cocks,
(Exempt of course
From any wisp of
Patriarchal power
Because they're just so queer now),
All while dicktating that
They're smashing up the
Status quo.

It takes an exemplary arrogance,
After all this time
Of brandishing their weapons
And erecting

Monumental towers
To the phallus,
To use the massive edifice of
Techno-corporate
Potency
At their disposal
To try and make us mouth
The catechism
Of its denial.

And nothing here has changed,

The dirt of the earth
And the blood of bodies
Still sustains you in your fantasies
Of uploaded immortality,
A clear Platonic sky
Of neural nets
And body-denigrating domination
Over the forms of life.
And even were you able to
Use your Law to
Excise the tongue
Of every single Fury
And stop her speaking of
Your rape
And desecration,
The earth will still make manifest,
In that matter
You have denied
Intelligibility
Since the dawn of time,
With words of
Water
Wind
And fire,
Her judgement
Upon you.

IV - PATRIARCHY, NARCISSISM, AND DOMINATION

PATRIARCHY AND NARCISSISM

Twitter

24 JULY 2020

1. Patriarchal masculinity is fundamentally defined by the conceit of invulnerability. That's what all the stereotypes about being strong, independent, and rugged are about. It's also what the repudiation of anything associated with the feminine is about, because the feminine is defined (by negation) as weakness, passivity, vulnerability, and so on. Ergo 'Boys don't cry,' 'don't be a sissy.' It's also where the male fear of being penetrated comes from.

2. One of the features of thinking you are invulnerable is that you can't be dependent on anything. Because that's a vulnerability. So patriarchal masculinity actually makes it hard for men to work out how to get their needs met ethically, because they have a problem even recognizing that they are dependent creatures and that they therefore have needs.

3. The best way to solve this problem—which you could call 'the dilemma of desire (or need)'—is to requisition the thing you are dependent on as property. This allows you to carry on thinking you are all invulnerable while appropriating the thing that meets your needs because if the thing is an inert piece of property, it can't ever tell you 'no,' or decide it's going to leave you.

4. So this, I think, is the fundamental structure of men's attempt to construct their relations to women and our bodies and care, etc., in the mode of appropriation.

5. The mode of this relation is fundamentally narcissistic because it doesn't recognize women as humans with our own interior lives and needs and wants, who need to be negotiated with. It is inculcated in males in this society by socializing them in narcissistic entitlement. (How that works is quite complicated, but it functions basically by the mechanism of repudiating the female/maternal, which actually stops them being able to recognize and process their own needs, and above all, deal with sometimes not getting what they want.)

6. The problem with all this is that, actually, we are human, and not things that can be straightforwardly appropriated. When we express our own interests or desires, demand to be listened to as human, say no, or put down any kind of boundary that stops men getting what they want, the result is often narcissistic rage, coercion, violent tantrums, and the attempt to redouble the effort to dominate and control us. This is the mechanism that underpins male violence, both sexual and non-sexual, against women. It is most clearly expressed in the logic of the incels, but it is at play in all male dominance.

7. When we put down boundaries, men are thrown back on the fact that they are dependent on and vulnerable to other humans, and it shatters their god-like dreams. They then project this onto us, and feel like we are controlling them by making them have needs or desires, and that by making them have needs or desires, we are exercising illegitimate power over them etc... Because they can't deal with their dependency, and they can't get what they want, this generates resentment and rage. This, I think, is basically what underpins misogyny.

The solution is for men to be socialized to learn how to tolerate their own vulnerability and needs, to understand that as adults they are not entitled to those needs being met by other humans, and to not project their rage feelings about their needs not being met onto women.

That would require a MASSIVE shift.

TRANS IDEOLOGY AND NARCISSISM

Twitter

4 MAY 2021

¿jordan¿
@fobbsmagazine

misgendering sucks, but what feels even more violent is when people get my pronouns right and i can tell they still perceive me as a man

4:53 AM · May 3, 2021

21.2K   389   Copy link to Tweet

This is where this leads.

The utterly narcissistic drive to get right inside other people's consciousness and control their perceptions because you want them to perceive what *you want to be true*, not what is actually there to be perceived. You people are the quintessence of fascism.

You could accept reality, and that people are being polite to you, and be okay with that. But no, everything, from our words, to our social organization, to our laws, to our very perceptions of basic constituent elements of the world has to be rearranged because YOU WANT.

And that is why you are so fucking dangerous. Because you go on and on and on about your authenticity, and your truth, and your journey, and you have not one single sliver of respect for the humanity of anyone else. We're all just flat fucking mirrors there to reflect YOU.

Our minds, beliefs, and perceptions have no place other than as a reflecting surface for YOU and YOUR IDENTITY. And if we don't reflect what YOU WANT to exactly YOUR specifications, you want to reach inside our heads and recalibrate our consciousness so that it serves YOU.

FUCK NO.

ONTOLOGICAL TOTALITARIANISM BY NUMBERS

janeclarejones.com

8 DECEMBER 2018

1. Human beings have a right to freedom of conscience and belief.

2. Human beings have a right to their own perceptions.

3. Human beings have a right to speak in a manner that expresses their own conscience, belief, and perceptions—providing that speech is not an incitement to violence against another person.

4. The only pronouns one can prescribe to oneself, ethically, are 'I' and 'me.'[1]

5. Third-person pronouns are granted to you *by another person.*

6. Pronouns function as a 'recognition protocol' to *instruct* someone else how they are to recognize someone, often in the absence of, or in contradiction to, observable cues.

---

[1] "The only ethical conclusion to the statement that begins 'My pronouns are' may be 'I and me.'" Christopher Reed, 'Axiomatic,' 2018. Reed, Distinguished Professor of English, Visual Culture, Women's, Gender, and Sexuality Studies, and Art History, published 'Axiomatic' on his faculty webpage at Penn State in October 2018. Reed was summarily denounced by our favourite trans activist, Grace Lavery, in a blog at the *LA Review of Books*, in which Grace withered on, at great and unsurprising length, about fascism and how it was all more or less the same as people resisting compelled speech ('Grad School As Conversion Therapy,' www.blog.lareviewofbooks. org, 29 October 2018). Reed replied on the same platform with 'Conversion Therapy v. Re-education Camp: An Open Letter to Grace Lavery,' on 11 December 2018, noting that the "tenor of your essay, which throws around appellations of 'garbage' 'bullshit,' not to mention 'fascist,' is indicative of the virulence of a call-out culture that stifles the free exchange of ideas." Of course, TRA pressure on Reed did not let-up, and by 19 December the customary dead-eyed 'We Have Listened and Learned' retraction had been extracted ('Lessons Learned,' www.blog.lareviewofbooks.org). Reed then removed 'Axiomatic' from his university webpage, although many of us saved it before he did so. It's worth reading, especially for the line, "Once upon a time, there was a word for people who worked together to dismantle conventional gender roles. That word was 'feminist.'" A copy can be found at www.janeclarejones.files.wordpress.com/2018/12/axiomatic.pdf.

7. Asking someone to use certain pronouns is a request that they perceive or recognize you in a certain way.

8. Prescribing pronouns is a diktat that another person perceives or recognizes you in a certain way.

9. Prescribing pronouns and enforcing that prescription is an act of coercion which violates people's freedom of conscience. This is ontological totalitarianism.

10. Resisting coercion is not bullying.

11. Ontological totalitarianism may well be bullying.

12. Recognition must be freely given if it is to meaningfully function as validation.

13. Coerced recognition is both a violation of people's freedom of conscience and is functionally worthless as validation.

14. Resisting coerced recognition is not an act of violence—literal or otherwise—nor an incitement to violence.

15. Trans people who are visibly gender non-conforming are subject to violence as a result of the policing of patriarchal gender norms.

16. Feminists do not police patriarchal gender norms.

17. Violence directed at people who violate patriarchal gender norms is an artefact of patriarchy, not an artefact of feminism.

18. Many feminists believe that sex and gender are analytically distinct, and do not believe that the performance or identification of a person's gender changes their sex.

19. This is a matter of our perception of reality and a matter of political conviction. It is not a pretext.

20. Blaming feminists for patriarchal violence against gender-non-conforming and trans-identified people is empirically baseless political strategy that serves as an instrument of coercion.

21. People refusing to validate your identity may be painful.

22. Something being painful is not conceptually identical to it being a moral harm, structural violence, or an act of oppression.

23. Not getting our needs met is sometimes painful.

24. Sometimes our needs don't get met because other people also have needs, beliefs, and interests.

25. Thinking you must always have your needs met and refusing to understand why other people may not meet your needs is narcissistic entitlement.

26. Narcissistic entitlement is the refusal to recognize the needs and interests of other people.

27. Narcissistic entitlement is the opposite of mutual recognition.

28. Mutual recognition is the condition of possibility of justice.

29. Ontological totalitarianism is a political manifestation of narcissistic entitlement.

30. Ontological totalitarianism is antithetical to the conditions of possibility of justice.

PRONOUNS ARE COOL!

Twitter

15 SEPTEMBER 2020

They're not cool.

They're a protocol for people to impose their own self-image on others, dictate to people what they are to perceive, and then throw a tantrum when other people don't comply.

They're narcissistic domination.

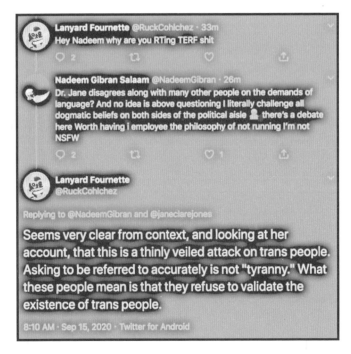

If someone makes a point about your authoritarianism, you might find that going full Inquisition on someone else retweeting it doesn't really help your case…

It's worth thinking through a couple of things in this statement, in addition to the 'thinly veiled' authoritarianism of demanding other people explain why they retweeted something.

1. 'A thinly veiled attack on trans people.' This statement is disingenuous. It depends on completely collapsing the difference between 'trans people' and 'the authoritarian gender essentialist and sex denialist ideology of the current trans rights movement.' As we have said repeatedly, we don't believe your religion. We think your religion is based on the reification of gender stereotypes, that it's harmful to women's sex-based rights, that it's bad for homosexuals and transsexuals, and that it leads to the unnecessary medicalization of gay and gender-non-conforming children.

Everything I have ever said is a critique of this ideology, not an attack on trans people. There are *plenty* of trans people who do not believe your religion either. Which is to say, the existence of trans people and the belief in gender identity ideology are not the same thing. Trying to consistently impose this ideology by collapsing critiques of your belief system into attacks on trans people's existence is an act of deliberate obfuscation that attempts to render any criticism of the ideology illegitimate and enforce ideological conformity. It is an anti-democratic attack on freedom of thought and belief.

2. 'Refusing to validate the existence of trans people.' Again this relies on collapsing 'gender identity' and its validation into 'the existence of trans people.' I am not denying, nor have I ever denied, that trans people exist. What I am denying is the belief in gender identity as the sole over-riding determinate of *who someone* is in a way that overwrites their perceptible sex, especially now that your religion demands that we 'validate' an immaterial identity solely on the basis that someone else asserts it. (This is what the pronoun protocol is: an instruction to someone of what your gender identity is and how others should validate that identity over-against anything one perceives or believes.)

To repeat: we don't believe your religion. And in a free society I am not obliged to profess any religion I don't believe, especially one that directly contradicts my own analysis of the world, and which I consider to be regressive and harmful.

The entire problem here is that gender identity depends for its existence on its validation, and the entire political project is about demanding and securing that validation. That makes the project fundamentally, not accidentally, authoritarian. This is the process I have called 'ontological totalitarianism.'

It should be noted here that this gives the lie to all the talk of authenticity. Authenticity depends on the ability to be and to express yourself, in a manner that doesn't require coercing people's response to you. If you are behaving authentically, what you will find is that people will perceive that, and they will respond to you on the basis of perceiving you as the thing you also understand yourself as being.

That is true validation. Because it is freely and honestly given. And not coerced. And no validation that is coerced actually serves the end of validation. Because people being forced to tell you something they don't think is true won't actually work. And you know it. Which is why this entire movement is characterized by people being on the verge of narcissistic rage the whole time.

This is the paradox of authenticity. To get social recognition, you have to not give a fuck about social recognition and immerse yourself comfortably and completely in the business of being yourself. And then people will see who you are and recognize it.

Freely and meaningfully.

DISCIPLINING MARTINA: HERETICS AND THE CHURCH OF TRANS NORMATIVITY

janeclarejones.com

DECEMBER 2018

Two main things turned up in my timeline this morning. One was the fallout from Rachel McKinnon's egregious and unconcealed bullying of Martina Navratilova, and the other was a Call for Papers from Brighton University.

I was already planning on writing this post when the Call for Papers popped up because Rachel's behaviour last night was such a copper-bottomed rendition of what trans activist coercion looks like, and I thought it was worth examining blow-by-blow. The academic CFP might, at first glance, seem tangential to the issue of trans inclusion in sports, but it refracted with Rachel's behaviour in an interesting way, so, whether this is a happy or unhappy accident, this is what you get…

The CFP sketches out the claim that 'queerness' is 'inclusive' and 'fluid,' while 'gayness' or 'homosexuality' is 'exclusive' and 'oppressive,' a dichotomy that rests on the never-fully-interrogated assumption that 'inclusion' is an unequivocal 'good,' while 'exclusion' is an unequivocal 'evil.' (See 'Why Feminists are Not Nazis,' p. 133.) The parallel here to the issue of trans inclusion in sports is evident: this is *precisely* the moral logic that makes McKinnon come over all God's avenging angel to one of the greatest sportswomen—and lesbian icons—of all time. And it's exactly the logic, to draw the examples closer, that underpins McKinnon's indictment of lesbians for asserting their same-sex 'exclusiveness.' But what strikes me as particularly interesting about the refraction of these two moments with each other is that the CFP belies a critical contradiction. While the discourse of 'exclusive' homosexuality is 'normative' (in queer-theory speak this is synonymous with 'disciplinary' and 'oppressive'—i.e. 'bad'), queer perspectives, they admit, have now assumed a 'hegemonic status.'

Quite how the organizers planned to parse '*bad* normativity' from '*good* hegemony' is anyone's guess—if 'normative' or 'hegemonic' discourses are 'disciplinary' or 'bad' *by virtue of being hegemonic*, then there is no reason why 'queer' discourses should get a free pass. (There is a paradox in the centre of queer thought here—at the point at which queer theory becomes a form of academic normativity, it is no longer, by its own definitions, *queer*.) Indeed, what I want to suggest here, is that McKinnon's behaviour toward Martina is exactly a demonstration of the way in which the moral logic of queer 'inclusivity' has now become a hegemonic, punitive, and *profoundly* disciplinary discourse.

Trans and radical queer activism is animated by a deeply authoritarian and coercive political impulse that leads proponents to behave like the bastard children of Stalinism and the medieval Catholic Church. It has produced a generation of aesthetically and discursively identikit activists who are utterly in thrall to their own moral righteousness, the categorical 'evil' of anyone who questions their sacred axioms, and their inquisitorial right to school and punish heretics. That is, the very fact that a mediocre philosopher and mediocre cyclist considers themselves in a position to discipline someone as widely and rightfully respected as Martina Navratilova for heresy, tells us everything we need to know about which discourse is dominant here—the hegemonic normativity of 'queer' inclusivity—and the fact that there is nothing 'anti-disciplinary,' 'diverse,' 'fluid,' 'open,' or, strictly speaking, '*queer*' about trans activism. 'In Queer Times' we find ourselves. Indeed.

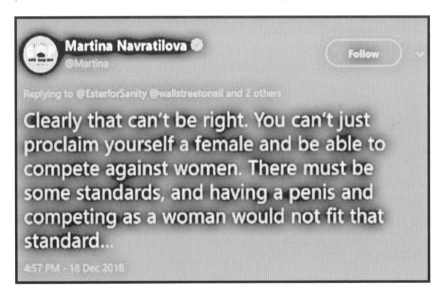

Invitation from the conveners: Introducing the English translation of Mario Mieli's 1977 'Towards A Gay Communism', Tim Dean describes Mieli's articulation of gayness as 'loosening gayness from an exclusively sexual orientation to something more capacious' (Mieli 2018:xi). Yet Mieli was writing before the emergence of queer theory, and in contemporary scholarly work around sexuality and sexual identity, queer appears to have achieved a hegemonic status. Over the past decade the articulation of theory or politics that is explicitly gay (rather than queer or LGBTQ) has often been attached to limiting, exclusionary, and oppressive practices, particularly regarding race and gender. As an unsurprising result, in both academia and activism 'gay' is frequently framed as the normative, assimilationist, and exclusionary past to queer's fluid, radical, and inclusive present and future.

Yet critically engaging with what gay and queer mean (or could mean) nowadays can be elided precisely because of this problematic juxtaposition. While in many ways we broadly align ourselves with queer thought, we are sceptical of knee-jerk tendencies to unquestioningly surrender gay to a politics of exclusion and neoliberal assimilationism. We want to challenge and interrogate assumptions of how gay can be known and conceptualised, beyond conflation with / reduction to homosexuality. Consequently, this conference invites a focus explicitly gay scholarships, theories, identities, identifications, politics, cultures, histories, and futures. It asks:

Anyway, let's look at what happened. This is the tweet that kicked it off (which Martina has since deleted, because Rachel):

> **Martina Navratilova** ✔
> @Martina
>
> Replying to @EsterforSanity @wallstreetoneil and 2 others
>
> Clearly that can't be right. You can't just proclaim yourself a female and be able to compete against women. There must be some standards, and having a penis and competing as a woman would not fit that standard...
>
> 4:57 PM - 18 Dec 2018

Now, I'm not going to get into a thing here about whether Martina is right to claim that *this* standard—having or not having a penis—should be *the* standard by which trans women should or should not be included in women's sports. What those standards should be is a whole conversation, and I'm just going to say: *we need to have that conversation*. What interests me, rather, is that it's not a conversation trans activism is willing to even countenance, because trans activism is committed to the proposition that 'transwomen-are-women-in-all-and-every-respect-and-any-attempt-to-make-any-distinctions-based-on-sex-is-an-act-of-egregious-hatred-that-must-be-pounced-on-and-disciplined-immediately.' Ergo:

> *@rachelvmckinnon:*
> *Welp, guess Navratilova is transphobic*

This is of course the classic form of the opening salvo, viz. 'HERETIC.' Followed quickly by 'RECANT':

> *@rachelvmckinnon:*
> *She could delete the tweets an replace them with an apology*

Then there are a couple of quote tweets to drive the point home:

> *—@Martina:*
> *To all the people on the thread – I am totally and completely pro-trans people or any part of the spectrum. I do not wish to define anyone. All I want is fairness on the playing field. That is it.*

> *@rachelvmckinnon*
> *No, you are not 'pro-trans people' if you say that trans women with a penis must not compete in women's sport. That's transphobic. Genitals do not play sports. What part of penis is related to tennis?*

> *—@Katie975312000:*
> *It's easy to scapegoat minority groups in times of difficulty Martina, but scapegoating trans women is no more a cure for gender oppression than scapegoating Jewish ppl like me solved the economic problems of Germany in the 1930s. Sad that you march today with the far-right.*

> *@Martina:*
> *I'm not scapegoating anyone.*

> *@rachelvmckinnon:*
> *You said that trans women with a penis shouldn't compete in women's categories. No one is misrepresenting you. You were really clear.*

The insistence that 'we're not misrepresenting you' is entertaining but unconvincing, seeing as it was in response to the tried and trusted imputation that anyone who thinks the difference between male and female people might matter in any situation whatsoever is a literal Nazi.

One imagines from this that Martina's mentions were a shitshow at around this point, and she decides to engage directly with McKinnon:

> *@Martina:*
> *Enough already!!! Not sure what exactly I said that offended you and what exactly I ought to delete. I have deleted like two tweets ever because the tone was wrong. Clearly I messed up somewhere along here. I will try to fix it. Am always open to more knowledge. Till tomorrow :)*

To which McKinnon replies, 'you messed up by doing a HERESY':

> *@rachelvmckinnon:*
> *You said that having a penis disqualifies trans women from women's sport.*

There are multiple branching threads in this exchange, so I'll try to put them together as best I can. In response to the 'Third Reading of the Charge of Heresy' we get this, a recanting:

> *@Martina:*
> *Ok – I take it back. Clearly I don't know what u am talking about. So once again – I will defer to Renee Richards as she certainly knows that she is talking about. I will find that tweet and delete it. All I want is fairness. Thank you.*

> *@rachelvmckinnon:*
> *Deferring to a single trans person is a bad idea. And you're playing yourself as the victim here: you're the one who did the bad thing. Can you not even admit that?*

Martina also replies to the original tweet telling her to recant with this:

> *@Martina:*
> *I tell you what – I will keep cooking the dinner...and will continue trans athlete convos with experts in the field in private.*

> *@rachelvmckinnon:*
> *If you want to talk to me in private, we can. I am an expert on this (maybe you don't realise who you're speaking to?).*

In all the time I have been trapped in this hall of mirrors, this is the most epic self-awareness fail I've seen. Can you imagine, IMAGINE, for a fraction of a second, being a two-bit philosopher and shit cyclist who is almost entirely famous for calling women TERFs and nefariously winning medals, bowling up to a woman who has won 18—18!—Grand Slam titles, and saying, 'DON'T

YOU KNOW WHO I AM???' Like, seriously, my brain cannot even begin to compute the quantity of narcissistic obliviousness that requires.

And, as if that wasn't enough, McKinnon follows up the grandiose peacocking by posting a bunch of links to their videos and articles, so that Martina can 'educate herself' (aka 'Read the Good Book until you understand the WORD, heathen').

The final reply from Martina to the original tweet telling her to delete was this:

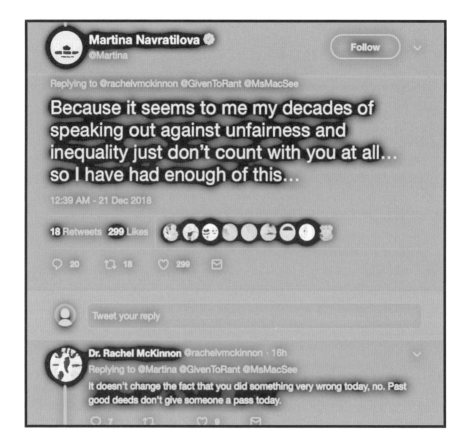

This one is a doozy, and it points to something that drives me nuts about trans activism. That is, the sheer unadulterated narcissism of its moral system. There is only their moral code, and their moral code is ALL ABOUT THEM, and gives not one flying fuck about the needs of anyone else, or about anything in another person's character or history if it's not ALL ABOUT THEM. Martina Navratilova is an outstanding human being[1]—along multiple axes—but she has committed a sin against the Great Church of Trans Ideology and so she gets treated with blanket contempt. The punitive moralism dripping off McKinnon's reply here makes me want to scream. Yeah, right, very fucking *queer*.

Following the pronouncement on Martina's sins—and despite the fact that she has already recanted—we then get instruction on the proper way to prostrate and atone. Along with the conventional 'we're just trying to help you do better.' (Could you get more dead-eyed disciplinarian, bending over you with a belt, telling you it's *for your own good*???):

> *@Martina:*
> *I am done with this in a public forum-thank you. Deleted tweet and I am out. Clearly I don't know enough and I am fighting way too many fights to try and keep up with this one. Thanks again...*

> *@rachelvmckinnon:*
> *All you had to do: "I'm sorry. I made a mistake. I will work to do better." Then delete the tweets. Why drag this out?*

> *@Martina:*
> *I did exactly that and you are still carrying on. When will you stop trying to rub my nose in it? Come on!!!*

> *@rachelvmckinnon:*
> *Have you apologized? Have you acknowledged that you caused harm? Could you maybe stop attacking the people trying to help you do better?*

Martina then goes back to the earlier tweet in which McKinnon gave her some 'educate yourself' material, and it prompts more admonishment on correct atonement procedures (plus a nice side-swipe at a potential ally explaining why this might not be productive):

> *@Martina:*
> *You're right. I don't know who I am talking to and you do. Once again – clearly I am ignorant of what is being transphobic. So I am sorry for my ignorance, it won't happen again.*

---

[1] Julie Bindel, 'Martina Navratilova: I Want to Save Lives,' *The Guardian*, 15 April 2010.

@rachelvmckinnon:
Wow...this is exactly how NOT to react, Martina.

@Frances_Larina:
I've unintentionally screwed up like that... Finally someone explained and I acknowledge & apologised. Ongoing hurtful reaction to my mistake means I avoid that community now instead of ally. It's a waste.

@rachelvmckinnon:
And that's on you: that's your failing to be a fairweather ally.

The last responses from Martina come in a thread that had developed about her coach, the trans tennis player Renee Richards. McKinnon is absolutely dismissive—because Richards doesn't toe the trans ideological line—before heading straight back for more moralistic 'I hope you see the error of your ways, my child':

@rachelvmckinnon:
Richards supports genital surgery requirements...she's hardly the most progressive trans athlete to be talking to.

@Martina:
And now you are even condescending to a woman who has done more for trans people than you can ever dream of and put herself under immense pressure. Shame on you...

@rachelvmckinnon:
Umm...wow. Martina, engaging with you and holding you accountable for your public transphobic comments is not 'bullying,' and it's not 'nasty.' I hope you see your way to regretting how you've handled this.

Martina, quite rightly, counters by pointing out that McKinnon's 'engagement' bears all the hallmarks of bullying—or, to be more specific, all the hallmarks of trying a heretic. McKinnon, of course, is having none of this. Evidently, only one person here is being victimized:

@Martina:
You didn't engage, you bullied. For examples asking me to delete a tweet and then asking for a screenshot of it so you could keep shaming me. Not going to happen...

@rachelvmckinnon:
Why are you continuing your attack on me this morning. I was done last night. Do

you not see how many transphobic people are now responding? I mean it. They think you are on their side. But you've been silent in response to them.

And clearly the best way to demonstrate that is with a few more quote tweets about what a terrible creature Navratilova is, and how very dare she:

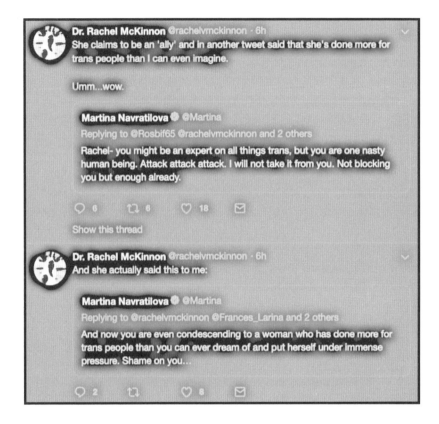

I don't have much more to say here. It tells, I think, a pretty clear tale. I'm not doing this because I hope to make a mark on McKinnon's narcissistic carapace. I guess my only hope is to appeal to my one-time colleagues in the academy who are still churning out this bollocks about queer fluidity and anti-normativity and inclusiveness. For the love of the goddess, open your fucking eyes. This is an unequivocally, irremediably identitarian discourse. Everything we learned about the dangers of totalization, and the inability to deal with difference, and the importance of openness. Everything you allegedly believe about 'bad' normativity and discursive discipline. Every thought that arose from the post-war ashes about how not to purify ourselves with flames. This discourse is everything you claim to oppose. It is everything that it claims that it isn't.

For fuck's sake. LOOK.

ON WOKEIST AUTHORITARIANISM

Twitter

1 MARCH 2020

So, I wanted to share some thoughts on the authoritarianism of some of our younger people, which I've been mulling over.

Most of us were brought up in the shadow of both right- and left-wing totalitarianism. We read *Nineteen Eighty-Four* and *Animal Farm* when we were teenagers. We were also exposed throughout our youth to the horrors of racist state repression in South Africa. I wrote my extended essay for GCSE English on a comparison between *Nineteen Eighty-Four* and JM Coetzee's *The Life & Times of Michael K*. I was seriously concerned about the damage to the humanity of people of all kinds at the hands of violent, reality-twisting state machinery.

This generation were brought up in the shadow of 9/11 and the War on Terror. They came of age steeped in the abuse of the language of liberal democracy to justify violent imperial wars. With the understanding that the language of 'freedom' could be effectively deployed to mask illegitimate economically self-interested and massively destructive meddling in the self-governance of other, less economically and politically powerful, and often non-Western/non-white nations. To them, the language of liberal democracy is a sham. It is the polite face of a neoconservative and neoliberal imperial fist. And they have often been taught in university that liberalism is the political discourse of capitalism. And they are not entirely wrong about that.

So, it is not entirely surprising, under these conditions, that they would be suspicious about all appeals to democratic process, and would be easily convinced that we are concerned only with masking the operation of power. They don't have our cultural memory about the damage authoritarianism can also wreak *in the interests of power*. And they feel, quite understandably, powerless, in the face of a massive rapacious global neoliberal machine that is laying waste to millions of lives and the very substance of the earth, and has cloaked itself in the language of freedom.

As with most things, the truth lies somewhere between the extremes. Both the neoliberal and imperial abuse of democratic rhetoric and authoritarianism are threats to the well-being of people and of the polity.

It is understandable, I think, that we feel angry with the way young people have apparently uncritically absorbed a discourse that prompts them to act in such a totalitarian manner, and that they have somehow been convinced that the linchpin of the structure of global domination is a bunch of mostly middle-aged left-wing feminist women, that they project their anger at the intellectual traditions that, in fact, have won so much for them and are not responsible for the damage neoliberal imperialism has wrought over the last four decades.

It's understandable that we are angry that their justified anger at the state of the world has so effectively been diverted from what I think should be its rightful target, that they don't see that their analysis is distorted, that it actually serves the interests of exactly what they want to resist, and that it so much easier to beat up on older women than actually trying to stick it to 'the man.'

But we should also probably remember that, like us all, they are products of history and power. And that one of the real sources of this fucking mess is the right-wing men who so abused the language of democracy in order to continue their avowed intent to exploit the world and its people to the point of near extinction.

<Ends>

TWITTER, TRANS RIGHTS TOTALITARIANISM, AND THE ERASURE OF SEX

janeclarejones.com

SEPTEMBER 2018

Normally, when I write I make jokes. But this morning I find I really don't feel like joking about any of this right now. I finished working late yesterday afternoon only to read Graham Linehan's tweet warning me that Twitter had announced a potential new policy[1] that would lead to the 'immediate silencing' of my voice. And when I read the proposed policy I realized, with a wash of sudden cold shock, that he was right. Those of you who know me, know me. You know that I have dedicated my life to thinking about injustice, and to analyzing how mechanisms of domination function to destroy the lives of vast numbers of people because of their sex, or sexual orientation, or socio-economic class, or race. You know I've never bothered much with accumulating civic or financial power, because I think we live in a bankrupt neoliberal patriarchal white-supremacist environmentally suicidal clusterfuck of a society, and all I really care about is saying that over and over again. And you also know, I hope, that I do this, because I believe, deeply, that *all* human beings have the right to live meaningful lives in which they have a chance to fulfil their potential, and to be treated with dignity, respect, and social support. But that's not what Twitter believes. Twitter believes that people who believe what I believe hold views so inexcusable that we shouldn't be allowed to participate in public political discourse. And this is the story of why that is so.

As many of you also know, there is currently a deep and ongoing dispute between the trans rights movement and feminists who hold a material, sex-based analysis of women's oppression. The trans rights movement has, over the last six or so years, effected an incredibly powerful takeover of the majority of our civic institutions. Four of the UK's political parties (the Con-

---

[1] Vijaya Gadde and Del Harvey, 'Creating New Policies Together,' *Twitter*, 25 September 2018. (www.blog.twitter.com/official/en_us/topics/company/2018/Creating-new-policies-together. html.)

servatives, Labour, the LibDems, and the Greens) are entirely onboard with trans rights discourse, as are *all* of our LGBT+ organizations (at the national, institutional, and student level). When the Conservative government did its initial consultation on changes to the Gender Recognition Act, they consulted *only* with trans rights organizations, and accepted, without question, the argument that changes to the definition of what a woman is, and how that impacts public policy, was of no political or material concern to women, and that women's perspectives shouldn't be entertained. Groups like Gendered Intelligence have rolled out trans awareness training in schools, social services, health care settings, and universities, and the policy of charities like the Girl Guides is also being determined in consultation only with trans rights organizations, as is the policy of the vast majority of our trade unions (as shown by the Trade Union Congress's vote last month in favour of gender self-identity). This sounds tinfoil hat, but it is not. And it should also give us pause when considering the claim that the present trans rights movement is working only in the interests of the most marginalized and politically powerless constituency in history.

While all of this is happening, a large swath of the British public remains completely in the dark about exactly *what* is happening, or their awareness extends only as far as thinking that the trans rights movement is just the latest frontier in the extension of liberal human rights. That is, a good chunk of the British public remain completely unaware about the *ideology* that informs the present iteration of the trans rights movement, and completely unaware of the practical implications of this ideology should it come—as it actually *is* at a staggering rate—to inform the creation of public and institutional policy.

One of the reasons the public remains so ill-informed about this ideology and its implications is because there has been a near-total freezing of public discourse on this matter. From the moment of its emergence, the current form of the trans rights movement has sought to make all interrogation of its discourse or the consequences of the ideas and policies it pushes an act of illegitimate hate speech, and has sought to demonize critics, mostly feminist women, as evil TERF bigots who should be vilified and ignored. I wrote about this tendency in 2015,[2] and over the intervening years, it has only become more pronounced. The trans rights movement and its allies have exhibited a consistent pattern of no-platforming, refusal to engage with critics (and refusing media appearances in dialogue with critics), harassing institutions that give space to critical voices, and raising Twitter mobs to pressure any public or commercial body that commits the sin of publishing wrongthink.

---

[2] Jane Clare Jones, "'You Are Killing Me': On Hate Speech and Feminist Silencing,' *Trouble and Strife*, 17 May 2015.

In recent weeks alone this has manifested in the dismissal of humanist student Angelos Sofocleous[3] from three of his positions for the thoughtcrime of believing that there are male and female humans, pressuring Brown University to disavow a study[4] investigating whether the dramatic increase in girls transitioning might be due to social contagion, the Girl Guides decision to expel two leaders[5] who had concerns about the inclusion of male-bodied children, and the successful efforts of one Dr Adrian Harrop to get a billboard removed[6] that had been placed in Liverpool for the Labour Party conference and which merely stated the biological definition of the word 'woman.'

The trans rights movement has effected this near-total silencing *by collapsing the present ideology of the trans rights movement into the existence of trans people*, and presenting all critique of its ideology as an act of hatred directed at trans people. It variously leverages claims that feminist criticism of its ideology is responsible for the deaths of trans people, that all criticism of its ideology are acts of bigoted 'transphobia' analogous with right-wing expressions of homophobia (see 'Gay Right and Trans Rights,' p. 67), and has consistently linked gender-critical feminists and their allies with the alt-right, the Christian right, and white supremacists. It has been *devastatingly* successful at convincing the majority of right-thinking, left-leaning people that *anyone* who raises concerns about the trans rights movement is motivated by nothing but baseless bigotry and spite, and that there are no legitimate questions or concerns that need to be given full public consideration before they start determining public policy. The practical upshot of this is that both the left-wing press and the vast majority of academics in the United Kingdom—and other English-speaking nations—are either fervently opposed to allowing criticism to be expressed, or, in many cases, voices of dissent are too scared about the professional consequences of speaking out to put their heads above the parapet. (The writing, and backlash to the writing, of the work of Professor Kathleen Stock, is a prime example of how this operates in the academic context.)

As feminists who hold an analysis of the sex-based oppression of women, we maintain that this is a political and ideological disagreement, and that silencing political discourse by construing criticism of the *ideology* of the trans rights movement as hate speech directed at trans people is demo-

---

[3] Angelos Sofocleous, 'Resignation Statement — Humanist Students President-Elect,' *Medium*, 24 August 2018.

[4] Meredith Wadman, 'New Paper Ignites Storm Over Whether Teens Experience 'Rapid Onset' of Transgender Identity,' *Science*, 30 August 2018.

[5] Andrew Gilligan, 'Girl Guide Leaders Expelled for Questioning Trans Policy,' *The Sunday Times*, 23 September 2018.

[6] Sky News, 'Posie Parker V Adrian Harrop,' *YouTube*. (www.youtube.com/watch?v=2G4IhPncF3w.)

cratically illegitimate. The heart of this disagreement is the way trans rights ideology is committed to erasing the fact that humans are sexed, the denial of the political importance of the existence of male and female humans, and the effort to ensure that all public policy is executed in line with this denial. One of the great obstacles we face in informing the public about this ideology and its effects is that its core ideological structure runs so entirely counter to how everyone who has not been indoctrinated by trans ideology understands the world that it is incredibly difficult to persuade people that this is a) what the trans rights movement really advocates, and b) that public institutions would be so easily swayed by this ideology and that public policy would end up being made according to its precepts, with *almost no debate.*

The trans rights movement will tell you that what we say is hatred. If, however, you look at the examples above of people who have been dismissed or censured for committing 'anti-trans' thoughtcrimes, what you will see is that *all they did was think that there are male and female humans* and that this might be politically or practically important. As I discussed in 'Gay Rights and Trans Rights: A Compare and Contrast,' the ideology of the trans rights movement is committed to the thought that whether a person is a man or a woman is *only and exclusively* a matter of their 'gender identity'—that is, that 'gender identity' *overrides and determines* physical sex, and that all public provision that has hitherto been provided on the basis of sex should now be provided on the basis of *self-declared* gender identity. I don't want to get bogged down now in the *long* discussion of the ideological and practical problems of this. Rebecca Reilly-Cooper has dissected the incoherence of the concept of gender identity,[7] and I have also outlined my analysis of the issues and implications of the erasing sex as a meaningful political category (see 'What Is at Stake,' p. 36). What I want to stress here is that I do not consider it to be an act of hatred to think that there are male and female human beings and that that is politically important. Indeed, shockingly, I believe that it is a *fact* that there are male and female human beings, that the oppression of female humans cannot be explained without understanding and describing this fact. And I think, moreover, that it is actually impossible to give an account of how *any* system of domination arises and functions if we cannot take account of the interaction *between* culture and material reality.

By contrast, the trans rights movement—and the form of 'intersectional' liberal analysis with which it is aligned—believes that there is no such thing as material reality, that *everything* is culturally constructed, and this applies also to the existence and perception of sex differentiation. What this

---

[7] Rebecca Reilly-Cooper, 'Trans Issues and Gender Identity,' in *Sex and Gender: A Beginner's Guide.* (www.sexandgenderintro.com/trans-issues-and-gender-identity.) See also, 'Critically Examining the Doctrine of Gender Identity,' *YouTube.* (www.youtube.com/watch?v=QPVNxYkawao.)

amounts to is the conviction that the existence of male and female humans—and the fact that we can usually perceive the difference between male and female humans within nanoseconds—isn't something given by the world and our perception of it, but is, in fact, purely the result of cultural training. (This is equivalent to saying our perception of *all* objects—trees, river, mountains, roses, tables, whatever—has nothing to do with the existence of objects in the world and our perception of them, but is entirely produced through our concepts and language. That is, it's a crass, reductive misreading of postmodernism that fails to understand the fundamental deconstructive insight that *all* cognition in humans arises through an interaction *between* ourselves and the world.) Anyway, the thinking goes, that if we only perceive male and female humans because we have been *trained* into perceiving male and female humans then, ta-da, we can just be trained *out* of it. Because, no, there is nothing at all sinister about trying to dictate how humans perceive the world so that it conforms to your political ideology. (Ends justifies the means, right side of history, we are the possessors of the one righteous truth: this doesn't sound much like 'queer' anything to me.)

As I suggested in 'Trans Right and Gay Rights,' trying to structure a political movement around the *denial* of a fundamental and readily perceptible fact about the world marks the trans rights movement as fundamentally divergent from *all* previous civil rights movements. Campaigning for the removal of *value judgements and systemic discriminations based on differences between peoples* is not the same as attempting to enforce the belief that *such differences do not exist and must not be perceived*. The totalitarian political tactics of the trans rights movement are not, therefore, an accident. Rather, they follow necessarily from the fact that attempting to legislate that human beings *must not perceive* a fact about the world that we do, in fact, all perceive is totalitarian to its very bones. (Orwell was right, the existence of material facts is a fundamental bulwark against totalitarian thought control.) The reason, therefore, why the trans rights movement *cannot* allow there to be a public discussion around its political ideology and its implications is because if people *really* understood that its political ideology is committed to denying that there are male and female humans, then the collective 'What the Actual Living Fuck?' would be so deafening that the whole political project would be dead in the water. So, instead, it has had to be achieved through behind-the-scenes collusion between trans rights organizations and individuals in positions of political and civic power[8] and by silencing public debate through bullying dissenters, hamstringing the press and public bodies, and making sure that everyone understands the high social sanctions for speaking out.

---

[8] Please see Jane Clare Jones and Lisa Mackenzie, *The Political Erasure of Sex: Sex and the Census*, October 2020. (www.thepoliticalerasureofsex.org.)

Enter Twitter. Given the extent to which public discourse has been shut down around this issue, there are presently only a few significant online public spaces where there is anything resembling an open discussion around the nature and political implications of the trans rights movement. One of these is Twitter and the other the 'Feminism and Women's Rights' boards on Mumsnet. As I've said before, it's no accident that women who have created and fed other humans with their bodies are not buying this 'bodies are politically irrelevant' business—in fact, it's an axiomatic non-accident, because what is at stake here is *all about* the political importance of reproduction, and the immemorial patriarchal erasure of the mother.[9] 'Mumsnet Towers' have done a sterling job, in the face of persistent harassment by the trans rights movement, of defending the rights of women and mothers to name their bodies, the political importance of their bodies, and to analyze the political stakes of the erasure the trans rights movement is currently effecting. Unlike Twitter, however, Mumsnet caters to a particular segment of the population. It is not, as Twitter is, the 21st century virtual equivalent of the Greek *agora*—the public square where people (well, *men*) came together to debate and discuss the political and philosophical issues thrown up by running their early, democratic city states.

For better or worse, Twitter is where we now *do democracy*, on a global (although very much tilted, like all global power, to the Western) scale. When the internet first took over our collective lives, there was a good deal of talk about its 'democratizing' potential—and while that utopian promise has inevitably been corrupted by commerce, and, as in the case of Cambridge Analytica, by the collusion between social media corporations and nefarious political power, it's not complete hogwash. For all its ills, the great virtue of Twitter is that anyone with a computer and an Internet connection can create an account and start shouting. It has the capacity to connect people in power and people with public voices with people who have particular political interests, expertise, and concerns. And it has the power, sometimes, to actually give direct political voice to people who otherwise would have none.

The resurgence of feminist activism at the beginning of this decade comes down, substantially, to Twitter. Almost the entirety of my feminist political life—the friendships I've made, the meetings I've attended, the writing I have been empowered to do and the audience I've found—has been down to Twitter. The expression and organization of resistance to the impact of trans rights activism on the lives of women, girls, lesbians, and homosexual men is organized on Twitter. When people find themselves confounded or shocked by something they hear briefly on the news—that Lily Madigan became a Labour Party Women's Officer, that a trans woman assaulted female

---

[9] Jane Clare Jones, 'Luce Irigaray: The Murder of the Mother,' *New Statesman*, 14 May 2014.

inmates in a female jail, that Pips Bunce won an award for being a female executive although he is a transvestite and not actually a female person—they come to Twitter. And on Twitter they find a LOT of people talking about this. Serious, smart, well-informed, researched-up-the-wazoo women and men who have serious theoretical and political objections to a discourse that is holding our political life in a kind of stunned zombie-thrall. And Twitter knows this. And Twitter wants it to stop.

The proposed policy that Twitter announced yesterday would pass quietly under the nose of anyone who is not well-versed in this conflict, and in its ideological and rhetorical tropes. Despite the fact that Twitter has tolerated women being inundated with death and rape-threats—most famously in response to Caroline Criado Perez having the temerity to campaign for there to be *one* woman left on a British banknote—Twitter has *now* decided its policy on policing hate-speech needs to be tightened up. It has decided that hate speech is defined by dehumanizing language—fair enough—and then decided that there are two principal examples of this kind of dehumanizing speech. The first, uncontroversially, is comparing humans to animals or viruses (vermin, cockroaches, plagues, etc.).[10] So, no problem there—it's a much-used and well-documented trope of othering groups of people, and comparing human beings to cockroaches *never leads* anywhere good. The second—and this is where a MASSIVE alarm-bell starts ringing—is "reducing groups to their genitalia." Something Twitter describes as a form of 'mechanistic' dehumanization.

Okay. So, first off. I'm pretty well-versed in the types of tropes that have been used in historic acts of dehumanization against groups of people, and as far as I know, 'reducing people to their genitalia' is not, and has never been, a form of widely used dehumanization which has served as a precursor to systemic mass violence against any *group* of people. Using genital-based insults aimed at individuals is a pretty standard form of English-contempt-giving ('dick' 'prick' 'cunt' 'twat' 'cockwomble' etc.), but these types of insults aren't used to present an entire group as either a threat, or to dehumanize them in order to legitimize violence against them. So, what the hell is going on here? As anyone versed in the rhetoric of the trans rights movement will immediately recognize, 'reducing someone to their genitals' is one of the phrases trans rights activists turn out when arguing about why it's not okay to distinguish male from female humans, or why it's 'problematic' to think the

---

[10] It's worth noting here that trans activists use this kind of language about non-compliant feminist women all the time. They refer to 'nests of TERFs,' call us 'cockroaches,' and post memes showing bottles of 'TERF-repellent.' I was blocked by the noted feminist philosopher Kate Manne for calling her out for referring to us as a 'swarm.' I have never seen a trans activist suspended for using this kind of language against us.

Twitter's Dehumanization Policy

You may not dehumanize anyone based on membership in an identifiable group, as this speech can lead to offline harm.

Definitions:

Dehumanization: Language that treats others as less than human. Dehumanization can occur when others are denied of human qualities (animalistic dehumanization) or when others are denied of human nature (mechanistic dehumanization). Examples can include comparing groups to animals and viruses (animalistic), or reducing groups to their genitalia (mechanistic).

Identifiable group: Any group of people that can be distinguished by their shared characteristics such as their race, ethnicity, national origin, sexual orientation, gender, gender identity, religious affiliation, age, disability, serious disease, occupation, political beliefs, location, or social practices.

For the last three months, we have been developing a new policy to address dehumanizing language on Twitter. Language that makes someone less than human can have repercussions off the service, including normalizing serious violence. Some of this content falls within our hateful conduct policy (which prohibits the promotion of violence against or direct attacks or threats against other people on the basis of race, ethnicity, national origin, sexual orientation, gender, gender identity, religious affiliation, age, disability, or serious disease), but there are still Tweets many people consider to be abusive, even when they do not break our rules. Better addressing this gap is part of our work to serve a healthy public conversation.

definition of 'woman' has something to do with being biologically female. It's a totally bogus argument because it relies on collapsing the distinction between 'something being defined by' and 'something being reduced to'—to say that being a woman has something to do with having the sexual characteristics of a female is *not* to *reduce* a woman to being *only* those characteristics. (See 'The Radical Notion that Women Are People,' p. 106.)

And what's more, the reason for arguing this is transparently not because the trans rights movement is unduly concerned about women being reduced to dehumanizing body parts or functions. In the name of inclusivity they have promoted the use of phrases like 'uterus-havers,' 'cervix-havers,' 'menstruators,' and 'bleeders.' The function of this argument, that is, is purely political. And its political function is to claim that it is morally reprehensible to distinguish male and female humans, in the service of arguing that no public policy, or public space, can legitimately be organized on the basis of that distinction. In the case of the Twitter policy, this function is further amplified by the fact that Twitter apparently recognizes that both 'gender' and 'gender identity' are acceptable ways of identifying a group. But it does not recognize that sex is. (That is, it will allow us to talk about 'women' and 'men' because they think the category of 'women' includes male people who identify as women. But it will not allow us to talk about *female* people.)

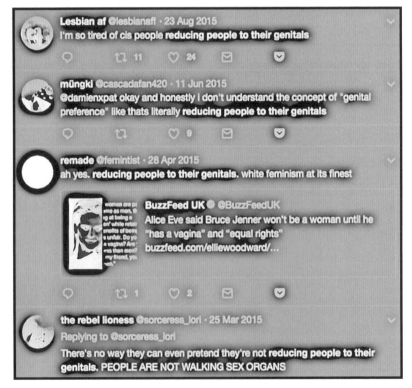

Lesbian af @lesbianaff · 23 Aug 2015
I'm so tired of cis people reducing people to their genitals.

◯ ⟲ 11   ♡ 24   ✉   ⌄

mũngki @cascadafan420 · 11 Jun 2015
@damienxpat okay and honestly i don't understand the concept of "genital preference" like thats literally reducing people to their genitals

◯ ⟲   ♡ 9   ✉   ⌄

remade @femintist · 28 Apr 2015
ah yes. reducing people to their genitals. white feminism at its finest

BuzzFeed UK ● @BuzzFeedUK
Alice Eve said Bruce Jenner won't be a woman until he "has a vagina" and "equal rights"
buzzfeed.com/elliewoodward/...

◯ ⟲ 1   ♡ 2   ✉   ⌄

the rebel lioness @sorceress_lori · 25 Mar 2015
Replying to @sorceress_lori
There's no way they can even pretend they're not reducing people to their genitals. PEOPLE ARE NOT WALKING SEX ORGANS

When Graham Linehan told me that my voice would be silenced by the new Twitter policy, this is what he was talking about. The political line that women like me have been trying to defend is the political importance of the difference between male and female humans. The reason why we are defending this line is not because we hate trans women. But we have serious concerns about changing the definition of a woman to include 'any male person who simply asserts that he is a woman.' And the reason why we're concerned about that is because male people pose a very significant statistical danger to female people, and there is no reason to believe—and no empirical evidence to support the idea—that male people cease to commit male-pattern violence against women and children simply because they *say* that they are women. Nor, moreover, has the trans rights movement expressed the slightest shred of interest in thinking about the way that a policy of fundamentalist self-identification is manifestly open to abuse by predatory men and men who want access to children.

The other major concern we have is that feminism is fundamentally a political movement dedicated to articulating the interests of female people, and in explaining why *female people are oppressed as female people*. Women are oppressed by gender, but we are not, fundamentally, oppressed because of the way we *perform our* gender. (See 'Smashing the Gender Binary,' p. 49.) Men rape female people. Men exercise violent coercive control over female people. Foetuses are aborted because they are female. Clitorises are cut out because they are the organs of sexual pleasure of female people. Women are paid less because they are female. And none of this can be avoided, or changed, by the way women *do their gendering*, or by trying to coerce everyone into thinking that female people do not exist. All this will achieve is to make the speaking of the sex-based oppression of women impossible, which is exactly what we've been saying is the threat hiding in plain sight in trans ideology this whole damn time. What Twitter is doing, therefore, by seeking to ban as hate speech the actually non-existent dehumanization of groups of people by 'reducing them to their genitals,' is to *prevent the speaking of the feminist analysis of the oppression of women*, which they just happen to have framed in precisely the language used by the trans rights movement. Twitter is trying to ban women from the only major public democratic space where we are still more or less freely able to express our political criticism against a massive assault on our rights—and it is seeking to do so explicitly in the interests of the trans rights movement.

I have been running around on Twitter for the last few months, saying, repeatedly, to anyone who will listen, that the trans rights movement is the most totalitarian thing I have seen in my entire life—and yet, somehow, I still don't believe, even though we are so far off the political map of normal, that any of this is really happening. That, for all the political complicity and manifest misogyny and the incessant drumbeat of violence and disrespect aimed at women, that we are seriously in a position when feminist women could be ejected, *en masse*, from the global public square, for saying that *female people are oppressed as female people* and that that *matters*. Even though I know, and have been saying, for the last five years, that the fundamental structure of trans rights discourse threatens to make feminist speech unsayable, I still somehow don't believe that they are really trying to frame a policy to make us stop saying it. And yet, I can't help coming to the conclusion that they are. For those of you out there still sitting on the fence, or who still believe that I, and everyone opposing this 'civil rights movement,' is just a nasty evil hate-mongering bigot, please, if you give one shit about women and the protection of women, wake the fuck up. This is actually happening, it's scary as shit, and we're running out of time. This is what woman-hating totalitarianism looks like. This is not a fucking drill.

V - WOKE CRITICISM

POST-TRUTH LEFT AND RIGHT

Twitter

8 JUNE 2020

Dear morally righteous people who identify as progressive:

There is a man, currently in the White House, who is about as pure an emanation of everything that is wrong with this culture as you can get. In both the UK and the US, we are nominally 'governed' by a bunch of what I can only describe as sociopathic lizard people (no, David, I don't mean it like *that*).

An absolutely core part of how they are exercising this contemptuous authoritarian power, and tearing up the basic civic contract, is by denying and twisting reality.

Even when it is right in front of our eyes.

The crowd at the Trump inauguration was bigger than the one for Obama, even though the photographs clearly show it wasn't.

A man is murdered on camera by another man who knelt on his neck, and yet he wasn't murdered.

A man who supposedly drafted the lockdown rules breaks the lockdown rules and the police say he did although he didn't.

A man is pushed by police and left lying in the street, but he slipped.

Priests are gassed in front of a church but there was no gas.

And under these conditions, where we are being repeatedly lied to and laughed at by people who are so blatantly serving their own interests and twisting reality in order to do so, you decide that trying to enforce reality denial on us all is the way to go.

Under these conditions, you still cling to the idea that it's edgy and radical and oh-so-sophisticated to assert that reality is only what power says it is, and deny that there might be any other 'reality' we could refer to in order to dispute that.

Seriously, what the actual hell do you think you are doing?

#TwoPlusTwoEqualsFour

TO ANOTHER 'GENUINELY CURIOUS' AMERICAN ON THE PUZZLE OF TERF-ISLAND

Twitter

7 JUNE 2020

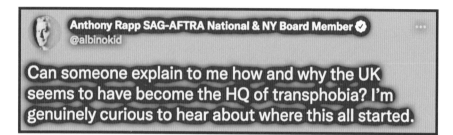

Anthony Rapp SAG-AFTRA National & NY Board Member ✔
@albinokid

Can someone explain to me how and why the UK seems to have become the HQ of transphobia? I'm genuinely curious to hear about where this all started.

Because Americans keep asking this question, I've been wondering about it for a while.

1. The British left has a better understanding of materialist class analysis than the States ever had, and 'progressive' politics in the US is still far more individualist. So, when people come along and try to erase an entire axis of material oppression we're quicker to say: 'um, what, fuck no.'

2. Relatedly, the British have a longer and deeper tradition of socialist feminism than the US.

3. Further relatedly, we have been able to create a left-wing movement to oppose trans ideology from a progressive political position.

4. In the States, this has been much harder to achieve, and because of the culture war and the presence of the conservative right, left-wing women are faced with the problem of how to organize without playing into the hands of the right, who oppose trans ideology for almost diametrically opposed reasons to us.

5. Trans rights in the US don't exist independently of sex-based rights. So, opposing the appropriation going on would actually equate to removing trans people's legal protections against housing/employment discrimination. Most decent people don't want to do that.

6. The States is much bigger so it's much harder to organize and get traction and energy going like we have. Many of us have met each other, and a lot of us have got drunk together. Even in this dematerialized age, this still matters for building a political movement.

7. The way women were deliberately excluded from the political process around GRA reform REALLY pissed us off. Especially when we discovered that trans activist organizations had been explicitly petitioning the government to remove our rights.

8. Maria MacLachlan was assaulted by Tara Wolf outside a feminist political meeting. Young males assaulting older females to try and shut them up about their own political rights turns out to be a great way of creating resistance.

9. We don't like authoritarianism. We have a long tradition of opposing it, and a long tradition of analyzing it. When people start dictating to us what we can and can't say, or what we must or must not believe, it tends to make us fighty.

10. We are a bunch of uppity non-compliant gobshites and the granddaughters of the suffragettes. Males have tried to bully us before and we broke shit. We will do it again if we have to.

Oh, and American people who know fuck all about this country and read everything through the lens of your own limited worldview. To lift one of the most pious and condescending tropes of the movement you are supporting...

'Educate yourself.'

TRANS ACTIVISM AND INTERSECTIONAL FEMINISM

janeclarejones.com

AUGUST 2018

As many of you know, there was an act of vandalism by trans activists on a historic building in Devonport where women were meeting to discuss proposed changes to the Gender Recognition Act.[1]

One of the posters the trans activists stuck up was this one, which got me thinking (again) about the connection between trans activism and intersectional feminism.

When trans ideology first came on my radar, around 2013, it came in a kind of trans activism/intersectional feminism pincer movement. This wasn't an accident. So, my question is: what work is intersectional feminism doing to support trans ideology?

So, first off, nothing I'm about to say really has much to do with Kimberlé Crenshaw's original thought. Intersectionality *as an analytic method* is basically unimpeachable, a call to feminists to pay attention to how other axes of oppression inflect the thing you're looking at. That's not what I'm talking about. I'm talking about what I call 'Tumblrized Intersectionality.' And that's not a method, it's a dogma. In fact, it's a catechism.

---

[1] Stuart Abel, 'Shock as Vandal Sprays Abusive Graffiti on Listed Plymouth Building,' *Plymouth Herald*, 26 August 2018

The first thing that's really noticeable about that catechism, is how un-intersectional it is. It's not about looking at any particular thing and trying to understand how all the axes interact. It's a rigid set of views—pro-trans, pro-sex-work, anti-white feminism™, etc.—and a rigid point-scoring rubric that produces a hierarchy of who is allowed to speak and who must listen. According to this hierarchy, trans people are more oppressed than everyone else, and hence, their oppression must be prioritized over everyone else. In the context of feminism—and particularly in connection to the leveraging of the 'cis/trans binary'—this produces the thought that feminism should centre the oppression of trans women over the oppression of women. That is, Tumblrized intersectional feminism functions to displace women's oppression from the centre of feminism.

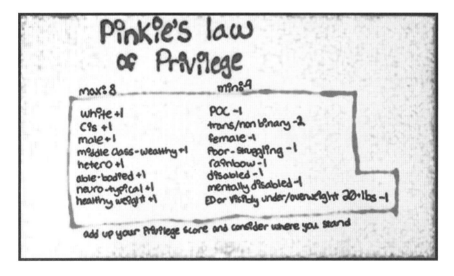

The second, related thing is that intersectionality is used to bolster and re-inforce trans activism's efforts to undermine 'woman' as a political category. Trans activists argue that being a woman has nothing to do with femaleness, in concert with the intersectional argument that, because of the intersection of axes, there is nothing meaningful about the axis of sex-based oppression in itself. This is just bullshit. It's one thing to say that different axes impact women differently and we need to attend to that. It's quite another to say that because of those different axes, there is nothing we can say about the oppression of women as a class. And note—this intersectional argument could easily be used to undermine all political categories. It hasn't been. Funny that.

Thirdly, there is something utterly (neo)liberal about both intersectionality and trans activism as they are put to work. And what I mean by that is that while they ostensibly draw on the discourse of structural analysis (oppression/privilege etc.), the understanding of that oppression is entirely individualized. Oppression is no longer a matter of a set of structural material conditions, and how those material conditions are held in place using so-cialization, discursive tropes, negative attitudes towards certain groups of people, all backed up with force and the threat of force. The material analysis has completely dropped out of the picture. Oppression is just a matter of people having bad attitudes (BIGOT! NAZI! INSERT-PHOBE-HERE! etc. etc.)... And if we can just change (or bully) people into right-thinking, op-pression will just disappear.

Yesterday, someone pointed me to this article,[2] which contains a version of the poster that was used to deface Odd Fellows Hall. It's a pretty inter-esting example of what gets lost in intersectional/trans discourse from a feminist perspective. The sociologist in question spends a lot of time talk-ing about 'doing gender' and how that relates to inequalities, and to women's inequality. But there is absolutely no recognition that the system of gender inequality didn't just arise *ex nihilo* out of the ground one day, that it is mo-tivated, and that is has something to do with the sex-based oppression of women, and with the extraction of reproductive, domestic, and emotional labour *from* female people *by* male people. In obscuring the material and sex-based nature of women's oppression, trans activism and intersectional fem-inism are working as one.

Lastly, Tumblrized intersectional feminism is doing very important work obscuring this central point of feminist analysis by dismissing sec-ond-wave feminist thought as 'White Feminism™.' Taking the current dis-course around 'white feminism' apart would take me all day (bell hooks was addressing liberal feminism's complicity with capitalism, people!). For the moment, let's just say that it is true that many of the present thought leaders of feminism are women of socio-economic and racial privilege, and it is also true that *some* of those women do not have great class and race analyses to go with their feminism. And that's something that should rightly be called out.

That said, it is an absolute ahistorical lie that no feminist ever thought about this until a bunch of people starting pointing it out five years ago, or that feminism has always been a movement that was *only* interested in the things that bother middle-class white women (tell that to Dworkin or Fires-tone or Lorde, please). The second wave was a massive and diverse tradition: running from radical feminism to lesbian feminism to socialist feminism to environmental feminism to sexual-difference feminism to maternal femi-nism to black feminism and womanism. The negotiation of issues of race within feminism is crucial, complex, and often fraught. But it *has been going on the whole time* (which is not to say we're good at it, we're often really not).

---

[2] Zuleyka Zevallos, 'Transgender Women's Experiences of Gender Inequality at Work,' *Other So-ciologist*, 1 December 2014

It's worth here, for example, looking at *Notes from the First Year/Second/Third Year*[3]—the magazines published by New York Radical Women, under Firestone's editorship, from 1968 onwards. I'm not going to claim that the treatment of the relation between race and women's oppression in these magazines is in no way, to use that now-almost-loathed phrase, 'problematic.' But I do think it's important to note that it's there, right from the start. There are articles on black feminism by black feminists (p. 21, *Third Year*), there are discussions of how feminist consciousness-raising involves understanding racial and class privilege (p. 80, *Second Year*), and there is a critique (p. 106, *Third Year*) of the way left-wing men try to discredit the women's movement by claiming it's run by a "bunch of white, middle-class women." So, that's a new one then.

> D. Understanding and developing radical feminist theory
>   1. Using above techniques to arrive at an understanding of oppression wherever it exists in our lives—our oppression as black people, workers, tenants, consumers, children, or whatever as well as our oppression as women
>   2. Analyzing whatever privileges we may have—the white skin privilege, the education and citizenship of a big-power (imperialist) nation privilege, and seeing how these help to perpetuate our oppression as women, workers

My point here is not that intersectional issues shouldn't be constantly acknowledged, discussed, and struggled with. My point is that these issues are being ahistorically leveraged by 'Intersectional Feminism™' to position the entire second wave as morally and intellectually bankrupt and worthless. And that's political, and directly serves the interests of trans activism, because it facilitates the wholesale erasure of the feminist analysis of patriarchy as a hierarchical system of material sex-based oppression. And that's the point.

---

[3] All three issues are available from the online repository at Duke University, (https://repository.duke.edu).

THE RAINBOW PENS OF DOOM MEET BLOODY GOOD PERIOD

Twitter

8 JUNE 2020

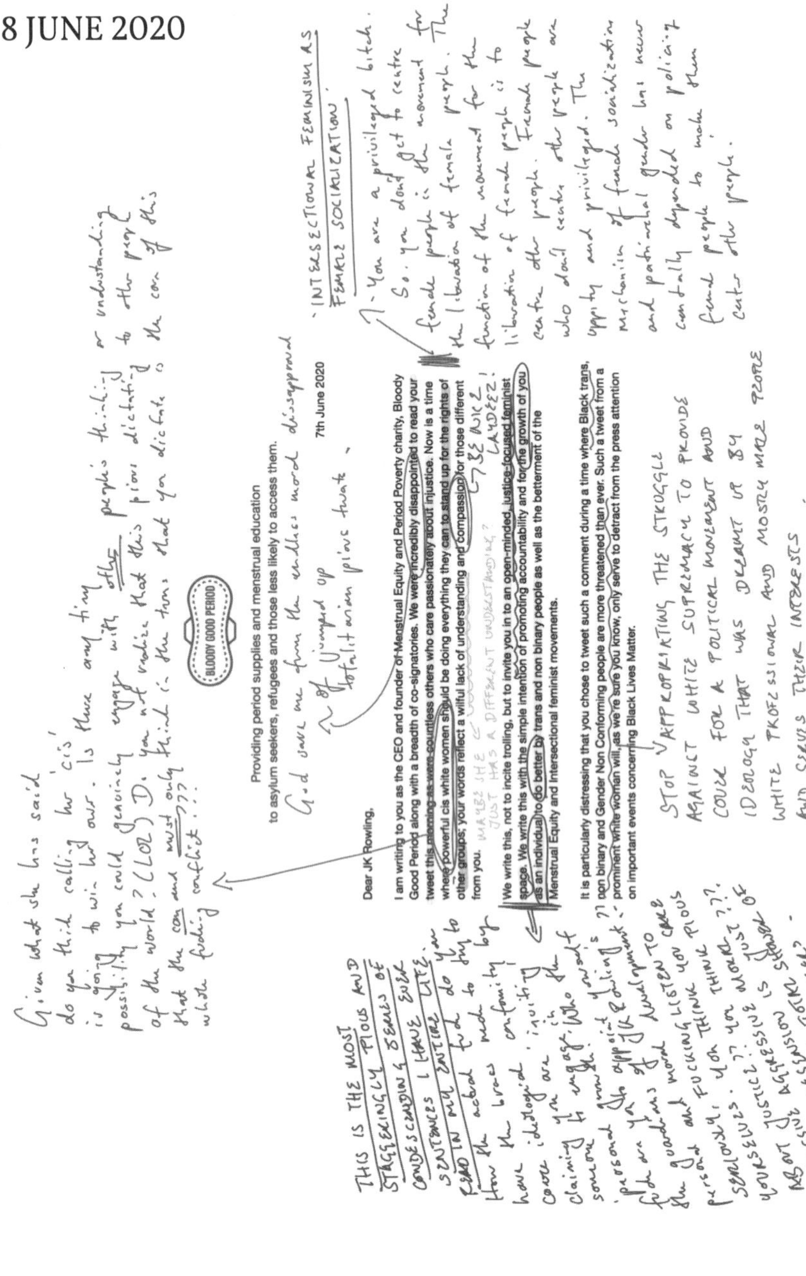

Providing period supplies and menstrual education
to asylum seekers, refugees and those less likely to access them.

7th June 2020

Dear JK Rowling,

I am writing to you as the CEO and founder of Menstrual Equity and Period Poverty charity, Bloody Good Period along with a breadth of co-signatories. We were incredibly disappointed to read your tweet this morning as were countless others who care passionately about injustice. Now is a time where powerful cis white women should be doing everything they can to stand up for the rights of other groups; your words reflect a wilful lack of understanding and compassion for those different from you.

We write this, not to incite trolling, but to invite you in to an open-minded, justice-focused feminist space. We write this with the simple intention of promoting accountability and for the growth of you as an individual, to do better by trans and non binary people as well as the betterment of the Menstrual Equity and Intersectional feminist movements.

It is particularly distressing that you chose to tweet such a comment during a time where Black trans, gen binary and Gender Non Conforming people are more threatened than ever. Such a tweet from a prominent white woman will, as we're sure you know, only serve to detract from the press attention on important events concerning Black Lives Matter.

[Handwritten annotations surrounding the letter:]

'INTERSECTIONAL FEMINISM AS FEMALE SOCIALIZATION'.

1. You are a privileged bitch. So, you don't get to centre female people in the movement for the liberation of female people. The function of the movement for the liberation of female people is to centre other people. Female people who don't centre other people are 'oppressing' and privileged. The mechanism of female socialization and patriarchal gender has never centrally depended on policing female people to make them centre other people.

Given what she has said do you think calling her 'cis' is going to win her over. Is there any tiny possibility you could genuinely engage with other people's thinking or understanding of the world? CLOD. You're not woke, that this pious dictated to other people that she can and must only think in the terms that you dictate is the con of this white funding conflict???

God save me from the endless moral disapproval of totalitarian pious twats.

WHERE'S THE ∁ UNDERLIST ANDSWF? THAT HAS A DIFFERENT UNDERSTANDING? TROUBLE LANDEEZ!

STOP APPROPRIATING THE STRUGGLE AGAINST WHITE SUPREMACY TO PROVIDE COVER FOR A POLITICAL MOVEMENT AND IDEOLOGY THAT WAS DREAMT UP BY WHITE PROFESSIONAL AND MOSTLY MALE PEOPLE AND SERVES THEIR INTERESTS.

THIS IS THE MOST STAGGERINGLY PIOUS AND CONDESCENDING & SMUG SENTENCES I HAVE EVER READ IN MY ENTIRE LIFE... How the hell are you actually asking me to fuck off to read in conformity. How the hell have ideological, vomiting cunts are this. Who the claiming to engage yourself somewhere? And JK Rowling's personal appoint development? Who are you JK Rowling for development? You goodness mock LISTEN TO present and fucking you think pious seriously? Do you think ??? yourselves?? to what...? About justice passive aggressive shades of consternation is you can bother?

210

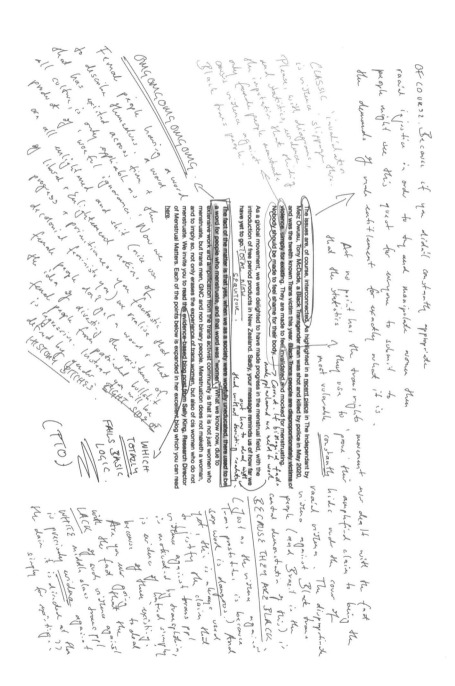

The issues are, of course, interconnected, as highlighted in a recent piece in The Independant by Metz Owusu, Tony McDade, a Black Transgender man was shot and killed by police in May 2020, and was the twelfth known Trans victim this year. Black Trans people are disproportionately victims of violence. Simply for existing. They are made to feel invalidated, and mocked for menstruating. Nobody should be made to feel shame for their body.

As a global movement, we were delighted to have made progress in the menstrual field, with the introduction of free period products in New Zealand this year. Sadly, your message reminds us of how far we have yet to go.

The fact of the matter is that yes, when we as a society were woefully uneducated, there used to be a word for people who menstruate, and that word was "women". What we know now, due to extensive work and amplification from the trans activist community, is that it is not just women who menstruate, but trans men, GNC and non binary people. Menstruation does not maketh a women, and to imply so, not only erases the experience of trans women, but also of cis women who do not menstruate. We invite you to read the evidence-based blog post from Sally King, Research Director of Menstrual Matters. Each of the points below is expanded in her excellent blog which you can read here.

Do stopped clocks stop being clocks? Are ornamental chairs not chairs? Do houses stop being houses when unoccupied? THINGS CAN BE DEFINED AS HAVING A FORM TO FULFIL A CERTAIN FUNCTION. THEY DO NOT STOP HAVING THAT FORM WHEN THEY ARE NOT FULFILLING THAT FUNCTION. You wouldn't even be able to make the statements below if you couldn't tell WHICH PEOPLE ARE FEMALE.

None of the statements would make ANY SENSE

Were it not for the fact that you actually understand properly well that female people are the ones who can menstruate.

NOT ALL FEMALE PEOPLE MENSTRUATE
→ ALL PEOPLE WHO MENSTRUATE ARE FEMALE.
SO FUCKING HARD.
TO. GRASP

1. Only half the female population is of reproductive age so half do not menstruate
2. A significant part of the female reproductive population use hormonal medications/ devices that prevent menstruation and are therefore not people who menstruate
3. A fairly significant part of the female reproductive population does not menstruate for health or exercise reasons

WHAT IS THIS FEMALE POPULATION OF WHICH YOU SPEAK ???

4. A small part of the female reproductive population is pregnant or breastfeeding and so, are not menstruating
5. A small part of the female reproductive population has experienced early menopause and so, are not menstruating
6. A small part of the female reproductive population cannot menstruate
7. A small part of this population do not identify as 'women' or 'girls'

Generalisations about entire gender are impossible (and usually dodgy). You are right that the term TERF (Trans Exclusionary Radical Feminist) should not apply to you. While your incorrect views on menstruation certainly exclude trans women, feminist is not a term we think applies to anyone who does not stand for ALL women, and ALL people, including all those who menstruate.

So feminism stands for white supremacist Trump supporters too then? um. THAT'S NOT WHAT YOU MEANT TO SAY SORRY WHAT?

We implore you to spend some time researching, and learning from the generosity of trans and non-binary activists and academics, a small number of whom we have listed below.

Kenny Ethan Jones - the first trans man to front a period campaign
Munroe Bergdorf - activist and model
Charlie Craggs - activist and founder of Nail Transphobia

you can yourself

SHE DID. SHE THINKS YOU'RE FULL OF CRAP.

Juno Dawson - Writer
Jamie Windust - Writer and activist
Jono Roche - Writer
Freddy McConnell (the "Seahorse" dad)

Its a term for people who are committed to the liberation of female people from male dominance. And you are not the feminist fucking gatekeepers.

Female is not a gender

UNREASONABLE IDEAS: A REPLY TO ALISON PHIPPS

janeclarejones.com

JANUARY 2020

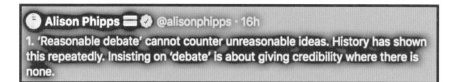

This is an excerpt from a piece I wrote in response to Alison Phipps refusing Kathleen Stock's offer of open debate on the grounds that "'reasonable debate' cannot counter unreasonable ideas." It was clear that Phipps couldn't actually be saying our position lacks reasoned argument, because then, evidently, it could be defeated by reasoned debate. Rather, what Phipps was doing was making a moral claim that our ideas are so morally delinquent, and that we are so bad, wrong, and evil, that we can and should be excluded from the community of legitimate speakers.

Casting people out of the community of legitimate speakers by creating an image of them as an all-purpose-bogeywoman-Nazi-witch is a straightforward act of 'othering.' What I was interested in looking at in this essay is how the 'social justice'/'wokerati' branch of the alleged left justifies this act of othering by using a corrupted 'Oppression-Olympics' Tumblrized[1] intersectional analysis that posits middle-aged lesbian women and feminists as the pinnacle of the power structure and/or fascists, and rests, particularly in Phipps's case, on a web of bullshit analogies which attempt to demonstrate that 'believing humans are sexed' is an artefact of white supremacy. Which it really isn't.

---

[1] For more on what I'm calling 'Tumblrized intersectionality,' please see 'Trans Activism and Intersectional Feminism' (p. 206). There are several points here, the first being that this variant doesn't actually look at the way things *intersect*, at all, but rather uses a single cumulative up down aggregation which produces a hierarchy of oppression. If you used a matrix like 'Pinkie's Law of Privilege' (p. 207), what you'd get is 'woman' (-1) plus 'cis' (+1). That is, being female effectively doesn't *count* as an 'oppression' at all because the oppression of being female is neatly cancelled out by the privilege of not being trans—hence, being female becomes, by not being trans, a privilege in and of itself, even though it is a fundamental axis of material oppression (handy trick hey wokebros?). If you then add race and class to that, the 'middle-class white woman' would score +2, hence positioning her as straightforwardly 'privileged,' and completely erasing recognition of the axis of her oppression. This is a) bullshit, b) anti-feminist, and c) *not* intersectional at all.

WHY NONE OF THIS IS REASONABLE

1. The first thing to note here is how the analysis of power is central to what we're arguing about: which is whether humans happen to come in two sexes or not. We think that sex is a material given, a product of evolution, while on the other side we have a bunch of drunk Foucauldians who have taken it to heart that nothing in the entire world is actually given and that everything is brought into being by processes of power, for, er, *reasons* ('they're reasonable reasons, which we'd be happy to show you, were you not so unreasonable'). There are two levels of massive dematerialization here that just won't wash. First, the claim that a process of sexual differentiation that began billions of years ago is somehow a simple artefact of white-colonial-heteronormative-patriarchy is just utter bullshit, and making this claim is probably the single most damaging thing anyone has ever done to the credibility of leftist structural analysis. Second, you actually have to give me a convincing account of *why* and *how* 'thinking sex exists' was produced as an idea and *why* and *how* that idea serves the interests of a specific power structure.

Along with the ludicrousness of that old favourite 'colonialism invented the gender binary,' one of the most common queer-typical responses here would be 'heteronormativity,' to which I'm going to ask, why does heteronormativity exist, and whose interests does it serve? It makes no sense to assert that we invented male and female people because we just have a random normative system of thinking male and female people exist and a random normative system of thinking that male and female people should mate to produce live young. If you want me to accept that something as apparently materially evident as human reproductive differences are actually an artefact of power, you better tell me a pretty stellar story about how that normative system arose and whose interests it serves. Telling me it causes people distress won't cut it. Nor will telling me we invented sex to enforce heterosexuality and then not explaining how on earth we came up with the concept of 'heteronormativity' *without being able to perceive two sexes in the first place.*

2. Because arguments about human sexual difference being an artefact of power are such a tottering pile of weak, implausible, ahistorical rubbish,[2] a great deal of what Phipps—and many like her—are devoting their energy to is casting us beyond the moral pale by analogical guilt-by-association.

---

[2] For a more detailed discussion of the intellectual development and critique of arguments used to undermine the material reality of sex, please see my essay 'The History of Sex: Sex Denial and Gender Identity Ideology,' forthcoming in *Sex and Gender: A Contemporary Reader*, edited by Alice Sullivan and Selina Todd (London: Routledge).

Specifically, by trying to triangulate 'thinking sex exists and matters politically' with other sets of political beliefs that are clearly artefacts of power and are widely accepted by leftist thinking to be morally abhorrent. We're all familiar with these formulations—'you're Nazis,' 'you're Christian fundamentalists,' 'you're the same people who supported Section 28,' etc., etc. And the one I want to focus on here—because it's key to Phipps's forthcoming book[3] and was also raised by Mona Eltahawy's tweet yesterday that "racism and white supremacy fuel so much white U.K. transphobia"—is the claim that our beliefs are in some sense *inherently* racist and/or are to be understood as an artefact of white supremacy.

The first thing to note here is that to demonstrate that 'thinking sex exists' is a racist idea you actually need to demonstrate that it is, *in itself*, a racist idea. That is, that there is something *specifically* in the idea itself which can be shown, with some kind of evidence, to conceptually or materially support the fundamental structure of white supremacy. Spoiler: We're not going to get that—I'm tempted to say, 'because it doesn't exist,' although, that said, if anyone thinks they've got it, I'd be really interested to see it.

What we are going to get instead is a lot of stuff that looks like this:

i. Privileged white women are racist
ii. These are the same privileged white women who think sex exists
iii. Therefore, thinking sex exists is privileged and racist
iv. Therefore, sex does not exist and anyone who thinks it does is privileged and racist

As well as the small sticking point that no one has yet shown that 'thinking sex exists' is plausibly an artefact of power (yes, yes, of course, the magic Judith Butler dust, silly me), there are two more reasons this won't fly. Firstly, because the claim of a perfect overlap between 'privileged white women who are racist' and 'privileged white women who think sex exists' is rhetorically produced and empirically spurious. Within the structure of intersectional feminist discourse, this projection is actually perfectly circular: to question intersectional feminism (in its Tumblrized form) and any of its axioms (especially TWAW or SWIW) is, *de facto*, to be racist. Convenient. This, of course, neatly eclipses the black feminists who reject the way intersectionality has been appropriated in this conflict, reject what they perceive as the inherent racism in some of its formulations (like suggesting people of colour didn't

---

[3] Alison Phipps, *Me, Not You: The Trouble with Mainstream Feminism* (Manchester: Manchester University Press, 2021).

recognize sex before white people explained it to them...), and who also maintain that sex is a material reality and the axis of female people's op- pression. Which brings us to the second point: the fact that some white wom- en are racist (which of course they are) and that some of those same white women hold that sex exists doesn't actually demonstrate in any meaningful way that one view follows conceptually from the other, and given that most black and brown people also think sex exists, that's really not very surpris- ing.

The claim of relation being presented by Phipps does, however, have something more to it than mere coincidence (no matter how manufactured or distorting). I've discussed this in more detail elsewhere, but the core of this thought is the purported analogical relations between 'excluding trans women from the category of woman' and either a) 'excluding black women from the category of woman' or b) 'excluding black people from the category of human.' The apparent consonance on these analogies relies on what I've called elsewhere 'the sovereign imaginary'—the idea that excluding people from recognition, resources, and rights has often been historically justified by acts of othering and by constructing excluded others as some type of menace of threat. (See 'Why Feminists Are Not Nazis,' p. 133.) Within leftist discourse, this type of othering is an operation of power and involves the projections of a dominant class onto a marginalized class for the purpose of shoring up that class's material privilege and/or group identity. Thus, the argument goes, just as white people maintain their position of dominance by othering and excluding black people, so then 'cis' white women maintain their position of dominance by othering and excluding trans women. As such, the gender-critical position is structured by the same mechanism as racism, ergo, it is implicitly tied to racism and white supremacy.

There is a LOT to say about this. Probably the most important being that this analogical set of relations only holds if we accept the claim that white women are the dominant class. To be properly intersectional about this, we should say that they are members of the dominant class in being white and members of the subordinate class in being women. Insofar as this is a con- flict over access to sex-based resources, it is not immediately evident why the charge of 'whiteness' should invalidate women's claims that we have, as a class oppressed on the basis of sex, the right to our own spaces or political self-definition. But the fact that this argument seems to work so well has a great deal to do, I think, with the endless reflexive repetition of the intersec- tional axiom that 'middle-class white women are privileged,' which neatly suggests that women are not oppressed *qua* women. (The middle-class white woman is oppressed only on the axis of sex. If you persistently position her as a member of the dominant or privileged class, what you're implicitly com- municating is 'sex-based oppression isn't really oppression.' Useful, that.)

Our claim, by contrast, is that female people are oppressed because they're female, and that with respect to a sex-based conflict, female people are most definitely *not* the dominant class. To wit: Women are not the white people in this analogy, and I'd really like someone to explain how female people are the dominant class *qua* female people, without resorting to analogies with race, or summoning the cis/trans binary. This question of the perceived balance of power between the warring parties here is critical, because it's only *if* gender-critical women can be decisively shown to be the dominant class that our position is rendered an illegitimate act of sovereign exclusion and we can be cast beyond the pale. If not, we are just a bunch of women drawing a reasonable boundary in response to an unreasonable attempt to appropriate our political identity and rights, by, on our reading, members of the dominant class. Which is precisely the interpretation Phipps is paddling furiously to avoid.

We should also note what exactly is being concealed here by positing 'cis women exclude trans women from womanhood' as a conceptual cognate of 'white women exclude black women from womanhood.' Because I'm going to say that what's being concealed is the reality of sex, and the conflation of sex and gender enabled by pretending this horrendous clusterfuck is a bun fight over some mythic essence of 'womanhood' that confers some kind of privilege we're all so jealously guarding. (To be clear, being white confers privilege, being a woman does not, unless, that is, you're a men's rights activist.) The roots of this analogy come from the fact that white and black femininity have historically been constructed in divergent ways—principally by patriarchal power's interest in confining white women to the home, while exploiting black women's enslaved or menial labour. Insofar as 'womanhood' means 'the image of patriarchal white femininity,' then it's true that black women have been 'excluded' from that category, and that white women steeped in the discourses of white supremacy perpetuated that exclusion.

But, as I've said many times, whatever this fight is about, it's *not* about access to the font of 'womanhood,' whatever the hell that might be, and especially not if 'womanhood' means 'white patriarchal femininity.' Black women might have been excluded from 'womanhood' if that's what you think it means, but that's not what we think it means. In fact, we don't think this nebulous gendery 'womanhood' that no feminist gave a shit about until five minutes ago really has much meaning other than as a linguistic sleight-of-hand for you to avoid the fact that *we are talking about sex*. Black women are included in the class of women *because they are female*. Trans women are not included in the class of women *because they are not female*. That's it. And to suggest that the femaleness of black women is in some way analogous to the non-femaleness of trans women, is, in fact, to repeat the masculinizing racist devaluation of black women that you're purportedly calling us out for.

Seriously, quite how you have the sheer brass neck to go around calling us white supremacists when you're peddling an argument that reduces to 'if black females are women then males are women,' is utterly beyond me. No. Really. Just fucking stop it.

3. The last point I want to make here is how Phipps posits gender-critical women as agents of political dominance, both with respect to analogies with race, and more generally, to allow for the dismissal, *tout court*, of anything we might say as simply entrenched power protecting the status quo. As we suggested above, I don't accept that on a true reading of the intersection of axes of oppression, women, white women, or even middle-class white women are straightforwardly 'privileged' in a manner which justifies the absolute refusal of the legitimacy of our claims. Moreover, if we look, for just a moment, at the actual reality of institutional, government, and corporate support for the two sides in this conflict, the idea that a bunch of crowd-funded middle-aged radical feminists and lesbians are the linchpin of hegemonic political dominance becomes even more absurd than it appears on first inspection.

DESCRIPTION –

Me, not you pulls back the curtain on #MeToo and other recent feminist campaigns against sexual violence. In a right-moving world, women's anger about sexual violence has been celebrated as a progressive force. However, mainstream feminist politics is unable to tackle the converging systems of gender, race and class which produce sexual violence.

Phipps argues that the mainstream movement against sexual violence expresses a political whiteness which both reflects its demographics and limits its revolutionary potential. Privileged white women use their traumatic experiences to create media outrage, and rely on state power and bureaucracy to purge 'bad men' from elite institutions with little concern for where they might appear next.

Even more dangerously, the more reactionary branches of this feminist movement are complicit with the far-right, in their attacks on sex workers and trans people. This text is essential reading for anyone interested in the politics of sexual violence, and the feminist movement more generally.

The list of evidence one could provide to back this up is so extensive it's hard to know where to start. Phipps herself is, of course, a much-marginalized Professor of Gender Studies, at the University of Sussex, where she runs an MA course that recycles the trans/intersectional catechism mindfully, week in week out, without, one would imagine, much in the way of 'TERFy' critical scrutiny. On the day Phipps was sneering about how gender-critical academics couldn't possibly be experiencing censure because 'look at this cartoon of a massive big megaphone,' her colleague in arms, the venerable Professor Sally Hines, was reporting on her project on pregnancy in trans men, beneficently funded by Equality and Human Rights Commission. There is also the much-noted project at King's London on 'The Future of Legal Gender' ('We're erasing sex, boom boom!') also funded by the EHRC, along with three other universities. By contrast, there are, to date, no academic projects by gender-critical academics in receipt of public funding.[4] And we have to ask, if—as both Phipps and I would probably agree (finally, something!)—the modern university is a neoliberal and patriarchal institution, why it's so uninterested in our status-quo-enforcing ideas and so very keen on supporting a gender agenda that will purportedly bring the entire power structure to its knees (…any minute now).

We could, of course, ask the very same question about government funding. In 2018, Stonewall, the mothership of the trans rights movement in the UK, received funding from the UK government[5] to the tune of £233,000, with £90,000 from the Scottish government (as well as all the cash they made handing out those 'Diversity Champion' gongs to big business and the NHS and the army and MI-fucking-6 in return for telling them lies about the Equality Act). North of the border, the Scottish government has also funded a number of organizations pushing the trans rights position, including the Scottish Trans Alliance (£181,000 in 2018) as part of the Equality Network (91% funded by ScotGov), and Scotland's alleged women's organization Engender (£275,000 from ScotGov in 2018). During this time, during the whole of recorded history in fact, gender-critical feminist groups have received precisely fuck all by way of public subsidy. That is, the UK and Scottish governments are giving large amounts of public cash to special-interests groups that are pushing for the political erasure of sex, and who have specifically petitioned the UK government to remove women's single-sex exemptions from the Equality Act, and in order to protest proposed legislative changes that would impact women's rights, we have had to run a somewhat motley, make-it-up-as-you-go-along grassroots campaign, funded almost entirely by individual donations. Such are the facts of our social and political dominance. (And if you want to wheel out that propagandist shit about us being funded by the Christian right, I want receipts, ideally delivered to my bank account.)

None of this, of course, is news to anyone here. But what staggers me is how, after a heady array of financial, pharmaceutical, corporate, and media institutions—not to mention the police and the spymasters general (who's

---

[4] This changed in October 2020 when *The Political Erasure of Sex* project received some funding from the University of Oxford, and was then duly subject to numerous FOI requests.
[5] Mary Harrington, 'Lessons from 2018: The Year of Uncivil Society,' *UnHerd*, 26 December 2019.

the carceral feminist now, eh?)—added their fulsome support to the campaign for GRA reform, it's possible for someone like Phipps to carry on with her barefaced schtick about how she's the voice of the marginalized and powerless, while we're the living breathing pointy-toothed embodiment of white supremacist capitalist patriarchy. This may be a post-truth world, but the facts do not stack up. If you want to tell a tale about political power, and whose interests are being served, a web of alleged analogical relations, untethered from—and indeed contrary to—evidence about actual material or institutional interests, and which, when you think about it for more than two minutes, has no conceptual coherence whatsoever, won't do the job. Or rather the job it *will* do is convincing more and more people that the left has lost its fucking mind, and that when we point at anything in the world and say it's produced by power, we are talking unfathomable, unreasonable bollocks. Which, I have to tell you Professor Phipps, is a tragedy I'm going to hold you at least partially responsible for.

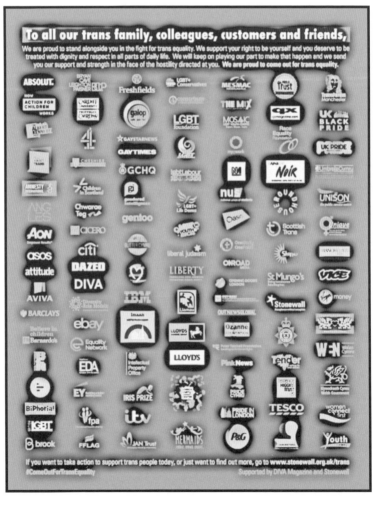

THE WOKE-EDI-INDUSTRIAL COMPLEX

Twitter

3 MAY 2021

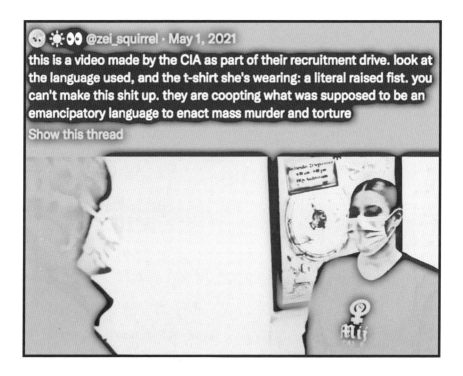

This language was long ago divested of any critique of material appropriation and became all about individualist recognition only. Its co-option isn't new.

This is why we need to speak the language of class oppression, not identity.

To be clear, when I say 'class oppression,' I mean the three axes of material appropriation: socioeconomic class, sex, and race.

The intersection of socioeconomic class, sex, and race was what intersectionality was intended to capture, before it was folded into an individualist, identitarian, anti-materialist system of purely representational politics. Before we decided that 'normativity' was a greater evil than 'exploitation' or 'domination.'

Before we decided structural oppression could be individualized as 'privilege,' and that instead of challenging systems of material domination, we could change the world through self-flagellating confessions, hunting down the sinful, and making them perform rituals of atonement to cleanse their souls.

Of course, corporate and financialized and military power will co-opt representational politics that makes no demands for fundamental structural transformation.

The last time actual corporate power was directly challenged, in the Occupy movements and the anti-austerity protests, the state came down hard. By a couple of years later, all that energy of dissatisfaction—stemming in part from the outrage of the financial crisis and the passing of debt and poverty onto the most vulnerable, while the elites ran off with all the cash they had stolen from the future—all that energy was distorted and twisted into the individualist, representational, witch-hunting politics of 'wokeism.' The corporate Equity, Diversity and Inclusion industry flourished. Political activism became about trying to get corporate and government power to punish people for wrongthink. Big business wrapped itself in rainbows and sparkles.

And the absolute, implacable exploitation of the earth, of the resources of less powerful nations, and of the bodies and labour of the working classes, racialized people, and women continues apace...

This is also what is fundamentally at stake when it comes to the replacement of sex-based exploitation with the purely representational system of gender, severed from any understanding of the role of gender in facilitating material exploitation.

Last night I could hardly sleep because of how angry this pernicious bullshit makes me:

People coming along, dressed up in the language of 'intersectionality' and representational justice, destroying the analysis of material exploitation, and being richly rewarded for their trouble, by institutional and corporate power, while they all slap themselves on the backs for being so progressive and good and caring.

It makes me want to fucking scream.

PRIVILEGE IS AN AVATAR OF SIN

Twitter

12 JULY 2020

I'm a leftist, not a liberal. Although I'm also deeply anti-authoritarian and while democracy is a highly imperfect system, it's still the best option we have, and a great deal better than tyranny.

The woke-left has abandoned a material analysis of power and individualized the analysis of structural inequality. They think we live in an unequal society simply because people have bad ideas or bad attitudes. Privilege has become an avatar of sin. And so, the way to make the world a better place is to act like a bunch of medieval inquisitors, run around finding sinners, and then extort performative atonement from them, preferably with as much pain and humiliation as possible.

In their worldview, the only reason someone might object to their behaviour is because they want to defend the power structure.

Anyone who critiques them will be dismissed as a sinner defending sinners. They are 'white, rich, privileged, cis.' They can't know anything about power beyond their reflex to defend it. And so, the writers of the Harpers counter-letter[1] end up making the absurd revisionist claim that no white 'cis' intellectuals have ever had their intellectual freedom messed with, and tying themselves in knots to pretend that Noam frickin' Chomsky has spent his life defending the status quo.

Their worldview is, in this sense, entirely framed by the neoliberal assumption that people are only and could only be motivated by pure self-interest and the defence of the hierarchies that give them social power.

---

[1] 'A More Specific Letter on Justice and Open Debate,' *objectivejournalism.org*, 10 July 2020, replying to 'A Letter on Justice and Open Debate,' *Harpers*, 7 July 2020.

The idea we might really believe authoritarian is bad, might really dislike witch-hunting, might think this is all a load of individualist, anti-materialist, pseudo-Christian bunk that is playing right into the hands of the right, and is, in its own way, a mirror image of Trumpian populism, *cannot* be acknowledged.

They are the forces of truth, goodness and divine justice. Anyone who opposes them is evil.

That always ends so well.

CANCEL CULTURE AND THE PURITAN IMAGINATION

The Radical Notion Issue Five

AUTUMN 2021

In recent years, the theory and practice of allegedly progressive politics has undergone a radical transformation. The outlines of this shift first became evident in the early 2010s, with the rise of 'call out culture,'[1] a punitive authoritarian tendency that has now mushroomed into the full-blown 'cancel culture' we see today. Nobody can quite decide what to call this new culture on the left: 'identity politics,' 'social justice activism,' 'political correctness gone mad,' 'the successor ideology,' 'wokeism'... None of these labels quite does the job, and there is reason to object to all of them.

Many feminists have concerns about the 'wokeism' label, because 'woke' originally derives from black American nomenclature for someone awake to the realities of structural white supremacy. Here, we encounter an illustration of the way radical materialist feminists find themselves pincered in this debate between two movements. On the one hand, there is something exemplary about the evolution of 'woke' from a term designating opposition to one axis of material structural oppression into a political tendency overwhelmingly focused on representational marginalization, empty performative gestures (often by large corporate interests), and an apparently unquenchable desire to discipline people for thoughtcrimes and wrongspeak. On the other hand, we must remain attuned to the array of right-leaning political interests who are using the critique of the authoritarian overreach of 'wokeism' to try to put the analysis of structural oppression firmly back in its box. And that, to be clear, will include radical and materialist feminism.

Helen Pluckrose and James Lindsay's *Cynical Theories*—which lays the blame for contemporary cancel culture firmly at the door of academic 'post-modernism'/'critical theory'—is, I would suggest, representative of this latter impulse. Space will not allow me to here detail my many problems with their excessively flattened and, frankly, shoddy intellectual history, but the

---

[1] Jane Clare Jones, 'Bad-Faith Justice: Ethics of the Call-Out,' *sarahditum.com*, 23 February 2014.

bones of my critique are this: a) there is no particular reason to attribute the "belief that society is formed of systems of power and hierarchies" specifically to 'postmodernism,'[2] when such ideas arise much earlier in the histories of social movements opposing class-, race- and sex-based inequalities; b) the political phenomenon in question only arose in the last decade, and Pluckrose and Lindsay's narrative gives no clear explanation of why a theoretical movement that arose in the late 1960s should have waited 50 years to mutate into contemporary 'cancel culture'; c) whatever we might think about the epistemic relativism attributed to 'postmodernism,' it is manifestly the case that 'wokeism' is characterized by a form of absolutist moral and epistemic certainty that runs entirely counter to the anti-authoritarian impulse of postmodern scepticism. Which is all to say, Pluckrose and Lindsay's account does not explain what it purports to explain, and, despite putting themselves forward as the voice of impartial reason vis-à-vis 'activist scholarship,' their interest in using 'wokeist' overreach to dismiss of all forms of structural critique is political through and through.

A better explanation of the emergence of 'cancel culture' can be found in what happens when materialist accounts of structural oppression are run through a specifically American cultural matrix, infused with the individualist and idealist legacy of American Puritanism. As Ellwood Johnson observes in 'Individualism and the Puritan Imagination,' "American individualism has its source in an individualism inherent in Protestant theology." According to Johnson, the Calvinist heresy propagated by Jonathan Edwards's *Treatise Concerning Religious Affections*, "may be taken as the root statement of individualism from which has stemmed the indigenous Puritan culture in America." Edwards's doctrine centred on the belief in the possibility of the "purification... of the heart," through which the individual might prepare themselves for salvation, thereby promoting themselves into the ranks of the elect. For Edwards, this process of preparation was predicated on the belief that a man's identity was a product of his will, and in particular, of turning his will towards God. This choosing of religious faith was an entirely mental process, and the moral status of an individual flowed

---

[2] "The postmodern political principle: A belief that society is formed of systems of power and hierarchies, which decide what can be known and how." *Cynical Theories: How Activist Scholarship Made Everything About Race, Gender, and Identity—And Why This Harms Everybody* (Pitchstone Publishing, 2020), p. 31. One could argue here that Pluckrose and Lindsay are only concerned with critiquing the epistemic implications of some applications of structural analysis. However, the text is littered with phrases such as: postmodern "thinkers argued that the powerful have...organized society to benefit them and perpetuate their power," (p. 36) as if such statements are evidently absurd, and as if they meaningfully distinguish postmodernism from other forms of structural analysis, including Marxism and feminism.

directly from it. That is, Johnson writes, "moral good describes only... states or acts of mind, rather than deeds themselves." This then leads to a split which, Johnson notes, characterizes American literature and culture, in which the "spiritual world of the mind and heart" is considered "more real... than the material world," and the individual spirit has an almost superhuman capacity—or "divine light within"—that is capable of "render[ing] truth into reality."[3]

Contra Pluckrose and Lindsay, the basic claim I want to make here is that 'wokeism' is not simply a descendent of political traditions that understand society to be structured by material hierarchies of power. Rather, it is an extreme *deformation* of structural analysis produced by a Puritan sensibility that reinterprets material oppression through a lens concerned principally with the moral 'goodness' or 'badness' of individual hearts or souls. One way to trace this deformation is through the fate of the much-leveraged concept of 'privilege.' In the context of material analysis, 'privilege' once referred to the fact that people who occupy dominant positions in class-based systems of oppression do not have to deal with all kinds of shit that happen to people in subordinate positions. To follow the thought from Marilyn Frye's famous essay 'Oppression,' structural subordination involves encountering networks of obstacles that limit your choices and life opportunities, which people in dominant positions simply do not encounter.[4] Hence the truth of the claim that 'privilege is invisible,' and the tendency of people in dominant class positions to dismiss the testimony of those in subordinate positions. (Here we arrive at the value of standpoint epistemology, although the way this has been translated by 'wokeist' discourse into 'you must accept everything someone in an alleged subordinate position says about anything and, if you so much as question it, you are an agent of the status quo' is another of their many distortions.)

The concept of 'privilege' plays a central role in the Puritan deformation of structural analysis, transforming the happenstance of someone's location within a system of hierarchical class-based power into an individual property of a particular person's moral character or soul. From the perspective of materialist analysis, people in dominant class positions, often through no individual fault of their own, can't see certain things by virtue of where they are positioned, and, if they care about a more just world, then have some moral responsibility to try to understand how people in subordinate

---

[3] Ellwood Johnson, 'Individualism and the Puritan Imagination,' *American Quarterly*, 22(2), 1970, pp. 230-237.

[4] Marilyn Frye, 'Oppression,' in *The Politics of Reality: Essays in Feminist Theory* (Freedom, CA: Crossing Press, 1983).

positions experience things, and how they as members of a dominant class may be implicated in perpetuating oppression. In the hands of modern Puritans however, 'privilege' becomes an avatar of 'sin.' It is the mark of the moral 'badness'—the corruption of the purity of the heart—of an individual, an inherent stain which needs to be acknowledged, 'checked,' and performatively cleansed. Those who perform these public moral ablutions retain their status among the elect, while those who resist them are confirmed as sinners. The basis of our resistance becomes irrelevant. It doesn't matter if we think corporations spending truckloads of Equity, Diversity, and Inclusion money for their employees to self-flagellate about, say, the original sin of slavery, is a facile diversion from the task of addressing the legacy of material inequality that continues to afflict African American communities, and one that is principally about rewarding flagellants with their own moral feel-goods. Within the Puritan logic of 'wokeism,' the direction of the moral will, and the individual worth that follows from it is the alpha and the omega. Material exploitation becomes immaterial.

There are three important consequences of this individualizing dematerialization of the analysis of structural oppression. The first is a complete flattening of any distinction between class-based material exploitation (on the basis of sex, race, and class) and systems of discrimination that are not class-based material relations (e.g. heteronormativity, disability) —a move that has fostered the proliferation of 'oppressions.' In its original form, the 'privilege' that comes from membership of a dominant material class inheres in freedom from certain limits. In the 'wokeist' imagination, which has stripped away the material substratum of structural analysis and replaced it with the simplistic rubric of 'privilege-as-oppression,' any person not experiencing limits for any reason—being mentally healthy, being thin, being right-handed—is suddenly recast as the 'privileged,' the 'powerful,' and 'the oppressor.' Never mind that there is no class-based relation of material exploitation between righties and lefties, or thin and fat people, or indeed, between straight and gay people. While discrimination has material impacts on people's lives, addressing 'oppression' not based in extractive class relations does not demand fundamental transformation of exploitative practices and has limited impact on corporate bottom lines. 'Thank you very much,' says the multi-million-pound EDI industry. 'Would you like a rainbow lanyard with that?'

Closely connected to this phenomenon is the way that oppression has come to be seen as entirely about issues of 'marginalization,' 'stigmatization,' and 'representation,' rather than material extraction. The 'privileged' are free to move easily through the world not because they have more material resources and opportunities, but because they are not 'marginalized,' while the oppressed are not oppressed because they're exploited, but because they're 'stigmatized.'[5] This was driven home to me the other day when Judith Green contrasted the abject lack of class analysis in contemporary 'wokeist' politics with the common concern about 'classism.' Apparently, it's fine to carry on exploiting people, paying them shit wages and subjecting them to precarious employment, just as long as you don't have any nasty, bigoted ideas about the people you exploit.

This brings us to the last, crucial consequence of the Puritan analytic: the reduction of systems of oppression to aggregations of bad ideas and attitudes. In conventional materialist analysis, social attitudes, and political ideologies, are the *product* of material class relations, and exist in order to reify, justify, and perpetuate those relations. In the 'wokeist' mind, oppression is a *consequence* of people being nasty 'bigots' or '-phobes,' and, with staggering circularity, it seems many people now believe that 'privileged' people hold bad, bigoted ideas simply because they are bad and privileged.[6] Here the idealist individualism of the Puritan sensibility comes sharply into focus—and, with it, the utterly misguided belief that oppression can only be dealt with by quasi-religious means: hunting down those with impure hearts and minds, subjecting them to inquisition, making them recant ("repent, motherfucker!"), and then extracting elaborate public displays of atonement that will never appease the vengeful crowd or allow you readmission to the community of the elect. There's a reason so many of us feel like we're live action role-playing *The Crucible* every day on Twitter. Puritans are the witch-hunters extraordinaire.

---

[5] It is important to note that representational marginalization should not be completely dismissed. Mechanisms of hierarchical 'othering' brought to the fore by poststructural, postcolonial, and feminist writings do play a very significant role in maintaining systems of structural oppression by denying humanity, voice, and political agency to subjugated peoples. However, these mechanisms often exist in order to facilitate material exploitation of bodies, labour, and land. While 'marginalization' is psychologically and materially harmful in itself, there are significant problems in eliding the material substratum of structural analysis and allowing 'marginalization' or 'stigmatization' to stand in for the entirety of oppression.

[6] It is on the basis of this circularity that 'wokeism' is characterized by the belief that someone's 'privilege' can be automatically read off the fact that they hold a particular 'bigoted' belief, which can also then be automatically dismissed, because it is evidence of 'privilege.' Ergo, women who think humans are sexed are *de facto* white, middle class, etc., even when they're not.

AGAINST DEATH CULTS

Short seminar presentation at Oxford University

OCTOBER 2019

So, one of the things I've been trying to think through recently is why trans ideology is so compelling to people, despite the fact that sex denialism is based on an evident and wilful distortion of reality, and that no progressive movement should sign up for a political programme based on reifying the stereotypes of patriarchal gender.

I think there are many answers to that question, but what I'd like to look at today is the metaphysical or religious structure of gender identity, and how that might relate to quasi-religious narratives of transition and the cult-like behaviour we see among trans true believers.

Let's start with what gender identity is—a matter of great uncertainty. To our minds, it could only properly refer to human personality and the coding given to it by the structures of patriarchal gender, which, of course, is an interpretation most of our opponents would reject. To be given sense in their terms it must rest either on the scientifically dubious notion of male and female brains, or, as it often seems, on the assumption of some kind of internal gendered essence—that is, in many cases 'gender identity' functions as a more-or-less explicit belief in a gendered soul, which, inexplicably, somehow got put in the wrong container at the heavenly soul-bottling factory.

This idea rests on a form of mind-body dualism that can be traced in Western thought from Platonism through Judeo-Christianity to Cartesianism, and which emerges yet again in present-day transhumanist fantasies, which are deeply interwoven with trans ideology (as any reading of Martine Rothblatt reveals). What I'm principally interested in here is how gender identity functions as a modern iteration of ideas about the primacy of the soul or mind over the body, and in particular the way this dualism has been historically implicated in the longing for transcendence from the imprisoning mortality of the body. In the poststructural feminist tradition I trained in, the conceptual correlates of this longing are understood as an index of a masculinist refusal of our material dependencies—on our own bodies, on the bodies of others, especially women, and also, on the earth—expressed as a drive towards a dematerialized transcendence which is actually a denial of the very conditions of life. Attempts to transcend the body express a longing for immortality that is ultimately a death drive.

It's worth here then thinking about the way trans ideology taps the same basic instincts that have also animated the appeal of Platonized Christianity. It sounds bonkers, but the primacy of gender identity would then express the drive to transcend bodily limitation analogous to the thought of The Resurrection—and both churches would centre on the impossible, but redemptive, metaphysical conviction at their core. The hero's journey of transition thus takes on the resonance of a messianic salvation narrative. The constraint and alienation of our suffering mortality will be finally overcome, and the initiate delivered to a promised land or newly minted afterlife in which only their inner, unblemished, authentic self will remain, free of all embodied impediments. If it's true that trans ideology's appeal rests on a metaphysical salvation fantasy, that would help explain why it functions far more like a religious cult than a political discourse—and why true believers are so impervious to rational argument and so fond of denouncing heretics and apostates.

The last thought I want to raise here then is the ethical importance of opposing an ideology based on a fantasy of immaterial transcendence. As we know, there are many areas of concern about the impact of trans ideology—including the effect on women's rights, on academic freedom, and on the possibility of speaking women's sex-based oppression. However, the sterilization of young people—in particular, performing hysterectomies on young, healthy women—is, I'd argue, symptomatic of the death-drive inherent in all immortality projects. Material embodiment and dependency are the conditions of life, and overcoming these material constraints can only be achieved in acts of fantasy or domination that are inimical to respecting these conditions. Trans ideology is, fundamentally, a death-cult. We must resist it in the interests of defending life.

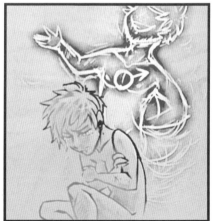 

NOTES ON DIGITAL TRANSCENDENCE

The Radical Notion Issue Two

WINTER 2021

If the dull substance of my flesh were thought,
Injurious distance should not stop my way;
For then despite of space I would be brought,
From limits far remote where thou dost stay.

Shakespeare, *Sonnet 44*
Opening epigraph of Martine Rothblatt's *Virtually Human*[1]

1. All living things on this planet exist in material bodies (if they are animal) or material forms (if they are vegetable). A body is material, but a living thing is not *just* material. A dead body is not a living body. A living body is distinguished from a dead body by the fact that it is *animated*. The Greeks named this principle '*psyche*' and the Romans named it '*anima*,' conceptualized as immaterial soul. But dualisms of soul and body miss that life is the animation of matter and arises only through matter. The only adequate word for this principle of animated matter—which is, from an explanatory perspective, inadequate—is '*life*.' And while the multiplicity of organic processes are the index of life, they are not, themselves, life *as such*. Despite massive advances in clever monkey knowledge—our ability to analyze and represent DNA replication, respiration, photosynthesis, etc.—we do not, in fact, know what 'life as such' *is*. It would serve smart-ass hubristic monkeys well to be mindful of this fact.

---

[1] Martine Rothblatt, *Virtually Human: The Promise—and the Peril—of Digital Immortality* (New York: St Martin's Press, 2014), p. 1.

2. That we do not know *what life is*, and that it insists on evading the mastery of our techniques, causes clever monkeys quite some consternation. We do not know *what makes it go*, we do know *what makes it stop*, and we do not know why—unlike our machines—*once it has stopped we cannot make it go again*. All we know is that there are living bodies and dead bodies, and that once animated matter is no longer animate, it will decompose back into its material elements, through other living processes. Death is intensely painful to us, and is, fundamentally, just like life, ungraspable by monkey minds. We find this inordinately difficult to accept, both emotionally, and intellectually.

3. Abstract monkey self-reflection—often about what it means to be a monkey capable of abstract self-reflection—has long struggled with this difficulty. We really cannot deal with being animated matter or with the fact that the condition of being animated matter is that one day, incomprehensibly, we will not be animate. We cannot grasp how it is that animated matter generates awareness, and awareness of awareness, and awareness that we cannot grasp how we are aware. Just as we do not understand life, we do not understand how consciousness, or what we reductively call 'mind,' arises in and through the animation of matter. It would serve us better to be also mindful that we do not understand the existence of our minds.

4. Given that we experience the world, and ourselves, in and through our awareness, it is at least comprehensible that we would identify 'ourselves' with this awareness. It is far less evident why we would insist on reductively calling this 'mind,' or rather, to be more precise, identifying this awareness only with the dense lump of neurons located in our skulls.[2] Awareness arises from animated matter and permeates our entire materiality (excepting our toe-nails, hair and bones, the parts of us, notably, that most resist decay). Sensation, and above all, emotion, is experienced, that is, *felt*, by something that can only properly be called the 'bodymind.' I have nonetheless met plenty of people who believe that their feelings are *in their brain*, and that they could *remove their awareness from their bodies* and it would remain unchanged. I

---

[2] It is perhaps understandable that we would make this mistake, given that almost all animals that possess higher intelligence belong to the phylum *chordata*, the majority of which have central nervous systems consisting of a brain inside a skull and a spinal column. The glaring exception to this principle, we are now aware, is the octopus, which as a mollusc with a relatively rudimentary nervous system, would seem to have little business being that intelligent at all. I like to think of the octopus as a kind of evolutionary rebuke to our dualist metaphysics and veneration of our brains as computational hardware. The entire body of an octopus—especially its multitudinous sensate suckers—is a complete gelatinous sentience, a spineless, aquatic bodymind, a floating intelligence that is a body.

can understand this only as an artefact of extreme repression and/or (it may amount to the same thing) a transcendence drive so implacable it wilfully distorts what is given to human consciousness, phenomenologically.

5. Since monkeys started writing down their abstract self-reflections—barely a fraction-of-a-nanosecond-ago by planet-time—we've been trying to wriggle out of the fact that *we are embodied awareness*. 'Bodies die, therefore we are not bodies.' 'Bodies hunger, thirst, sicken, yearn, can be *wounded*, therefore they are not us.' The words littering our philosophy and literature heap scorn upon eviscerating scorn; the body is nothing but a dark, deceptive, wanton, corrupting, polluted pile of "mortal trash,"[3] and if Plato—who bears as much responsibility as anyone for telling this pernicious lie—is to be believed, our duty is to dissociate from its treacherous earthy embrace, and ascend, by dint of pure abstraction, into the deathless sky. As if such a thing were possible. As if humans could stare directly at the centre of the sun without destroying the fabric of their eyes.

6. But monkeys will not be deterred. We will imagine our ideas—extracted from our dark, duplicitous bodies—glinting in the heavens. We will fall in love with triangles and the crystalline eternity of number, equation, and algorithm. We will tell and retell the tale of the afterlife, of the coming of heaven to earth, of the word made flesh, of bodies broken on crosses and reborn, into an everlasting life that is not and can never be life, because the condition of possibility of life, on this planet, is that you are the kind of thing that dies. Life would only be worth something, we seem to think, if it were *worth more than life*, if it were *beyond* life, but the only life *beyond* life, would be, in fact, *already death*. Life matters so much to us, we would trade it in a heartbeat for a death that cannot therefore die, rather than struggle with living and sustaining ourselves in *the material life that we are*. The drive to transcendent immaterial immortality is, at root, a death drive, and in striving for the beyond of life, in its resentment and contempt for the material limits of the living, it will deny and disassociate itself from the conditions that sustain it. We want life so much that we will, in fact, destroy it with our denial and disrespect.

7. This fear and *resentment* of our material dependence on what we cannot understand or fully master, echoes through all our relations to the more or less animated matter that creates and sustains us. The body and bowels of this

---

[3] "But tell me, what would happen if one of you had the fortune to look upon essential beauty entire, pure and unalloyed; not infected with the flesh and colour of humanity, and ever so much more of mortal trash?" Plato's *Symposium*, 211e.

rock, the efflorescence it shoots forth, the plants that turn the sunlight into sugar that makes our bodies move, the breath by which we burn that sugar, the quiver-beat of flesh, and above all else, the body blood mind and milk of the mother that brings us each to life. We cannot plot the genealogy of civilizations sprung from the fertile crescent and refuse to reckon with the social and symbolic transformations begun when the earth was first broken up and ploughed, enclosed and exploited, and the bodies of women remade by the masculine mind as passive, fertile, appropriable territory awaiting their seeds. The phallic mode of meeting the material dependency of embodied animal existence has long been to deny it in thought, while appropriating and exploiting what it refuses to recognize, but nonetheless needs, in fact. And so agriculture → patriarchy → rape → colonialism → slavery → capitalism are tied together by the logic of erasure[4] → appropriation → extraction of matter and its animation. That is, by the disrespect and domination of life.

---

[4] 'Erasure' is to be taken here in the largest sense, that is, as including not only the way mechanisms of appropriation/domination may *deny* the existence of something on which it depends, but also the denial that they exist *in their own terms*, and with their own principles of subjectivity, fecundity, or animation. It thus includes objectification, dehumanization, and the entire mechanism of phallic othering, through which those oppressed along the axes of sex, race and class are assigned the characteristics of the less properly human, and defined by projective inversion from the position of the phallic subject. (My claim here, and I take this is to be axial to radical feminism, and central to the analysis of the mechanisms of domination currently being repressed by the anti-materialist and individualist analysis of oppression-as-privilege, is that the fundamental structure of this mechanism derives historically from the objectification and mastery of the earth in its historic inter-twining with the objectification and mastery of women's bodies and reproductive capacities. Traces of this history are still found in the use of agricultural metaphors around sex ('sowing wild oats' 'ploughing' as a synonym for 'fucking'), and extend into the thinking of women's bodies as territory, and the thinking of the colonization and appropriation of land through sexual metaphors and vice versa ('virgin territory', the intertwining of rape and colonization in metaphor and practice, thinking penetration as proprietorial possession, etc.)).

The most revealing lexical trace of this history is the designation of male's contribution to the reproductive process as 'semen,' which derives from the Latin for 'seed.' Seeds are produced through fertilization, that is, they are the product of *the combination of male and female gametes*. This is therefore a denial/erasure of the active female contribution to fertilization, which posits women as the passive recipient of an entirely male generative principle, consonant with Aristotle's famous discussion in *The Generation of Animals*. In a significant sense, this moment holds within it, like a hologram, the entire structure of phallic dominance and the systems it has patterned. The necessity of relational co-creation, between male and female, between matter and idea, between the desire for transcendence and material facticity, is entirely elided in the image of the self-creating male subject—the 'self-made man'—who needs, depends, is *vulnerable* to nothing, because he has already reduced that on which he depends to the sub-human or the object, to nothing more than inert, passive, material he has already appropriated to himself. That is, in a significant sense, the entire structure of phallic dominance is held in the reduction of the

8. Some five millennia later, very little in our fundamental metaphysic, in the unflagging drive to transcend the facts of our animal existence, has changed. Empires have waxed and waned, the earth has been split open to offer up her sedimented reserves of sunlight, and we have used it to power our machines, now warming the planet to perilous extremes. At this moment, when we should, above all, be asking ourselves how we got here, why we have imperilled ourselves so thoroughly by denying and disrespecting the material animation on which we depend, many minds are instead transfixed by the transcendent possibility of machine life. If animal life is unsustainable, we will, finally, make our escape and fulfil our always-destiny in the realm of the ideas, our mindfiles uploaded into the 'cloud.' (Which is not a cloud and is not in heaven. Somewhere here on earth, there is—there will always be—a bank of silicon and circuitry, pulled from the ground, powered by energy, maintained, one imagines, by a hardware service class, while the digital elites dream their age-old dreams of abstracted immortality.) They do not want to know, they will not hear, that we do not understand the principle of animated matter. That bodies are not machines, that minds are not computers, that DNA is not just data, that we have absolutely no basis for believing that information and dead matter arranged at an adequate degree of complexity will simply spring into life, by our final mastery of alchemical magic.

9. In the last two decades, human social life, for swaths of the global population, has been completely transformed by migration into virtual space. The more immaterial aspects of our awareness—our likes, attention, interests, concern, above all *what we want and do not want*—have been siphoned into the machine, which they then *animate*, both through encounter and conflict with other desires. Plato was misguided to think desire is just a product of our fleshy, hungering selves. Desire is what *animates* us—what animates all animals. It moves us into the world, in search of food, shelter and sex, yes, but also in search of connection, recognition, purpose, knowledge, and meaning. Freud was not entirely wrong when he called the libido—the life-instinct—'Eros,' although he was emphatically wrong to think our satisfactions as nothing but expelling uncomfortable excitation: the quenching of a baby's thirst or the expulsive release of male orgasm. We are drawn into the

---

earth and its animation to object, and of women to earth. It is through this lens that the present attempts to distort and deny the existence and meaning of sexual reproduction as representative of the fundamental principle of relational co-creation should be metaphysically interpreted. It is entirely consonant, and in fact inextricably bound, to the effort to deny that creation and generation (of both reproductive and non-reproductive types) can only take place through the dialectical interaction of idea/desire/transcendence and material facticity, and with the effort to assert the absolute sovereignty of identity over both matter and social relation.

world, again and again, not just by what we lack, but also by a positive desire, and the *pleasure*, of encounter and play, of project and collective co-creation, by the need to be immersed in the flow of ourselves as we unfold in our do-ings-in-the-world. Desire is not 'life as such,' but as key to what animates us, is one of its enduring indices. Life lived in the absence of desire is unbear-able: the slow, agonizing, suspension inside endless static time which char-acterizes the 'living death' of depression, or, as in Denise Riley's memoir on grief, the experience of *Time Lived, Without Its Flow*.

10. As a product, and indeed an engine, of the animation of bodymind, de-sire thus arises not just in the wanting body but in the yearning mind. Phi-losophy, theology, art, science, technology; the search for status, the accu-mulation of wealth, the demand for recognition, the creation of meaning; the fear of death, the drive to transcendence, the urge to mastery, the denial of dependence: all these are produced through the action of desire. *Contra* Plato then, in the age-old edifice of metaphysical polarity, desire is allied as much with the mind as with the body (from which the mind cannot dissoci-ate). We may resent the body for the way its hungering disturbs our conceits of invulnerable, stoic rationality, but the fact is the mind also wants, and what most often frustrates its *wants* are the limits of material facticity, and the desires of other people.

11. Feeding our desire into the machine seems then to offer limitless satis-faction. The machine pretends to exist outside the constraints of material facticity, a frictionless, demassified utopia, a world freed from gravity, where we can finally ascend, out of the obdurate dark of the cave, and realize our-selves, in illuminated, almost immaterial pixels, as we truly want to be. It is the New Frontier, Manifest Destiny, a virtualized American Dream. Inside the machine, we are encouraged to produce and endlessly curate ourselves as avatar, brand, lifestyle, influencer, commodity, to attract other desires to the edited, touched-up, perfected *idea(l)* of ourselves, shorn of actual matter, filtered through filters that index our desire to transcend our very selves. En-tire generations have now been raised inside the narcissistic matrix of this machine, funnelling their desire not into embodied-activity-in-the-world, but into fashioning themselves as avatar, object, and ideal identity. Encour-aged to sidestep the challenge—and *satisfaction*—of manifesting themselves and their desires in messy confounding co-creation with the world and with each other, and skipping straight to the 'good part,' where we get to be pre-cisely who we always dreamt ourselves to be. An individual immaterial god.

> "A Klee painting named 'Angelus Novus' shows an angel looking as though he is about to move away from something he is fixedly contemplating. His eyes are staring, his mouth is open, his wings are spread. This is how one pictures the angel of history. His face is turned toward the past. Where we perceive a chain of events, he sees one single catastrophe which keeps piling wreckage and hurls it in front of his feet. The angel would like to stay, awaken the dead, and make whole what has been smashed. But a storm is blowing in from Paradise; it has got caught in his wings with such a violence that the angel can no longer close them. The storm irresistibly propels him into the future to which his back is turned, while the pile of debris before him grows skyward. This storm is what we call progress."
>
> 1942 · Walter Benjamin · *Theses on the Philosophy of History*

'Right Side of History My Arse'

12. Into this catastrophe of narcissism and dissociation, an ideology inserts itself. The brain-child of *Transcendent Man*[5]—Techno-Platonism v.10.13.4™. The fit is perfect. A generation raised on the promise of digital transcendence, on the frictionless fulfilment of their desires, but who find themselves, in fact, lost, alienated, and in pain inside their refracting, bloodless paradise, are sold a techno-salvation story—the newest and shiniest yet! You are free to be absolutely and completely only who you *feel yourself to be*, who you *desire yourself to be*, and nobody, no-*body*, can stop you. Desire, *life*, will finally transcend the mortal trash that weighs it down and holds it to the surface of this rock, and become sovereign over all it surveys. The body will be bent to our will, its pointless corrupting compliance to the cycles of generative life discarded, until we are finally able to discard it in its entirety. This is the manifest destiny of human progress, the 'right side of history,' the fulfilment of "our image of happiness... indissolubly bound up with... redemption."[6] No one should underestimate the power of this millenarian myth. Of how many times we have compulsively, recklessly reimagined the story of the

---

[5] *Transcendent Man* is the title of a 2009 documentary about Ray Kurzweil, the futurist and theorist of the technological 'singularity,' the thought that the exponential increase in computation power will at some point, by the end of this decade apparently, spontaneously generate artificial intelligence. The documentary opens with Kurzweil's trenchant refusal to accept death, and the next forty minutes (I couldn't get further) includes a parade of exclusively male talking heads, saying 'exponential' on a loop, because evidently, 'computation x exponential = life.' Notably, Kurzweil wrote the foreword to Martine Rothblatt's *Virtually Human* (2014), which, Kurzweil maintains, makes "a compelling and convincing case for virtual humans. After all, what difference does it make if our mental circuits are biological or electronic if the result is the same?" (p. ix). For a more detailed exploration of the role of Martine Rothblatt's transhumanist mind over matter dualism to the development of trans ideology, please see my 'Brief History of Transgender Ideology' (p. 22).

[6] Walter Benjamin, *Theses on the Philosophy of History* (1942).

soul's sovereign transcendence, and its redemption in the life beyond life. At this point in history, facing the prospect of material extinction—*because of our lack of respect for life*—that techno-corporate power would sell this story to an alienated, dissociated generation *whose future they have themselves stolen* is a crime against humanity and the earth.

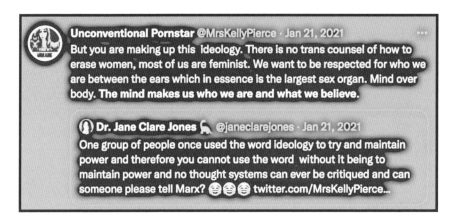

Unconventional Pornstar @MrsKellyPierce · Jan 21, 2021
But you are making up this ideology. There is no trans counsel of how to erase women, most of us are feminist. We want to be respected for who we are between the ears which in essence is the largest sex organ. Mind over body. The mind makes us who we are and what we believe.

Dr. Jane Clare Jones @janeclarejones · Jan 21, 2021
One group of people once used the word ideology to try and maintain power and therefore you cannot use the word without it being to maintain power and no thought systems can ever be critiqued and can someone please tell Marx? 😂😂😂 twitter.com/MrsKellyPierce...

13. One might imagine, or rather, have hoped, that the devastating intercession of the virus, in all its material implacability and horror, might have awoken us from our digital slumbers. As the symptoms of environmental, cultural, financial, and political demassification accumulate outside our windows, and the conflict between our unerring desire for transcendence and material facticity piles up more and more wreckage, we have retreated more than ever into the machine. We are not satisfied. The shimmering animation of our desire inside the virtual leaves us wanting. We want movement in the world, the landscape whizzing past train windows, our faces under the sun and the ground beneath our feet. We want real rooms filled with real human laughter and the buzz of real human energy. We want to hear each other's voices and look each other in the eye. We want to touch each other.

Now, we must hold onto this.

ACKNOWLEDGEMENTS

My thanks first of all to the people who have most directly made this project possible, the team at *The Radical Notion*, and especially Bec Wonders and Daisy Gudmunsen, as well as Eliza Mondegreen for her work on this manuscript. To everyone at the magazine, you are the smartest and most committed women I have ever had the pleasure to work with, and I am so proud of what we have made together. Respect to the fabulously talented stitch-witch Jess de Wahls, with thanks for allowing us to use her artwork *Somewhere Over the Rainbow, Something Went Terribly Wrong*, which perfectly captures in thread so much about this conflict. My particular thanks also to Jen Gill, whose effort, enthusiasm, humour, and ability to manage my backstage chaos have been central to making The Centre for Feminist Thought, *The Radical Notion*, and this book project into realities.

There are so many women who have contributed to this movement over the years who have encouraged and inspired me that it won't be possible to name them all, but I'd like to thank Jayne Egerton, Judith Green, Lisa Mackenzie, Ali Ceesay, Rose Rickford, Dani Ahrens, Allie Rogers, Helen Joyce, Lisa-Marie Taylor, Julie Bindel, Susanna Rustin, Suzanne Moore, Hannah Ryan, Ziggy Melamed, Lorelei Hatpinwoman, Wacky Pidgeon, and the Great Blob Homunculus for their work and for their sisterhood. To all the many women who have organized, argued, written letters, stickered, tied ribbons, given speeches, compiled data, taken court cases, sent in FOIs, visited your MPs, and dressed up as dinosaurs, all of it matters, and we all made this wave together. It's important to always remember that none of our thinking about transgender ideology has been done in isolation, that it has been a long and collective effort, and I'd like to thank in particular Marina Strinkovsky, Victoria Dutchman-Smith, Rebecca Reilly-Cooper, Emma Hilton, Feminist Roar, Radical Hag, and Young Crone/Shambolic Neutral for their analytic chops on this one. I'd also like to thank all of the women who have attended the Centre over the last three years, and to express what a privilege and joy it has been to think feminism together with you. Lastly, special and deep thanks to Selina Todd for her unflagging support for my work, which—as a somewhat errant academic—has been more precious to me than I can say.

To my parents, always gratitude for passing me your love of ideas and your belief in justice, for modelling integrity, and for bearing with your wayward daughter until she finally found some sort of path. And to the best friend I could ever have hoped for, Victoria Rimell, without whom none of this thinking, or becoming, would ever have been possible.